Unruly Spirits

M. Brady Brower

Unruly
Spirits

The Science of
Psychic Phenomena
in Modern France

UNIVERSITY OF ILLINOIS PRESS

Urbana, Chicago, and Springfield

Manufactured in the United States of America
1 2 3 4 5 C P 5 4 3 2 1
∞ This book is printed on acid-free paper.

Library of Congress Cataloging-in-Publication Data
Brower, M. Brady.
Unruly spirits : the science of psychic phenomena
in modern France / M. Brady Brower.
p.   cm.
Includes bibliographical references and index.
ISBN 978-0-252-03564-7 (cloth : alk. paper)
ISBN 978-0-252-07751-7 (pbk. : alk. paper)
1. Parapsychology—France—History. I. Title.
BF1028.5.F8B76   2010
130.944—dc22   2010018141

For Henry and Stella

Contents

Acknowledgments

Nineteenth-century spiritists believed that through table rapping, automatic messages, and other methods they had discovered ways of communicating with a vast spirit world and tapping directly into an unlimited reservoir of human knowledge. While no tables were turned in the making of this book, it, too, was a product of a long series of communications with mentors and colleagues who helped to shape my thinking about the historical problem posed by the intersection of science and popular religion. I may not have always deciphered the messages of these interlocutors accurately, and in many cases, no doubt, I have distorted their meaning by projecting my own interests and concerns onto theirs. Nevertheless, the experience of such exchanges helped animate my efforts by reminding me that, even as they feign to speak for the dead, historians realize their task only in addressing themselves to the living.

From its earliest stages this work was supported, influenced, and guided by the efforts of Bonnie G. Smith and Joan Wallach Scott, each of whom read multiple drafts and prompted me to fashion an amorphous set of concerns into something more coherent. It was Bonnie Smith's inclusive view of cultural history that made it possible for me to recognize what a crucial role the marginalized or undervalued term plays in any historical relationship, just as Joan Scott's uncompromising honesty encouraged me to remain faithful to the interest that I had initially seen in my topic and to approach it as a genuine epistemological problem and not simply a historical curiosity.

Other teachers, colleagues, and friends provided essential moral support and intellectual guidance. Martha Hanna, Susan K. Kent, and Robert Pois helped shape my early thinking about the relationship between trauma and identity in the context of the First World War, as did my good comrades Jared Poley, Richard Keller, and Tim Brown, who shared my preoccupation with the Belle Époque and its unraveling. Benjamin Brower provided encouragement, insight, and friendship throughout the production of this work. While not exactly producing a *dédoublement de la conscience,* our exchanges seem always to indicate similar concerns. Matt Matsuda, Brian Crim, and Lia Paradis patiently helped me to contain my initial *fluidomania* and compelled me to consider the implications of my topic as it began to appear in its early, prehistoric forms. Brian Connolly, Jennifer Pettit, Louisa Rice, Max Likin, and Sandrine Sanos offered their insights on early chapters and helped me to rethink the relationship of historical scholarship to its object. Donald Kelley's encyclopedic knowledge of European intellectual history presented a constant caution against naive presumptions. Elizabeth Ann Wilson deserves high honors for reading and commenting on an early complete draft and helping me to think about the constitutive exclusions and tensions that sustain the field of psychology. Amy Jamison brought her customary diligence to bear on various drafts of this work and provided the underlying moral conditions in which it was possible for me to bring it into being.

As psychical researchers were so painfully aware, intellectual pursuits require material resources, and I was fortunate enough to find generous support for my research from the Fulbright Program, the dean of the Graduate School at Rutgers University, and the Hemingway Faculty Development Trust at Weber State University. Much of the current work was written while I was employed as a research assistant at the Institute for Advanced Study, where, when reading envious accounts by nineteenth-century French scientists about the advantages of well-funded American institutions, I had a pretty clear idea of what they were talking about. Good people are of course what really make the institute what it is, and I thank all those who helped to make my time there stimulating and productive.

While researching this project in Paris I was fortunate to have as my unofficial protector Steven L. Kaplan, who pointed out the best bakeries in the *quartier* and graciously provided, through his colleague Alain Boureau, a guide to the resources of the École des Hautes Études, in particular, the seminar of Jacqueline Carroy, which served as a useful introduction to the history of French psychology. Tzvetan Todorov and Alain Corbin also took pity on my ignorance and suggested approaches and resources that had, to that point in time, escaped my attention. My exchange of research tips with Sophie Lachapelle, Renaud Evrard, and John Warne Monroe led to the discovery of sources that I would not have stumbled across on my own. Extra thanks also goes to John, who, along with Ian Dowbiggin, offered many thoughtful suggestions for revision of the final manuscript. Mario Varvoglis, director of the Institut Métapsychique International, welcomed me into the institute's archives and assisted me in the happy work of restoring to usefulness this important collection of documents. Marcia Tucker, Deborah Stephenson, Misty Allen, Amélie le Pendeven, and dozens of other archivists and librarians also played their part in making this work possible.

Unruly Spirits

Psychical Research and French Science

I fear that those to whom I confided my intentions have thought of me more than once as a victim of a bizarre and, in short, a rather futile curiosity. On what path have I put myself? "This curious by-path of yours," a friendly Englishman once told me in no uncertain terms. I, however, continued to believe that it was a detour worth following and it seemed to me by experience that it would lead rather far. With something that had, until the present, been nothing more than an anecdote, I supposed that I could make history.

—Marc Bloch, *Les Rois thaumaturges*

If "psychical research" is an expression that has limited currency among contemporary Anglophones, the French equivalents, *les sciences psychiques* and *la métapsychique,* are even less obvious to French ears. A quick analysis of any of these terms would not be incorrect in concluding that they have something in common with the field of psychology. A survey of the membership of the field of psychical research would reveal a number of prominent figures associated with the development of psychology in the late nineteenth century. For those who invented both the expression and the field of study to which it referred, "psychical research" was, in fact, a study of mental phenomena, and in this respect it was closely aligned with the nascent field of scientific psychology, whose aims and principles were, in the last decades of the nineteenth century, still very much disputed by the philosophers, physiologists, neurologists, neuroanatomists, psychiatrists, alienists, and all those who were eventually to become "psychologists." Some of these early figures in the field of psychology maintained that the mind could be studied scientifically only if links could be established between mental processes and their organic supports. Others insisted that consciousness could be studied on its own terms through introspection and that psychology need not limit itself to studying the neurosystem or the physiological processes of sensation and reflex. Within this debate psychical research offered an extreme argument for the autonomy of the mind by presenting itself as an investigation of "phenomena which are often . . . attributed to minds apart from material organisms."[1] At the same time, it proposed that the mind, as presented in certain phenomena, could nevertheless be studied using the objective methods of the experimental sciences. In psychical research the mind was objectivized but without recourse to the body.

The raw material for this endeavor was to be found in a set of practices and beliefs born out of the religious enthusiasms of the mid-nineteenth century and adapted to the secular and democratic values of the age. Usually given a precise date of origin in the discovery of mediumistic powers by the teenaged Fox sisters in Hydesville, New York, in 1848, Modern Spiritualism became an international movement in the early 1850s as millions of practitioners throughout America and Europe engaged in communication with spirits of the dead. In France *spiritisme* would debut in the spring of 1853 with the proliferation of "talking" and "dancing" tables, remarkable phenomena in which ordinary household furnishings moved by mysterious means around middle- and lower-middle-class salons. These movements often corresponded to verbal commands given by séance participants, and it was soon learned that the tables could respond with extraordinary accuracy to participants' inquiries by rapping out letters of the alphabet. Eventually, these communications, like the American form of the practice, highlighted the intervention of "mediums," individuals who were seen as especially skilled at contacting the spirit world and could, in the most talented cases, produce a whole host of strange mental and physical phenomena, ranging from clairvoyance and telepathy to the materialization of spirit forms. Adepts of spiritism argued that these phenomena could not be explained away with references to mundane causes. They also argued, however, that these phenomena were not the product of supernatural forces. Spirits belonged, they insisted, fully to the order of nature. Communication with the spirit world was not an occult practice limited to those with access to secret knowledge. Spirit phenomena could be produced and observed by anyone willing to follow a few simple procedures.

In the 1880s elite researchers from the fields of physics, chemistry, physiology, medicine, literature, and philosophy began taking these claims seriously enough to subject them to close scrutiny. The reasons for this interest among scientists and intellectuals varied. In most cases, the individuals involved in psychical research felt an obligation to render, for the benefit of science and the concerns of the general public, an account of mediumistic phenomena that conformed to the scientific understanding of the natural world. For extreme skeptics, the engagement with mediumism might be sparked by the expectation that the medium would, in the course of close scrutiny by cautious and disciplined observers, be exposed as a fraud. For credulous researchers who accepted the so-called spirit hypothesis, the study of mediums was understood as a means of publicly confirming the survival of the soul as a fact of nature. For the many critical but open-minded researchers who occupied a place between these two extremes, the admittedly remarkable events of the séances were curiosities, alluring in that they suggested faculties of mind and properties of matter that remained, as yet, hidden from the light of science. In the movement of distant objects, materialization of spirits, telepathy, precognition, and other phenomena produced by mediums, psychical researchers saw evidence of an agency that defied mechanical notions of cause and prevailing scientific understandings of time and space. Spiritists and psychical researchers agreed to the extent that the phenomena observed in the séances were natural in origin and that they didn't exhibit the "fatalism" associated with other processes of nature.[2] The events studied suggested instead "intellectuality, will, *intention*" as well as "choice, purpose, [and] decision consistent with volition."[3] Rejecting the divine provenance of the soul, psychical researchers set out to demonstrate that intelligence was a faculty of nature. At the same time, however, they were drawn to phenomena that indicated that intelligence was, in its willfulness, creativity, and capriciousness, not completely bound by the deterministic forces that much nineteenth-century science had attributed to the natural order.

In this sense, the Nobel Prize–winning physiologist and psychical researcher Charles Richet would find his ideas in agreement with the pioneering French spiritist Allan Kardec. Just as Kardec had argued that "every intelligent cause has an intelligent effect," Richet would insist that the physical and mental phenomena of mediumism were "attributable to forces that seem intelligent or to some unknown, latent powers of human intelligence."[4] But while Kardec had made his claim in a period in which the mind was still considered unitary and self-identical (thus giving rise to an explanation dependent on the action of disembodied spirits), the intervening history of psychology would insure that Richet's statements resonated with theories of the mind in which this unity could no longer be assumed. As the historian Henri Ellenberger argued, psychical research would play an important role in psychology's theories of a decentered and fragmented subject.[5] Psychology would draw abundant evidence for subconscious activity, the subliminal self, and unconscious mental processes from the often staggering feats of mediums.

As a specialized field of elite practitioners, psychical research formally debuted in 1882 under auspicious circumstances with the advent of the London-based Society for Psychical Research (SPR). Bolstered by the prestige of the Cambridge moral philosopher Henry Sidgwick, the SPR was formed with the purpose of establishing a permanent institutional basis for an area of inquiry that had, to that point in time, been pursued either too informally or too sporadically to offer any meaningful contributions to science. The SPR's research program built upon and continued the studies performed roughly a decade earlier by the London Dialectical Society, studies that were, in turn, only a formalization of the countless personal investigations, interested and disinterested, credulous and skeptical, undertaken in the countless séances that had been held since the advent of Modern Spiritualism at midcentury. Based on the reputations of its core members, the British-based movement quickly drew a prestigious international membership. The internationalism of the field was realized with the emergence of other organizations like the American Society for Psychical Research in Boston and later in New York (1885–present), the Institut Général Psychologique (1900–1933), and the Institut Métapsychique International (1919–present). International cooperation reached its apogee in the decades following the First World War with a series of international congresses involving participants from dozens of European, Asian, and American countries.[6]

As members of a field of research that emphasized the mind's independence from matter, psychical researchers self-consciously occupied a heterodox relation to what they termed "official science," describing their field as a study of phenomena that "lie on or outside the boundaries of recognized science."[7] Claiming the status of a science in their methods and attitudes, the practitioners nevertheless opposed themselves to the narrow and routinized practice of science that they saw developing around them. Emerging in a period when broad proclamations about the mastery of science and technology over nature were common, psychical researchers were quick to point out those facts that continued to elude scientific knowledge. By doing so, they sought to preserve the speculative character of the scientific enterprise by staking out an area of free inquiry in which existing scientific paradigms were undeniably inadequate.

If the field willingly adopted a marginal relationship to the established sciences, its core members—men like Frederic William Henry Myers in England, William James in America, Théodore Flournoy in Switzerland, Cesare

Lombroso in Italy, and Henri Bergson and Pierre Janet in France—were hardly foreigners to the scientific establishment they so often criticized. The great paradox of psychical research was that, while it maligned the stifling effects of "official science," many of its practitioners were members of the very faculties and scientific academies that this term presumably encompassed. These men nevertheless resented the silences that science, in its institutionalized form, seemed to impose on those anomalies that refused to fit its established paradigms. As men already respected for their individual contributions to their respective fields, psychical researchers would make their effort to sustain the heroic age of discovery in an era increasingly characterized by the regimentation and specialization of scientific work. William James would, for instance, note in a reference to anomalies ignored by official science: "Only the born geniuses let themselves be worried and fascinated by these outstanding exceptions . . . [y]our Galileos, Galvanis, Fresnels." In the meantime the "more passive disciples" would continue to look upon their science as a "closed and complete system of truth."[8] For scientists who refused to adopt this "passive" relation to knowledge, psychical research seemed to hold out the opportunity for creative new insights worthy of the adventurous spirit of science. For these researchers, this also meant taking on an ambivalent and uncertain relationship to what they took to be the institutional sources of scientific authority. The result was that, as Richard Brown has pointed out, psychical researchers "request[ed] admission into orthodox science with their left hand while rejecting it with their right."[9]

While opposed to the constraining effects of institutionalization, the figures who founded the field of psychical research nevertheless drew upon the great personal prestige that institutional recognition lent to their various efforts. Indeed, the attention directed toward psychical research had much to do with the presence of so many highly credentialed scholars in the field. While the reputations of these individuals tell us nothing about the objective value of their personal observations, the concentration of social capital does confirm the importance of mediumism to those elites who would otherwise wield great influence over the intellectual currents of their time. While these men sought to claim mediumism as an object of elite scientific study, the practice was ultimately disassociable from the popular, democratic circumstances at its origins. Even as prominent men of science claimed that mediumism was a legitimate object of study, the practices of table rapping, clairvoyance, spirit materializations, and telepathy would continue to bear strong associations with middle- and lower-middle-class religiosity. Just as this popular aspect tended to color attitudes toward psychical research in its own time, so too does it continue to confuse historical discussions of the field, which tend to equate psychical research with an assortment of presumably premodern and nonscientific practices like magic, mysticism, and occultism.[10] While psychical researchers were diligent in defending themselves from such associations, they were never entirely successful in doing so. Spiritists eagerly embraced the legitimizing aura of elite science by drawing parallels between their religious beliefs and the findings of psychical researchers. For their part, psychical researchers sometimes found it rhetorically useful to draw upon the legitimizing principles of democracy by making reference to the fact that the phenomena they studied had been witnessed by tens of thousands of amateur observers on numerous continents. Due to the antagonisms between psychical research and official science, they also found it useful on occasion to draw upon popular enthusiasm to procure material resources for their research. What was at issue in these transactions between the elite world of psychical research and the world of popular spiritism was not the question of what sort of phenomena it was proper for science to study or what questions it was permitted to ask. The question was, rather, by what distinction science claimed its special authority over public knowledge, given the democratic nature of modern society.

My examination of the scientific heterodoxy represented by psychical research proceeds on the assumption that a field of knowledge as general and far-reaching as "science" achieves its identity only in relation to that which it excludes, prohibits, and otherwise invokes to differentiate itself from competing systems of knowledge. In the nineteenth century such distinctions were more difficult to inscribe between the disciplines as science expanded into new areas, producing knowledge of objects that had formerly been deemed improper to a field dedicated to an objective study of nature. The most notable expansion in this respect was in those undertakings in which the human being's consciousness, beliefs, behavior, and patterns of association were deemed fully knowable objects of scientific inquiry. Scientific psychology, sociology, anthropology, and modern linguistics all arose in the last decades of the nineteenth century as part of this general effort in the sciences to produce socially useful knowledge about man.

In late nineteenth-century France this expansion of scientific knowledge was promoted as a central component of the ideology of the Third Republic not only because it offered a means of excising the supernatural surplus in man—the soul that had given the church its jurisdictional claims to worldly affairs—but, more importantly, because it provided secular society with a scientific basis by which human motives and conduct could be determined, accounted for, and accommodated within the republic's efforts to rationalize social forces and achieve a durable social peace. This approach became particularly relevant after the disastrous defeat of France by Prussia in 1870 and in the wake of the terrible fratricidal violence of the Paris Commune. While one event presented a political catastrophe for the French nation, the other marked a moral catastrophe for French republicanism. The survival of republican ideals lay not only in overcoming the monarchist electoral challenges posed by the "Government of Moral Order" but in finding more effective means of governing that might contain revolutionary expressions of liberty without making men less free. Established in the wake of the Second Empire and the Commune, the republic needed to find better ways of representing the interests of its citizens. Given the lessons of their recent past, sincere republicans could no longer look for reasonable expressions of popular sovereignty in the streets or at the ballot box. In place of these measures of public interest the Third Republic would offer the "daily plebiscite" of social peace, achieved by "modest empirical solutions" permitting government to found a social order not, as the monarchists proposed, on metaphysical illusions but rather on an improved scientific understanding of "man, his desires and needs."[11] Writing as an influential ideologue, Ernest Renan assumed that these desires and needs could not only be recognized and fulfilled but that they could also be used to reconcile republican faith in individual autonomy with the need to preserve social order. It was in the context of this project that Renan's call for government to "organize humanity scientifically" would resonate so deeply with the ideals of an entire generation of republican leaders.[12] For Renan, as for Paul Bert, Marcelin Berthelot, Jules Ferry, Léon Gambetta, Hippolyte Taine, and the other *savants* and politicians committed to the survival of republicanism in France, the sciences offered not only an understanding of immutable natural laws but also a set of universal moral imperatives. Awareness of these would come from the example provided by social elites (*les classes dirigeantes*) through a universal system of education designed to integrate and draw support from an emerging middle class (Gambetta's *nouvelles couches sociales*).[13] While conservatives like Maurice Barrès decried this growing class of knowledge producers as an "academic proletariat," progressive republicans saw the movement of lower-middle-class students into the academy and the professions as a sign of successful democratization.[14]

The scientific spirit of education in French primary and secondary schools was thus an essential part of the republic's efforts to combat traditional claims to authority that undermined the secular ideals of republicanism. The church was not, however, the only institution threatened by the new scientific faith.

Within the already secular domains of higher education, the expansion of science into fields like psychology posed an additional threat to the philosophical tradition that had serviced the liberal monarchy of the 1830s and 1840s. The "eclectic spiritualism" of Victor Cousin (not to be confused with the French term *spiritisme* or the Anglo-American Modern Spiritualism) would remain firmly entrenched in degree-granting institutions like the Sorbonne until the last decade of the nineteenth century, creating an obstacle to the expansion of scientific forms of knowledge into the area of psychology. Spiritualist philosophers had long made the study of "psychology" part of their field, but they meant by this term an introspective practice by which philosophers interrogated their own states of consciousness. As the academic accompaniment of the July Monarchy's doctrine of the *juste milieu,* Cousin's philosophy proved useful for most of the century by affirming the liberal principle of a unified and autonomous self. In the first decade of the Third Republic, however, the representative powers of Cousin's philosophy proved ultimately too narrow, and many scholars looked to scientific positivism for alternatives. By 1879 the idea of scientific psychology had taken up a position strong enough to present a real challenge to the followers of Cousin. Critics who disliked Cousin's methods because they lacked objectivity could point to the pioneering efforts of German psychologists like Gustav Theodor Fechner and Wilhelm Wundt and proclaim them a model for the future development of an experimentally based psychology in France.[15]

In the same span of years the rediscovery of provoked somnambulism and its legitimation as "hypnosis" presented French doctors and scientists with a means of provoking certain mental states and altering faculties like memory and sensitivity. With this renewed interest in what the eighteenth century had called "animal magnetism," French scientists and doctors began to encounter evidence of "occult" faculties of mind described by the ancient magnetists—such as clairvoyance and the transmission of thought. The encounter with these "supernormal" faculties subsequently led researchers to the investigation of mediums drawn from the popular religious practice that the French called *spiritisme.* In spiritism's "medium" French researchers found all of the characteristics that had interested them in hypnosis. The medium exhibited the same symptoms of involuntarism, automatism, and disaggregation that had been observed in the somnambulant state produced by hypnosis. The medium also evinced a great variety of supernormal faculties, which researchers described either by borrowing terminology directly from the literature on animal magnetism or by inventing an entirely new vocabulary. In the study of both somnambules and mediums French psychical researchers presented an ambitious agenda to the new psychology by pointing to instances in which the mind, rather than being determined by the body and its material environment, seemed to possess the inverse ability to influence and transform matter.

Emerging in the midst of enormous optimism about the potential of science to bring prosperity, national strength, and social peace, psychical research nevertheless reflected a deep ambivalence about the project of extending scientific methods into domains formally structured by nonscientific assumptions and methods of inquiry. Psychical research was, as Michel Pierssens has suggested, the product of a larger "crisis of anticipation" by which faith in scientific progress produced the expectation of a limitlessly expanding certainty.[16] The relationship between the forward movement of scientific knowledge and its goal of universality was classically paradoxical. As Claude Bernard would explain in his seminal 1865 work in physiology, *Introduction à l'étude de la médecine expérimentale* (Introduction to the Study of Experimental Medicine), "the intellectual conquest of man consists in diminishing and pushing back [*refouler*] indeterminism to the extent that he gains ground on determinism with the aid of the experimental method. This alone should satisfy his ambition because it is through this that he extends and will extend his mastery over nature." Bernard's optimism was, however, qualified by the admission that "we will certainly never attain absolute determinism in all things; man could no longer exist."[17] Science could thus satisfy its ambitions in increasing its mastery over nature while remaining secure in its faith that universal determinism would not compromise the existence of man as an autonomous entity within nature. Bernard was not, of course, embracing mystification as the means by which to defend man's freedom. While he accepted that the *unknown* would persist, he categorically rejected the heresy presented to science by the *unknowable:* "Our reason encompasses, scientifically, the determinate and the indeterminate, but . . . it cannot admit the *indeterminable,* for this would be only to admit the marvelous, the occult, the supernatural, which must be absolutely banished from all experimental science."[18]

Psychical researchers embraced Bernard's definition of science and thus internalized its basic paradox. Their faith in the expanding empire of science would lead them to propose that scientific methods might unravel the occult mechanisms of mediumism. On the other hand, they, like Bernard, worried about what the universal determinism proposed by science implied for the freedom of man. In particular, the great concern of psychical researchers was what this projected scientific mastery of nature implied for the creative nature of the scientist. Confronted by the prospect of a closing scientific frontier and a corresponding loss of creative agency, psychical researchers energetically highlighted those indeterminacies revealed by mediumism and somnambulism. Partaking of the optimism expressed by Bernard and others, psychical researchers understandably assumed that the unknown aspects of mediumism were the result of a lack in the positive content of knowledge that could be resolved by more systematic efforts and refined methods. While the explicit goal of psychical research was to explore these spaces still virgin to science, to conquer and colonize them with scientific reason, the effect was quite the opposite. The ambivalences of the field toward the project described by Bernard were to be revealed in the fact that psychical research simply confirmed the mystery surrounding mediumism in promising to dispel it.

While individual scientists formed opinions about these phenomena, no consensus ever developed among either psychical researchers or the scientific community as a whole as to their causes or mechanisms. Without attempting to foreclose the question, it seems unlikely that the facts accumulated by this field will find explanation in the work of its inheritors in the field of parapsychology. Few in number and even more marginalized in their efforts, parapsychologists have, in any event, largely turned away from the spectacular phenomena of mediumism and focused their interest on objects of study more adaptable to the routines of laboratory science.[19] What influence the findings of parapsychologists will ultimately have on our general knowledge of the world, no one can be sure. What is certain is that the history of this field, like the history of science in general, is a story with no predetermined trajectory and no definitive ending.

This is not to say that psychical research was without discoveries. Indeed, as part of a general movement in late nineteenth-century psychology, psychical research did give rise to one persistent and indisputable fact—that of its own uncertainty. While the types of uncertainty varied, the cause of this uncertainty derived from the fact that, whatever form they took or whatever specific methods they employed, the experiments of psychical research depended on the medium to produce the phenomena that formed the object of study. As a result, the question of objective cause thus devolved into a question of subjective intent in which both the mediums and those who observed them were implicated. Fraud and self-deception were always a possibility. Researchers hoped to eliminate these causes of error by using ever more sophisticated means of controlling mediums and ever more accurate methods of recording the phenomena they produced. The researchers' optimism proved misplaced. Not only were they unable to discount the possibility of fraud on the part of their subjects, but they also had to concede the possible errors of their own perceptions and judgments in moments of fatigue and inattention. Memory proved another pitfall, as did efforts to transcribe experiences into narrative accounts. Finally, there was the possibility of hallucinatory autosuggestion, which contributed to doubts both about what was witnessed and about the effectiveness of the controls imposed on the medium. At the center of these doubts was a subjectivity that the techniques of experimental science failed to account for. As Henri Bergson would point out in his 1913 presidential address to the Society for Psychical Research, "It is the essence of the things of the mind not to lend themselves to measurement."[20]

None of these doubts were, however, considered fatal to the enterprise of psychical research. For nearly three decades French researchers enterprisingly devoted themselves to devising better means of isolating subjective causes in the hopes of identifying objective ones. In their efforts to do so they found that the source of doubt was simply displaced elsewhere. Even when scientists were convinced that both fraud on the part of the medium and errors of observation on the part of the researcher could be eliminated from all consideration, those who had no direct part in the experiments—the large public that closely followed the researchers' published accounts—found themselves inclined to question the motives of those who were. Given that most researchers felt themselves to be working in the interest of public understanding, popular disbelief in the sincerity and accuracy of their observations proved devastating. This popular skepticism persisted even in cases involving the most reputable mediums and the most esteemed scientists. In other words, regardless of the improvements made in the procedures of control and observation or the standing of the participants, uncertainty continued and continues to surround their experiments. If doubt was the most decisive finding of these experiments, most psychical researchers would fail to recognize it as such. It remained for most of them a problem to be overcome and not a positive discovery in its own right.

The mystery of mediumism proved, in the end, to be less a borderland into which scientific knowledge might successfully penetrate than an internal enigma that, in refusing to be rendered intelligible, had the paradoxical effect of sustaining the general field of knowledge. As the psychoanalyst Olivier Flournoy would note in reference to the role played in the field by his grandfather Théodore, psychical research aimed not so much at the achievement of a new "scientific era but paradoxically the preservation of the celestial habitations. It is a little like the way in which today we endeavor in the name of science to create here and there natural preserves, national parks, to combat the predatory effects of science itself."[21] The point of comparison evoked by Olivier Flournoy is of course the one presented by his own field of psychoanalysis, which, beginning with a similar collection of late nineteenth-century psychological bric-a-brac, transformed the doubts that Freud had about the representative qualities of hysterical discourses into a fully articulated theory of the subjective uncertainty. In contrast to psychical researchers who professed the doctrine of determinacy, psychoanalysis argued that subjectivity was to be found in an agency of uncertainty, which was revealed in the distortions of dreams, lapses of memory, and slips of the tongue. While psychical researchers sought to minimize and control the influences of such representational errors, the techniques of psychoanalysis allowed them to proliferate and made them the very material upon which the analysis was to work. The impasse that psychical research reached in its inability to untangle objective causes from subjective motivations was in psychoanalysis overcome by a not-too-scientific reconceptualization of the relation of indeterminacy to knowledge in which the failure to achieve certainty was regarded not simply as an irregularity within a particular system of representation but as a symptom of its true inner working. In psychical research one finds nothing like the founding instance of doubt ("I no longer believe in my neurotica") that transformed a quest to discover the traumatic historical event at the origin of hysterical symptoms into a question about the unconscious relations between the investigator and the object of his research.[22] In shifting his attention from the objective content of his patients' speech to the circumstances of its enunciation, Freud would set his field at odds with the general ambitions of scientific psychology and, eventually, with the very definition of science itself. If, as his grandson argues, Théodore Flournoy embraced the spirit of exact science in order to preserve "celestial habitations," Freud would, by contrast, make recourse to the "mythology" of the drives ("magnificent in their indefiniteness") to build for psychoanalysis a kingdom of a very worldly nature.[23]

This realm would not, however, be easily established on French soil. The efforts of Freud's early francophone disciples to gather a community of psychoanalysts in France would not see any great success until the 1920s. In the meantime, the heterodoxy of psychical research, with its combined affirmation of determinacy and preservation of uncertainty, would prove a much better complement to the universalist ambitions of French science. It was not until the end of the First World War that the optimism once expressed by men like Renan would begin to falter amidst widespread doubts about the future of French civilization and its rational, scientific heritage. While efforts to promote psychical research in the years immediately following this catastrophe were momentarily buoyed by the appeal that mediumism held for those millions seeking hope and redemption from their losses, French psychical research would within a matter of years find itself stalemated by counterattacks from the realms of official science and popular skepticism. Its momentum lost, the field would gradually diminish from public view after the mid-1920s. For most of the twentieth century, psychical research and its inheritors would find themselves isolated from the general trends in French thought that would, by the 1930s, give genuine consideration to the implications of the psychoanalytic unconscious.

1

From Religious Enthusiasm to Reluctant Science

Psychical Research, 1848–1882

On 29 May 1853 the famed physicist François Arago submitted a letter to the assembled body of the French scientific elite reporting a most unusual phenomenon. The letter, written by the celebrated rail and bridge engineer Marc Seguin, began with a reference to the astonishing rumors then circulating throughout Paris of mundane household objects being moved by a mysterious invisible force. Upon first hearing them, Seguin admitted that the rumors seemed "so extraordinary and so inconceivable that I did not hesitate in rejecting them." Seguin's position changed radically after he conducted a series of personal investigations in the course of which he found himself so "convinced by the evidence" that he felt it "necessary" to bring the attention of the Académie des Sciences to bear on this "serious matter."[1]

Several days earlier, Seguin, his cousin Eugène de Montgolfier, and a small group of their associates followed the procedure that was becoming routine throughout Parisian salons of forming a "human chain" while standing around a small wooden table slightly over a meter high and less than a meter across. Each participant laid his or her fingertips lightly on the table's surface and touched the small finger of each hand to the corresponding finger of his or her neighbor to each side. The table, weighing about three kilograms, then began tipping, turning in place, and sliding from one end of the apartment to the other. These movements corresponded to verbal commands issued aloud by members of the chain. After several hours of experimentation, the group discovered that even with a single person (Montgolfier) "directing" it, the table continued to perambulate about the room with great energy across the rough parquet. Seguin found he could not interrupt the table in its movements even when he applied enough force to dislodge one of its legs. "All the while M. de Montgolfier only lightly touched the table's surface with the tips of his fingers."[2]

Seguin's letter, reproduced in the printed account of the academy's weekly proceedings, was just one of many that French readers would have encountered in the spring of 1853 as reports of *tables tournantes* and *tables parlantes* caught the attention of France's popular press and scientific elites. Seguin's account was, in many respects, quite typical. Expressing varying degrees of curiosity and disbelief, participants would gather around a small table (or, alternatively, a hat, a vase, or a sewing basket) and place their hands on the uppermost surface of the object with no obvious points of leverage. The séances often started slowly with little activity in the first ten or fifteen minutes, and many attempts might have to be made to achieve the correct configuration of the chain by changing the positions of the participants. A successful séance was marked by the movements of the table, which tipped, turned, and lifted partially or even entirely from the floor—sometimes, it was reported, without any contact whatsoever.

More surprising than the simple movements of the tables was their apparent intelligence. The tables not only responded to verbal commands but also answered questions with an astonishing degree of accuracy. Over the long history of such séances this feature proved the most convincing to skeptics. The tables, which most often communicated in the form of audible knocks interpreted through a prearranged code, could accurately convey the time of day, indicate the first letter or word from the page of a book selected at random, guess the participants' ages, approximate the amounts of their personal fortunes, tell the number of their siblings or children, answer questions about their health problems, or even, it seemed, read their unspoken thoughts. Other early adepts of the tables improvised other methods of communication; for example, a pencil inserted through the bottom of an upside-down sewing basket would trace out responses to their queries directly onto a piece of paper.[3] The *planchette,* a device in which a moving indicator pointed to letters of the alphabet arrayed across the table's surface, also proved popular. Eventually, séance enthusiasts began to attribute a prominent role to a single individual in the group, the medium, who proved particularly adept at inciting responses from the table. Many mediums used the technique of automatic writing, in which they took the pencil directly in hand and wrote responses to the questions posed onto a piece of paper. Some used direct voice by simply speaking the responses. While many saw these activities as a harmless diversion, comparable to other popular parlor games like the mind-reading game called Cumberlandism, others insisted on the seriousness of the tables, shaken as they were by their inability to assimilate the facts of the séances into a more general understanding of the world.

For some, like Seguin, the phenomenon of the turning table indicated not some supernatural influence but rather a mysterious force of nature comparable to other unseen forces like those produced by electricity and magnetism. Seguin's report speculated, for instance, that the phenomenon represented an "electricity of a particular nature," a tactic clearly designed to appeal to Arago, who, seven years earlier, had been engaged in a widely discussed investigation of Angelique Cottin, the *fille électrique* of Normandy who appeared to have the ability to move objects without touching them. Having found no positive indications of an electrical force in the simple-minded Angelique, Arago would refuse to show any interest in Seguin's mysterious electrical force and would dismiss Seguin's account by making reference to a physiological phenomenon in which muscular activity could remain imperceptible to the subjects exerting it and still move large objects when many such efforts were coordinated with one another.

Cynics responding to the sudden craze for table turning would find a less technical explanation by reaffirming Seguin's initial suspicions of charlatanism. The famed wit Honoré Daumier would, for instance, caricature the turning tables as a cheap parlor trick, the puerile pastime of a bored bourgeoisie or a stratagem by which young rakes permitted themselves to caress the hands of other men's wives in dimly lit rooms.[4] Daumier's series of drawings, entitled *fluidomanie,* emphasized the presumed charlatanism of the turning tables by invoking the disreputed practice of animal magnetism, which had similarly swept through Paris seventy-five years earlier only to be refuted by the Académie Royale des Sciences. Rather than discrediting table turning, however, the reference to the ideas that the Austrian physician Franz Anton Mesmer had introduced to France in the twilight years of the great Age of Reason only reproduced the uncertainties that had continued to surround Mesmer's claims. Indeed, adepts of the 1853 vogue in table turning embraced the naturalistic language of "fluid" as an effort to legitimize their enthusiasms. If Seguin saw in the gyrations of his *guéridon* the effects of "electricity," this was only to dissimulate the fact that enthusiasts elsewhere were invoking the proscribed theories of Mesmer and his "universal fluid."

Echoes of Animal Magnetism

If the tables of 1853 were firmly rooted in their own social and political moment, practitioners nevertheless sought to understand their experiences in terms provided by the controversies of the past. What seemed a natural lineage was, in actuality, an echo, one that framed table turning's challenge to orthodoxy in terms that reproduced the controversies surrounding Mesmer's arrival in Paris in 1778. In spite of the opposition it inspired, Mesmer's theory of animal magnetism was perfectly tailored to the ideals of his age, describing as it did a universe in which humans were literally immersed in an all-encompassing flux of nature. Just as the gravitational pull described by Newton influenced the tides, the universal fluid described by Mesmer produced, it was claimed, its own effects in the human organism. Systematically exposed to a magnetism contained and directed by Mesmer himself, the physician's fashionable patients found their various physical and nervous ailments alleviated. By touching a patient's arms and abdomen in what were called "passes," Mesmer claimed an ability to redirect the magnetic fluid in his patients' bodies, provoking *crises,* which some compared to epileptic fits. He also devised a more efficient and very profitable method for treating large groups by charging a large, enclosed tub with the healing fluid. Seated around this *baquet,* patients applied protruding iron rods to locations on their bodies while listening to the ethereal sounds of a glass armonica playing in the background. It was both the scandalous nature of Mesmer's cure (which often involved inducing convulsive states in young aristocratic women) and his claim that animal magnetism was a property of nature linking living beings to the celestial order that drew the attention of the gatekeepers of scientific legitimacy in Paris. In 1784 the Académie Royale des Sciences organized a commission to test the phenomenon as demonstrated by Mesmer's adept, Charles Deslon. Chaired by Benjamin Franklin (international expert on natural "fluids") and composed of notables such as Antoine Lavoisier, Jean d'Arcet, Jean Sylvain Bailly, and Joseph-Ignace Guillotin, the body ruled that the invisible fluid claimed by Mesmer did not exist and that the *crises* brought about by his cures were simply due to the effects of imagination, imitation, and the intimate touching occasioned by the magnetic passes.[5] In the phenomenon of animal magnetism, the late Enlightenment acknowledged an exception to what the French Revolution would later enshrine as the abstract individual.[6] In the Franklin commission's secret report to the king this individual was still very much in possession of his or her various attributes, including those of his or her sex. The woman, the report noted, is always magnetized by a man: "The relations then established are no doubt those of a patient toward her doctor, but this doctor is a man; whatever the nature of the illness, it does not divest us of our own sex, nor does it entirely remove us from the power of the other sex."[7] It was, by this account, the sexualized nature of both the patient and her doctor that would deny the disinterestedness required for making public representations of fact.

Although Mesmer would leave Paris the following year, the Franklin commission's verdict hardly marked the end of his influence in France. Indeed, the doctrine and practice of mesmerism would continue to spread in the years following the academy's rebuke. Most students of the history of mesmerism attribute its lasting influence in France to the writings and teachings of the distinguished French nobleman Amand-Marc-Jacques de Chastenet, marquis de Puységur.[8] Puységur, who had learned of Mesmer's healing arts through his elder brother, began experimenting with animal magnetism at his sprawling estate in the northeast of France. Treating the peasants in his service, the marquis discovered that, instead of Mesmer's convulsive *crises,* his magnetic passes produced a strange sleeplike state, which he called *somnambulism.* Not only did Puységur's subjects display in this state unusual levels of attention and bodily discipline, they also seemed to possess an extraordinary capacity of perception not accounted for among the functions of the normal physical senses. Dubbed *clairvoyance,* this capacity seemed to allow Puységur's somnambules to see through opaque objects (including their own bodies), read their magnetizer's thoughts, and even foretell future and distant events. When the trance was broken, the somnambule lost all recollection of what had transpired. Puységur's teachings marked what Anne Harrington has described as a Romantic turn in the history of animal magnetism by effectively downgrading the importance of Mesmer's impersonal "fluid" and agitated *crises* and emphasizing the interpersonal "rapport" between the magnetizer and his subjects and a calming state of half-sleep.[9] For peasants who gathered around the elm tree that Puységur magnetized near his estate in Buzancy, animal magnetism reinstated a mild and provident version of the feudal dependencies that were to be so fundamentally shaken by the social and political crises of late eighteenth-century France. It is not surprising that it was Puységur's pastoral and quasi-mystical version of mesmerism that would move into the foreground during postrevolutionary efforts to restore the ancient terms of legitimacy to the social order.[10]

While still heterodox and in many cases clandestine, mesmerism did indeed flourish in the early decades of the nineteenth century, particularly among members of France's medical community for whom it conveniently filled a number of gaps in the underdeveloped science and techniques of medicine. This continued enthusiasm would bring another round of investigations in 1825 under the auspices of the Académie Nationale de Médecine. Proponents of these studies argued that the concepts associated with the practice had evolved since the Franklin commission had issued its report. Few practitioners still claimed the existence of the pervasive natural fluid and instead emphasized Puységur's notion of rapport, now understood mostly in psychological terms. Observers of this phenomenon argued that it did in fact produce discernible psychological and physiological changes and thus deserved thorough study by medical science.[11] Henri-Marie Husson's report, delivered to the Académie Nationale de Médecine in 1831, found positive evidence of changes in pulse, respiration, levels of physical sensitivity, memory, levels of strength and even of clairvoyance, internal sight, and prevision.[12] Perhaps even more important to the development of psychology, the report rhetorically reframed the role of imagination, seen by the 1784 commission as a cause to dismiss Mesmer's claims, as an element influencing the human organism and thus worthy of scientific attention. While Husson, chief of services at the Hôtel-Dieu, had hoped to legitimize the study of somnambulism, his report ultimately failed to receive the support of the academy, which, for its part, continued to undermine the claims made of the phenomenon by emphasizing those aspects most difficult to prove. The series of studies initiated by the academy in 1837, for instance, tested primarily for the capacities of clairvoyance and double sight. These trials, conducted in connection with the Prix Burdin (a three-thousand-franc reward for anyone who could demonstrate these abilities), resulted in repeated failures.[13] By 1840 communications to the Académie des Sciences dealing with animal magnetism were formally prohibited. The practice itself would, however, continue in Paris and several regional cities, drawing practitioners from the world of medicine. With the turning tables, "magnetic" phenomena would return in force to the popular imagination but in a form that was quickly to depart from the exclusively naturalistic bent it had inherited from Mesmer. In 1853 the *tables parlantes* spoke not of fluids but of souls.

The Development of Spiritism in France

If the eighteenth-century doctrine had emphasized the impersonal, mechanistic forces of nature in tribute to Newton, with the sea change in European thought marked by Romanticism, the nineteenth century would increasingly emphasize and even celebrate the creative agency of the spirit. Practitioners of magnetism argued that the altered states of consciousness produced by somnambulism put the subject into communication with an obscure intelligence and that it was only this fact that could explain the action of the magnetist's unspoken will on the subject. Spiritualist magnetists argued that such transformations could only be regarded as the direct influence of one mind on another.[14] Charles Fourier suggested that what mesmerism demonstrated was an "ultrahuman" faculty permitting communication between souls, a fact that seemed confirmed when he returned during an 1853 séance to communicate with his followers sixteen years after his death.[15] By 1847 the somnambule Adèle Maginot was facilitating regular dialogues between her magnetist, Alphonse Cahagnet, and the spirit of the eighteenth-century scientist and mystic Emanuel Swedenborg.[16]

These ideas would also extend to the United States, then in the midst of its own efforts—cultural and spiritual—to come to terms with the transformations brought by economic and social modernity. Just as Fourier's utopian ideas would find avid followers *outre-mer,* so too would Puységur's influence be felt across the Atlantic. His acolyte, Charles Poyen, would personally bring news of somnambulism to New England during an 1836 tour and gather a number of important followers. One such adept, J. Stanley Grimes, would play a decisive role in the intermingling of somnambulism and American religious thought by demonstrating the phenomenon to a young Andrew Jackson Davis, later to become famous as the Poughkeepsie Seer. Davis's trance writings serve as an important precursor to the 1848 spirit rappings of the Fox sisters of Hydesville, New York.[17] Situated in what historian Whitney Cross would later dub the "burned-over district" of western New York, the circumstances surrounding the Foxes seemed ripe for the kind of religious populism represented by their spirit communications.[18] The region had for decades played host to a variety of experimental doctrines, social reform movements, and religious enthusiasms and, through itinerant lecturers like Poyen, was already well versed in the doctrines of mesmerism.[19] Although Margaret, age fourteen, and Kate, twelve, were unlikely to have been schooled in these teachings, others around them undoubtedly were, a fact that lent intellectual interest to what might have otherwise been readily dismissed as an adolescent prank.

Awakened by rapping noises in the bedroom where the family slept together, the Fox sisters discovered that they could provoke the rapping by clapping their hands or by asking simple questions. Using a rudimentary code, it was determined that the sounds were produced by the spirit of an itinerant peddler who had been murdered and buried in the house prior to the Foxes' arrival in Hydesville. It became clear that Margaret and Kate were key elements in the rappings after the girls moved to their sister Leah Fish's home in Rochester and the phenomenon recommenced there. The notoriety garnered by press accounts of their performances at Corinthian Hall in Rochester led the sisters to New York City for a series of exhibitions. By the end of their visit to New York the Fox sisters had established themselves as the first professional mediums in what was to become, in a matter of months, a new religious movement dubbed Modern Spiritualism.

Some argued that it was this American practice that was imported to France as the *tables tournantes* of 1853. While some would continue to mark this episode as a revival of the "fluidomania" inspired by the natural philosophy of eighteenth-century mesmerism, others saw the pernicious influence that American religious freedom was having on French culture. For Parisians who seemed not immediately to notice that they were engaged in a discourse with spirits, the newspaper *Le Siècle* felt obliged to draw their attention to happenings in the New World, noting that "while Parisians . . . place their hands on the gueridon and marvel at the effects of the magnetic fluid on simple material objects, Americans invoke the dead and engage in familiar conversation with spirits . . . a sort of religious sect, of which the principal purpose is the invocation of souls that reveal themselves to man in the form of rapping spirits."[20] Another account from later in the year highlighted the danger of French naïveté regarding the practice, noting that "Europe only gradually learned that these marvels, almost unheard of for her, which passed before her eyes on a daily basis, were nothing more than a feeble emanation of other marvels, quite noteworthy and ominous, that, for five years, have troubled the most enlightened people of America."[21] The ominous aspect was to be found in French attitudes to what Tocqueville had called the "spiritual insanity" of American life, obviously of great concern to those pledged to defending traditional forms of religiosity and spiritual authority in France.[22] What was most at issue in these warnings were the populist implications of American spiritualism. These conflicted not only with the principles of organized religion but also with those of the organized mesmerist movement in France, which saw the spirit communications as dangerously unorthodox. As John Warne Monroe has noted, the belief that the actions of the turning tables was due to the influence of otherworldly spirits caused a significant rift among theorists and practitioners of animal magnetism in the 1850s.[23] Thus, even as mesmerism had been publicly ridiculed and officially rebuked, mesmerists would in turn denounce spirit rapping as too popular and undisciplined. Among other things, mesmerists were disturbed by the comparative level of autonomy that mediums enjoyed in comparison to their preferred instrument, the somnambule.

For French observers, the great threat of the Fox sisters' practice, and the source of its popular appeal, seems to have been its relative simplicity and lack of philosophical pretension. Spirit rapping placed into evidence the raps themselves, which invited, by their very form, verification through firsthand observation.[24] Summarizing the forty-year history of the international spiritist movement in an 1892 essay, the psychologist Pierre Janet would emphasize the power of its simplicity in drawing popular adherence. "Spiritist beliefs," he argued, "certainly wouldn't have developed with such rapidity if they hadn't been supported, at least in the beginning, by a few easily repeated observations sufficiently true to convince the incredulous."[25]

While in its empiricism the practice explicitly mimicked scientific forms of knowledge, in its populism it questioned an older form of scientific authority rooted in elite ideals of social respectability. It also countered a newly emerging ideal of science based on the insulated and exclusive space of the experimental laboratory. Implicit in the challenge of spirit rapping was a civic ideal that found its basic pattern in post-Jacksonian American democracy, in which legitimacy was based less on the promise of elite expertise than on widespread participation. Table turning required neither any special training nor any apparatus aside from those available in any ordinary domestic setting. All that was required was a group of curious participants willing to testify to the evidence of their senses. The production of the phenomenon involved the active participation of every member of the circle, each of whom had the right to pose questions to the table and shared in the task of dictation and interpretation.[26] The importance or validity of the responses was measured by the members of the circle in open discussion, and no one person wielded authority over the interpretation of the responses.[27] In America spiritualism was perfectly adapted to traditions of antielitism and intellectual self-reliance, by virtue of which, as the historian Henri Ellenberger has noted, "every man claimed the right to think for himself and used this right with more vigor and freshness than intellectual discipline."[28] French adepts of the tables clearly hoped to capture some of this spirit in their séances.

If American spiritualism was the product of "freedom's ferment," the expression of this democratic impulse was, however, unlikely to be reflected in political reality in France during the spring of 1853, given the notorious police apparatus of Napoleon III's Second Empire.[29] Historians have argued that in this setting spiritism offered a viable, if ultimately disempowered, expression of dissent rather than a truly antiauthoritarian practice. While the real exercise of freedom became impossible during the first decade of the repressive Second Empire, political dissenters were still inclined, as Régis Ladous has argued, to "play at being free." Ladous contends that the banquets of 1848 had become the séances of 1853.[30] Skeptical observers of the craze would go even further, cynically suggesting that the sudden craze for table turning was actively encouraged by the "French police, who want to distract the public attention from the shamefulness of the government."[31] In fact, during the period of the Second Empire the regime of Napoleon III mostly left practitioners free to develop the doctrine of spiritism in private and even extended, in recognition of their apolitical nature, official recognition to the spiritist organizations that would develop by the end of the decade.

If the state saw the séances as innocuous, not all French conservatives were convinced that they were harmless. For France's Catholic leaders, spiritism represented a dangerous new form of liberty that threatened the spiritual protection offered by the church and its teachings. Those who conversed with spirits through the tables were, they argued, easily deceived as to the meaning and nature of the communications. In a pamphlet from May 1853 Eugène Panon Desbassayns, comte de Richemont, writing simply as *un catholique,* perceived the spiritual danger in table turning by identifying its relationship to the Protestantism widely practiced in America, "the nation where," he cautioned, "liberty reigns so limitlessly."[32] Already in America, Desbassayns continued, "the enemy is in place, and in a Protestant country where the principle of authority doesn't exist, the consequences are inestimable."[33] The message from the other side of the Atlantic was clear: "The truth is that, although a certain number of them call themselves Christians, the obvious goal of these spiritualists . . . is to destroy all of the Christian sects, the diverse dogmas of which are treated indifferently as embarrassing superstitions."[34] The problem for Desbassayns was not simply the importation of American pluralism but the increasing difficulty that the church in France, once "the sole depository of truth," had in making itself understood and obeyed.[35]

If the turning tables did not exactly march in the streets, the spiritist movement in France did offer terrain to reformist and utopian thinking that drew upon the traditions of socialism and republicanism. As an organized movement, spiritism also promoted a philosophical system that emphasized moral and intellectual self-improvement. As Lynn Sharp points out, the doctrine of reincarnation, which would become central to French spiritism and distinguish it from its Anglo-American counterparts, drew heavily upon the doctrines of the early French socialists Jean Reynaud and Pierre Leroux.[36] In emphasizing the egalitarian spirit of the political Left, spiritism attracted followers not only from the educated bourgeoisie but also from the upper echelons of the working classes, including artisans and skilled workers. This was especially true in the industrial cities like Lyon, where spiritist organizations tended to manifest themselves as workers' mutual aid societies.[37] Spiritism also extended the Left's suspicion of the influence of Catholicism in France and specifically adopted the positivistic approach to knowledge that characterized the post-1848 era in France.[38] Spiritism would in essence proclaim itself a scientific faith. In response to the dilemma of individualism sponsored by republican doctrine, spiritism offered a cosmological system that emphasized equality and that placed spirits into communion with one another. Spiritism's doctrine of a future life emphasized social responsibility by making individuals answerable to their peers and to their future selves. In response to the socialist discourses that sought to alter a bourgeois social order rooted in the sanctity of private lives and property, spiritism emphasized the emotional bonds of the family as the best guarantor of individual moral development.

The individual most responsible for transforming table rapping into a fully articulated science of revelation and moral creed was Allan Kardec. Born Hippolyte Léon Denizard Rivail, Kardec emerged from a well-known family of jurists and lawyers from Lyon. Traveling to Paris as an educator schooled in the principles of Jean-Jacques Rousseau, Rivail earned a living writing theoretical works on pedagogy as well as practical guides for teaching grammar, spelling, and arithmetic.[39] He interested himself in magnetism and phrenology and in 1854 was introduced to spiritism by a group of associates that included the dramatist Victorien Sardou. From these séances Rivail was transformed into "Allan Kardec" by a spirit revelation of his former life as a Celtic druid.

In 1857, only four years after the initial eruption of table turning in France, Kardec published the hugely successful spiritist treatise *Le Livre des esprits* and, with it, effectively launched the organized spirit movement in France.[40] Derived from séance transcripts given to him by Sardou and the editor Pierre-Paul Didier, Kardec's book presented what would become the basic tenets of French spiritism. These revolved principally around the concept of a "perispirit," a physical fluidic envelope that acted as an intermediate substance between the material and spiritual natures of the human being. The perispirit permitted the spirit to maintain material existence after the death of the body, a fact that accounted for the ability of souls to interact with physical objects in their worldly communications. Once disincarnate, the spirit progressed to a higher state to await its next incarnation. Through reincarnation, the spirit was afforded an opportunity to continue its progress, which moved it closer to moral perfection, represented by God.[41]

While Kardec acknowledged the lineage of spiritism from ancient religions, his theories did not entail a rejection of the fundaments of Christian belief. He described his writings as simply another revelation in line with those recorded by the Judeo-Christian tradition and argued that the compatibility of spiritism with Christianity was evidenced by the numerous instances of mediumship and spirit phenomena in the Bible. In spite of the censure imposed on his teachings by the Catholic hierarchy, Kardec's ideas were formulated in close association with existing forms of Christian piety.[42] Spiritist religiosity was realized by the introduction of ritual and prayer into the spiritist gathering, and many French spiritists continued to describe themselves as Catholics even if they disputed points of Catholic dogma.[43]

Kardec also presented spiritism as a decidedly modern practice appropriate to an age of science and reason. Just as science had progressed by seeking causes in nature formerly characterized as magical or mystical, so too had religion evolved through the investigation of what Kardec deemed the natural characteristics of the spirit. Mediumism, stripped of its magical or diabolical import, could be understood as a natural potential possessed by all human beings.[44]

To critics who would see spiritism as only another form of mysticism derived from religious belief, spiritists responded in terms that refused the distinction between science and religion. Generally averse to the representation of nature as an agglomeration of impersonal mechanical forces, spiritists were nevertheless inclined to argue that the events witnessed in the séances were the product of natural phenomena. What some looked on as the "supernatural" was, from this perspective, simply a force of nature that had yet to be properly understood. Spiritism thus claimed to reintegrate the elements of science and religion with experimental proof of the soul's survival of bodily death. If Kardec characterized spiritism as "scientific," he was also careful to qualify his use of this term with the understanding that scientific knowledge was not restricted to descriptions of the material world and could, in fact, respond to questions of moral or metaphysical importance. This was not to say that the spirit world was immaterial in the way that philosophy and religion had presented it. Rather, in Kardec's understanding, something was not necessarily either material or not but could in fact present differing degrees of materiality.[45] In short, by joining the mundane to the transcendent, spiritists developed a strategy for refusing both the moral bankruptcy of materialism and the dogmatic mystifications of religion. Spiritists thus found themselves among those who, although enthusiastic about the promise of science, were wary of the ways in which it threatened to undermine moral concepts rooted in religious belief.

Kardec's *Le Livre des esprits* was reprinted in revised form in 1857 and would go into more than twenty editions, becoming the standard work of reference for French spiritists to the present day.[46] His monthly journal *La Revue Spirite,* appearing in January 1858, would similarly help in solidifying the foundations of the new religion, which would continue to benefit throughout the 1860s from the expansion of literacy and the appearance of dozens of new books and periodicals on the subject. In 1867 the *Catalogue général de la librairie française depuis 1840* listed 123 titles under the topic heading "Spiritisme," a number that may be put into perspective by comparing it to the 107 titles listed under "Socialisme" produced in the same period.[47] In April 1858 Kardec instituted the first regularly convening spiritist society, the Société Parisienne des Études Spirites, giving spiritism an institutional basis. Although he wielded great influence over French spiritism through the organization, in his writing Kardec continued to emphasize the democratic principles of the movement, and, in fact, spiritism would remain a decentralized practice.[48] The spiritist circle composed of perhaps four to twenty-five people would remain the basic unit of organization.[49] The effect was that spiritism never achieved the unity of belief that characterized other religions. In the late 1880s it could still be described as "complete cacophony," a movement characterized by disagreement and discord.[50] Yet Kardec's influence in the movement was far from negligible, and, in fact, provided spiritism with its greatest intellectual leader. The hundreds of followers that gathered each year at Kardec's grave at Père-Lachaise to mark the anniversary of his death would find a persistent reminder of French spiritism's most influential doctrine inscribed high upon the dolmenlike monument: "To be born, to die, to be reborn again and endlessly progress, such is the law."[51]

If spiritism stated that progress was an inevitable feature of nature, it also encouraged moral and intellectual progress through the applied effort of individuals. Spiritism's emphasis on literacy extended, in a form designed for an increasingly popular audience, the print culture of the Enlightenment with its constitution of a "public" and its institutionalization of human thought in the disembodied language of the printed word.[52] Spiritists valued and emphasized the edifying effects of knowledge and filled the pages of their publications with dialogues involving questions of great philosophical importance. Literacy was central to the rituals of spiritism. The rapping of tables offered only the most primitive form of expression in an idiom that, in its similarities to Samuel Morse's code, was also decidedly modern in its import. Through such methods spiritism, like electric telegraphy and the daily newspaper, served to erase distances (telepathy was another faculty common among spiritualist mediums) and create a sense of community with the beyond. As a modern form of communication, spiritism went further by eliding the temporal remove dividing past from present and drawing into this community voices whose only presence prior to the advent of table rapping had been in the dusty pages of books written long ago.

For members of the popular classes, spiritism's two-way communication offered a means of mobilizing resources of cultural value normally out of reach. The spirits of departed cultural elites who visited the séances provided models for self-improvement by demonstrating the durable social value and individual pleasure afforded by a cultivated self. This prospect was undoubtedly appealing to those social groups that were particularly sensitive to the perishable nature of their accumulated "capital." Pierre Bourdieu's description of a "cultural capital" that "presupposes embodiment" and that "cannot be accumulated beyond the appropriating capacities of the individual agent" was mitigated by a doctrine that presumed a life that continues beyond death or renews itself through reincarnation.[53] The doctrine thus provided a sense of compensation to individuals who, in accepting the principle of progress implicit in self-improvement, also feared that their share in the knowledge produced by a progressing humanity would remain incomplete. In his *Legitimacy of the Modern Age* Hans Blumenberg has suggested that such notions of immortality in an otherwise secular era offered an essential means of coping with the "knowledge drive" that, for Feuerbach, distinguished this period of history from those preceding it. Manifest in individual life as a moral injunction to suspend personal gratification in the pursuit of a social good, the terms of this knowledge drive also cruelly promised to deny individuals access to its object. Increasing degrees of specialization within the social production of knowledge and the incomplete nature of the project of accumulation meant that mortal, embodied individuals were required to bequeath the products of their labors to future generations without being able to enjoy the full benefits of those products. Spiritism's communications with the spirit world and promise of a future life offered one type of solution to this dilemma both by giving individuals direct access to the accumulated wisdom of the ages and by ensuring that they would be around in future lives to enjoy whatever benefits might accrue as a result of their contributions to this wealth of knowledge. In these forms spiritism facilitated an exchange of values between the social and the personal, public and private, and the individual and the collective by permitting universal benefits to accrue from isolated labors and, conversely, by allowing individuals future access to the social product in its entirety by eliminating the temporal limits of an embodied life.

Intimate Spirits

The most obvious indication of the ways in which spiritism mediated between these worlds is evident in the physical space that served as the site of its most important ritual. While open in their reproducible, empirical, and democratic nature, spiritism's séances were, by virtue of their usual location in the domestic salon, semiprivate affairs, and, given the restrictions placed on political expression throughout the 1850s, this location offered a protected space in which social and political ideals could be articulated. For many middle-class practitioners, spiritism tended appropriately enough to focus on the growing commitments of family and even offered a mechanism for coping with the emotional ambivalences that structured relations in the private sphere. On the one hand, spiritism's moral dictates reaffirmed a bourgeois ethos of deferment by emphasizing the accumulation of moral value enjoyed by those souls that practiced disciplined self-denial and worked to pay their social debts forward. Spiritism even offered a powerful reminder of the obligations due the sacrifices of the past in the oversight that a dearly departed mother or father continued to exercise in one's daily life.[54] In spiritism the proscriptive functions of the bourgeois family achieved a pervasive authority over the individual's life.

Spiritism, however, could have hardly succeeded as a religious movement if its only role had been to intensify feelings of guilt or shame. Indeed, like more traditional religions, spiritism also offered means of transgressing the prohibitive moral framework of the bourgeoisie either in carnivalesque fashion or ecstatic states of sublime union. In the spiritist séance practitioners often found themselves in the presence of uncouth *esprits farceurs.* These spirits offered a negative lesson against the desublimated pleasures of the body while simultaneously permitting forms of expression that were otherwise prohibited in polite bourgeois circles.[55] In his account of a séance witnessed in one of the most tasteful and elegant districts of Paris, the chemist Michel Eugène Chevreul found, for instance, that he could not bring himself to transcribe the word by which the table, "happy to satisfy the desire" of the two beautiful young women operating it, had responded to their inquiries.[56] For the young ladies of this account, the séance offered a way of indulging in crude pleasures while preserving their position of innocence (of which Chevreul seemed ultimately doubtful).

A more powerful means of transgression came in a form that mimicked the sublime and erotically charged communions of the Catholic tradition but that reconfigured these in terms more relevant to the emotional intensities of bourgeois family life. The most persuasive evidence of the existence of spirits that any séance could provide came in the form of revelations of a highly intimate nature that only members of one's immediate family or intimate circle of friends could have provided. This amounted to what was, in essence, a sanctification of the relations of trust that structured the intimacies of the private sphere. For the spiritists, the survival of the soul was simply easier to believe than the possibility that the confidences of the private sphere might be subject to abuse. This lesson was made obvious to Auguste Vacquerie when he took part in the series of séances in which Victor Hugo famously participated during his period of exile on the island of Jersey after the fall of the Second Republic. Hugo was introduced to the mysteries of the *tables parlantes* by his friend Delphine de Girardin in September 1853 and spent more than a year dictating communications from the beyond in the company of his wife, his children, Vacquerie, Théophile Guérin, and a series of other associates who traveled to Jersey to pay homage to the great man of letters.[57] If the initial experiment with table turning had begun as an evening *divertissement,* the expectation of trust among the participants quickly transformed it into a more serious matter. Vacquerie, "determined to doubt until the point of offense," explained how his early skepticism and suspicions about Madame Girardin were ultimately thwarted by a communication from Hugo's daughter Léopoldine, who had drowned ten years earlier along with her husband, Charles Vacquerie (Auguste's brother).[58] "Here defiance renounced itself; no one would have had the heart or the impudence to transform this tomb into a theater before us. Mystification was already difficult to admit, but infamy! The suspicion itself would have been greeted with contempt. The brother questioned the sister who had returned from death to console the exile; from the mother poured forth tears of indescribable emotion which seized the hearts of each one of us."[59]

That the communication from the beyond might represent such a cruel betrayal of confidences was more incomprehensible than the actual presence of spirits. In any event, the effect of such communications did not indicate malicious intent but instead offered comforting confirmation of the lingering emotional investments between the dead and the living. In these early dialogues Hugo's encounter with the spirit world suggested the prospect of a form of love untroubled by the cruel privations of embodied life. Hugo's youngest daughter, Adèle, transcribed the exchange with the spirit of Léopoldine in which her brother Charles acted as medium:

> MME DE GIRARDIN: *Who are you? Tell us of yourself.*
> LA TABLE: *Death.*
> MME DE GIRARDIN: *Who are you?*
> LA TABLE: *Soror.*
> VICTOR HUGO: *That means "sister" in Latin.*
> LA TABLE: *Death.*[60]

Général Le Flô and Charles Hugo, who magnetized the table, were overcome with emotion, as were the bystanders.

CHARLES HUGO: *I lost a sister.*

GÉNÉRAL LE FLÔ: *As did I. . . .*

VICTOR HUGO À LA TABLE: *Tell me, are you happy?*

LA TABLE: *Yes.*

VICTOR HUGO: *Are you happy when each evening I mention your name in my prayers?*

LA TABLE: *Yes.*

VICTOR HUGO, overcome with emotion: *Where are you?*

LA TABLE: *Light.*

VICTOR HUGO: *What must one do to go to where you are?*

LA TABLE: *Love!*

For Hugo and other cultural elites who engaged in the practice, such appeals to the emotional life of the bourgeois family served only as a first step in reconceptualizing the social order in similar terms. For the remainder of their engagement with the talking tables, Hugo and his circle would converse with more abstract entities (La Critique, L'Idée, and La Drame) and with the great thinkers of the past (Socrates, Plato, Chateaubriand, and others), who gave voice to a variety of aesthetic and political concerns.[61] Some have argued that the intimacies revealed in Hugo's engagement with the spirits was simply a reflection of those universal social bonds that Hugo was now characterizing in the utopian terms of spiritism. The world of spirits in which souls remained in constant communion was, in Walter Benjamin's analysis of the episode, only a reflection of Hugo's belief in the mystical forces that linked the fate of the otherwise weak and atomized individual to the messianic destiny of the masses.[62] From the *procès-verbal* of the Jersey séances, it is clear that the failure of the Second Republic and the hope of a future republic figured largely among Hugo's mental preoccupations. Would there be another republic? The table answered in the affirmative.[63] In her examination of this episode in Hugo's literary and political career, Jann Matlock has argued that the prosopopoeia operating in Hugo's transcriptions functioned as an appeal to a collective ideal in which republicanism might prosper. "If the dead can be made to speak," Matlock argues by way of explaining Hugo's involvement, "then surely a dead country, made up of republicans with deadened souls, can also be awakened to their future."[64]

Policing Heterodoxy

If spiritism provoked a variety of hostile responses from institutions of academic and ecclesiastical authority in its first instances, it was largely left to its own devices even during the period of censorship and police oppression that characterized the first half of the reign of Napoleon III. Largely tolerated during the Second Empire, spiritist circles had the appearance of private gatherings and were thus exempt from police restrictions on public meetings.[65] Larger organizations like Kardec's Société Parisienne des Études Spirites had been authorized by the government on the condition that participation in the séances remain restricted to members of the organization.[66] Kardec himself understood that the ability of his organization to conduct its activities and publicize its philosophies depended on avoiding explicitly political activities. If an isolated practitioner like Hugo could find encouragement in the spirit world for his political ideals, as an organized movement spiritism would consciously avoid direct political action with the assurance that, given the immutable law of progress, social and political reform was going to come anyway.[67]

Spiritism's greatest threat was not to the institutions of the state but to the expert knowledge that the technocratic regimes of the second half of the nineteenth century became increasingly dependent upon for their legitimacy and effectiveness. Although the Second Empire could effectively abandon policies of police coercion in its last decade, the decline of the traditional reliance of the state and its opposition on violence would not occur until after the brutal suppression of the Paris Commune in the spring of 1871 by the nascent Third Republic. In this context the more explicitly political aspects of the spiritist movement after Kardec's death in 1869 were largely irrelevant, as the moment for a politics based on the revolutionary model had effectively passed. The end of the Commune and the rise of a circumspect republicanism marked a decided shift as the state came to draw more and more on science to legitimize its efforts to reorganize and regulate the social order. Just as asylums and prisons had provided the French state with normalizing discourses and institutions of social control in earlier periods, new developments in, for example, the physiology of labor, criminology, and the psychology of crowds would offer the Third Republic a means of optimizing the rational, productive forces of society by combating counterproductive irrationalism in all of its forms.[68] In this context the danger of spiritism and magnetism came not from some potential to stir popular enthusiasm on the barricades but from the more indirect challenge that they presented to the state in its efforts to reaffirm its position through scientific forms of knowledge. Spiritism was to science what midcentury bohemianism was to the canons of French art and literature. In claiming that they too were scientific, spiritism and magnetism attempted to place the definition of "science" uncomfortably beyond the control of the official, state-dominated institutions.

Given the capacity for institutions of science and medicine to define normative states, it is not surprising that the primary strategy for combating these heterodoxies was to pathologize them as dangers to individual and public reason. These explicitly repressive measures, which were indeed tied to police efforts, were, however, only one form of the response emanating from scientists and doctors. The accompanying approach involved a more ambitious effort of appropriation in which the phenomena of somnambulism and mediumism were legitimated within the sciences so that the practices, and the knowledge acquired through them, could be placed under the control of authorized institutions. The legitimation of animal magnetism as "hypnosis" was one outcome. The emergence of mediumism as an object of scientific study within psychical research was another.

These primarily discursive responses to magnetism and spiritism would evolve slowly in the last decades of the nineteenth century. Prior to the 1880s the effort to combat the pernicious influence of these practices mostly focused on the prosecution of fraud. Spiritists themselves helped to set the terms for this conflict by happily producing evidence of an objective nature that could be readily scrutinized outside of the spiritist séance itself. Because of their objective but highly technical nature, spirit photographs presented an appealing target to skeptics. The commercial practices associated with spirit photography also presented a convenient legal rationale for the regulation of what spiritists considered part of their religious observances. The crowning moment of this effort came in 1875, when Parisian police took into custody the spirit photographer Édouard Isadore Buguet on charges of fraud and implicated along with him Kardec's Société Parisienne des Études Spirites, then under the leadership of Pierre-Gaëtan Leymarie and Kardec's widow.

Spirit photography had grown in the 1860s and 1870s into a popular form of spirit representation and had become the foundation for several commercially successful studios in America, England, and France, including Buguet's atelier on the boulevard Montmartre.[69] The practice was similar to ordinary portrait photography except that, as well as being skilled in the techniques of photography, the photographer exercised his talents as a medium in order to call into being the departed relatives of his clients. When the photographic plates were developed, images of ghosts appeared in the photographs beside the flesh-and-blood sitter. The investigation of Buguet produced tremors within the spiritist community. While spiritists would defend their movement by claiming that, as a religion, it was protected by laws guaranteeing freedom of conscience, most were also obliged to admit that Buguet, otherwise an authentic and talented medium, had quite probably been seduced by the prospect of wealth and fame.[70] Buguet's confession, which he later withdrew, earned him a year in prison. Leymarie, the editor of the Kardecist organ *La Revue Spirite*, had financed Buguet's studio and was thus fined five hundred francs and also sentenced to a year in prison.[71] Commercial fraud became the basis on which the state authorized its prosecution of spiritists and magnetists alike. As the police informant reporting on these communities at the time of the Buguet trial noted, these communities presented a "strange world . . . led by a few clever people who live by it and exploit public credulity by way of medical and other consultations for which one must pay dearly."[72] In these years, during which the Third Republic was in the hands of a loose coalition of monarchist parties, the prosecution of spiritists and magnetists was fueled both by concerns about popular irrationalism stemming from the turmoil of the Commune and from the monarchist republic's alliances with the Catholic Church in its Government of Moral Order. The attack on spiritism was undoubtedly satisfying both to Catholics seeking to suppress this heresy and to sober rationalists engaged in an ideological battle with all forms of superstition.

With the transition of the Third Republic to a ruling majority of republicans in the Chambre des Députés, the campaign against spiritism and animal magnetism was made part of a more general campaign against all threats, both ancient and new, to the rational underpinnings of the republican ideology. The legal and scientific opposition to spiritism and magnetism drew in these years upon the anticlerical traditions of French republicanism and upon the doctrines of philosophical positivism. The sentiment expressed in works like Larousse's *Grand dictionnaire,* which would pronounce the miracle officially dead and encourage the "correctional police to take upon themselves to drag the jugglers of Lourdes and La Salette into the light of day," would lead most famously to the secularization of France's educational institutions in the 1880s and the separation of church and state in 1905.[73] Spiritism and animal magnetism would share in the animus directed toward the Christian miraculous. If Catholicism and Protestantism could be deprived of their political import through a process that excluded them from the public sphere by rendering them matters of private conscience, spiritism and magnetism, popular and unorthodox practices without the protected status of a recognized religion, were subjected to another set of procedures. Curiously, these involved a recognition that the phenomena described by magnetists and spiritists were real if not in a physical, then at least in a psychological sense and that they needed to be duly regulated and their practice restricted to men of medicine authorized by the state. This turn provided a scientific basis for implementing the terms of the law of 19 Ventôse Year XI prohibiting the illegal exercise of medicine.[74] By associating mediumism with hypnosis, the French medical and scientific communities also generated grounds for proscribing spiritism.

The transformation of animal magnetism into a matter of serious medical consideration began in the 1870s as James Braid's theories on hypnotism were beginning to gain currency in France.[75] Braid, a relatively obscure Manchester physician, was introduced to animal magnetism by the Swiss magnetist Charles Lafontaine in 1841. His own experimentation with the phenomenon caused him to overcome his initial skepticism and begin building a theory of animal magnetism as a subjective phenomenon. Braid's work highlighted the importance of fixed visual attention, whose effects he noticed by accident while observing the behaviors of his magnetized subjects. He published his experiences on what he called "hypnotism" in 1843, and it was this account that was brought to the attention of the French doctor Eugène Azam, who, in June 1858, turned to hypnotism in his treatment of hysterics at the hospital of Bordeaux.[76]

By this point, hypnotism had already received some attention among French readers as a result of Victor Meunier's scientific articles in *La Presse* (1852) and from Charles Robin and Émile Littré's entry (1855) on the subject for a new edition of Nysten's *Dictionnaire de médecine*. In Paris on academic business in 1859, Azam learned from the secretary general of the Société Nationale de Chirugie, Paul Broca, that a mutual friend, Eugène Follin, had performed surgery at the Hôpital Necker on a woman with a large and painful anal abscess using only the anesthetic effects of hypnosis. The next day Broca drafted a letter to the Académie des Sciences explaining the procedure.[77] Broca's correspondence caused a sensation in the academy, and Azam was later solicited by the editor of the *Archives Générales de Médecine* for an account of his experiments with hypnotism. Azam's treatment of the subject was buttressed by other similarly well-regarded accounts. These explanations benefited from a correlation to knowledge about the effects of light on the eye and the nervous system, but, as Azam would later suggest, the word "hypnotism," free from any associations with charlatanism, was itself probably enough to restore Mesmer's discoveries to their deserved prominence.[78]

In less than a year's time, for reasons difficult to explain, this sudden showing of enthusiasm in the milieu of official science would diminish and fade. In the end, none of those involved in the rediscovery of animal magnetism in 1860 were adequately equipped in their professional reputation or in their temperament to achieve sustained recognition for hypnotism. The editor Victor Masson, who had encouraged Azam in 1860 to prepare a translation of Braid's work for publication, abandoned the project after sensing that the audience for such a work had disappeared.[79] The public, which looked to the scientific academies to guide its understanding in these matters, remained confused. In 1860 the scientific popularizer Louis Figuier expressed his disappointment in the academy, which he hoped would, during its brief period of interest in "braidism," also apply itself to the mysteries of spiritism. Citing "academic indifference," Figuier chastised "official science" for its unwillingness to "enlighten the people on the question of turning tables; one can almost say that it has altogether abandoned them to their own impressions. Continuing its customary errors, [official science] began by completely denying the reality of the facts, calling them absurd and impossible *a priori*."[80]

It was not until a decade later that the subject of hypnotism would return to the academy, and even then interest was limited. Paul Bert (a leading champion of positive science and future minister of public instruction) would express his frustration after an unsuccessful 1870 conference at the Sorbonne on the subject that prophesied that hypnosis would become "one day the most used and the most fruitful experimental procedure of the new psychology."[81] Over the course of the 1870s Bert would gradually be joined in his enthusiasm by a group of adventurous thinkers, including Charles Richet, whose 1875 article on "provoked somnambulism" in the *Journal de l'Anatomie et de la Physiologie* began by acknowledging that "it takes a certain amount of courage to pronounce the word somnambulism."[82] While risky for a young medical intern still awaiting his *agrégation,* Richet's gesture was apparently well timed and executed and effectively established his professional reputation.

Richet is often credited with bringing hypnotism to the attention of Jean-Martin Charcot, who in 1878 would begin lecturing on the subject at the Salpêtrière in its association with his studies of hysteria.[83] Most accounts of this phase in the study of hypnotism point to Charcot's intervention in the late 1870s as the moment when hypnosis began to achieve real traction in the domain of official science. The decisive moment in most accounts was Charcot's 1882 communication to the Académie des Sciences, which argued that the effects of hypnosis could indeed be observed in the neuromuscular effects that accompanied the various nervous states that it provoked.[84] That the specific manifestation of these states (catalepsy, lethargy, and somnambulism) was already partly known from Charcot's studies of hysteria only reinforced his claims on behalf of hypnosis. In Charcot's work the powers once attributed to the universal fluid of animal magnetism were beginning to be recognized as phenomena that offered real insights into the conditions of nervous illness.

As a consequence of the status that animal magnetism was achieving in the 1880s, prosecution of magnetists in republican France began to focus more and more on the danger that the practice presented to public hygiene.[85] Because of its historical association with magnetism, spiritism too became a target of this new strategy of attack. For the medical community, the relation of spiritism to hysteria made the conduct of the séances more than a simple exercise in duping the public. Spiritism presented an unhealthy social practice that courted mental illness in epidemic fashion.

In 1885 Charcot addressed the subject of spiritism by attributing the development of hysteria among children in one instance to the household practice of spiritism.[86] His lecture, which described the family of the administrator of a military penitentiary, began by noting in detail the difficulties of life in a house of incarceration. The wives of the guards and administrators, who lived with their husbands in the prison complex, organized regular séances as a diversion from the dreary monotony and soon introduced their husbands and children to the practice. This exposure proved disastrous for the children, who were subsequently troubled by hallucinations of attacking "thieves" and "assassins" and overcome by cataleptic seizures. For Charcot, the case indicated "the danger of the constant tension of mind that necessarily exists in those who are addicted to spiritualism or to gratifying a love of the marvelous—a love that has such a remarkable hold on the minds of children."[87] Such incidents of madness were, he argued, higher among those who believed in spiritism because as a practice it tended to attract the weak-minded or those with a hereditary predisposition to mental illness.[88] In the larger medical literature on the subject, spiritist madness was characterized not only as an individual affliction but also as a form of collective social madness that undermined good reason and common sense and was generally seen as a sign of social degeneracy.[89]

If Charcot's presentation only intimated the pathological underpinnings of all religious belief, Paul Duhem, a doctor at the sanatorium of Boulogne-sur-Seine, was much more specific about the connection between combating spiritism and promoting secularism.[90] His 1906 account of a young patient who had naively sought the aid of a spiritual magnetist named Philippe for digestive problems focused on what Duhem described as his patient's religious obsessions—his states of spiritual exaltation, visions, compulsive praying, and excessive devotion to the Virgin Mary. For Duhem, the lesson to be learned from this young man's plight was clear and applied equally to magnetism, spiritism, and, apparently, all forms of religious belief:

I thus place M. Philippe, his method of cure, and all analogous services in the same ranks as the séances of spiritism—they are etiological elements of certain mental illnesses. I consider it a veritable danger to let them continue any longer in the present moment when the efforts of science are trying to dislodge from their final refuges those superstitions, whether of religious origin or not, that our brains have been more or less impregnated with from childhood. Spiritism and occultism in particular have already claimed too many victims, and I imagine that it will become almost the duty of the alienist to intervene in accordance with public powers in the effort to achieve the prohibition of all manifestations of this type.[91]

Issued in the wake of the intense debates surrounding the 1905 Law of Separation (Loi de Séparation des Églises et de l'État), Duhem's medicalized account of obsessive religiosity clearly coincided with a larger political struggle against the Catholic Church.

While Charcot and Duhem pointed to the obvious dangers inherent in spiritism and magnetism, some felt that these practices had a more limited impact on public reason due to the fact that they were most commonly practiced by women, understood to be incurably mystical by nature. In 1882 the Parisian prefect of police, Ernest Camescasse, a close associate of Prime Minister Léon Gambetta, renewed the effort to rid the city of the insalubrious trade conducted by magnetists.[92] While applauding Camescasse in general terms, some questioned whether the prefect's efforts could ever prove successful, given the desire for mystification among the weak-minded. "Do these modern witches really do so much harm to Paris?" Camille Delaville asked in the pages of *La Presse*. "I think not. . . . To start with, their activities only reach women, an attenuating circumstance. . . . At every step of the social ladder, that which has no common sense attracts women; against this, the vigilance of M. Camescasse can do nothing."[93] The limited range of topics dealt with (love and personal finances) by the somnambulant clairvoyants practicing throughout the city made the problem seem less than urgent. Others, however, were not convinced that the feminine nature of the occupation rendered commercial somnambulism innocuous. Some argued that while the somnambules themselves were almost exclusively women, their customers were actually much more varied than Delaville suggested. The neurologist Georges Gilles de la Tourette would note that it could not be assumed that "it is only women, weak-minded and blinded by jealousy, that populate the *cabinets* of the somnambules."[94] Those who consulted mediums and somnambules represented every class of society, and men as well as women were falling under the influence of these delusional women and their handlers.

In spite of what some considered to be an urgent public health issue, the actual pursuit of commercial magnetists and spiritists remained difficult. An 1892 note to the head of the municipal police from the prefecture of police reported that the commercial practice of mesmerism, hypnotism, and spiritism continued unabated in public forums throughout the city in spite of the formal proscriptions against them. The problem, it seemed, lay with distinguishing between authorized performances of prestidigitation, designed to entertain, and exhibitions of magnetism that, critics claimed, abused the public's confidences.[95] It was recommended that all demonstrations by magnetists be prohibited in public establishments under the surveillance of the police and that every theatrical performance that incorporated elements of magnetism be reported directly to the prefecture.[96] For Tourette, demonstrations in spiritism and magnetism designed as entertaining spectacles were, in fact, the greatest contributors to the late nineteenth-century plague in "provoked neurosis." Such performances, which exposed the public to the harmful effects of magnetism and spiritism, brought the somnambule and her magnetist together with potential clients for further, private consultations. These demonstrations also promoted membership in local associations and, most dangerous of all, inspired a host of amateur imitators among members of the audience. For critics, this *propagation vulgaire* produced the most tragic consequences both in its geometric proliferation of hysteria and in the further abuses that it facilitated. In his analysis of the vulgarization of hypnotism Tourette reiterates the Franklin commission's concerns with the sexual danger surrounding the relationship between the magnetist and his somnambule by recounting an incident in Switzerland in which a girl was reportedly raped by a person who, having attended a demonstration by the itinerant performer Donato in 1880, managed to reproduce the demonstrated techniques for his nefarious purposes.[97]

If science could argue for the regulation of animal magnetism based on the real effects produced by hypnosis and the dangers that these posed to society, popular magnetists could also argue that their practice had been legitimized by science and was thus protected from all charges of charlatanism. This was the tack taken by the prominent somnambule Madame Auffinger in 1895, when her activities brought her to justice for the illegal practice of medicine. In her own defense Auffinger would argue at length in the press that somnambules and card readers were afforded certain insight and sensitivity and that this was a scientific fact: "To forbid one today to predict the future is quite simply to retreat one hundred years into the past. And scientists don't protest; shame on them! For to let science be strangled is to let ourselves be led into darkness." Madame Émilie, a healer convicted and fined along with Auffinger, defended her practice in a similar manner: "We demand only one thing . . . that we be left in peace to practice our science, because it is a science and not charlatanism, as some are inclined to say."[98] The prediction of the future through somnambulism was, Auffinger argued, no different from an astronomer's use of a barometer to predict the weather: "It's obvious that somnambulism, which is the natural phenomenon of magnetism in the opinion of all the doctors who study it in the hospitals, in their laboratories, and in their clinics, provides a great service . . . and rests on a science that is today recognized, magnetism."[99] Auffinger went on to invoke the names of scientists who had acknowledged somnambulism as a special state of consciousness: Richet, Albert de Rochas, Dariex, Marillier, Janet, Gibier, Ochorowitz, Binet, Féré, Delboeuf, Liébault, Liégeois, Bernheim, and "so many other learned men."[100] The appeal to the prestige of science clearly had great rhetorical value for the defenders of magnetism and spiritism.

The association of great men of science with these practices would remain a problem for the scientific community, which, in its effort to co-opt the study of somnambulism and mediumism, also risked a damaging association with less-than-reputable magnetists and spiritists. This was particularly true in the mid-1880s, when scientists went beyond the simple affirmation of hypnosis as an induced form of mental pathology and began to study in earnest and find positive indications of some of the more remarkable phenomena associated with somnambulism. Psychical research was a product of this effort.

As the career of Charles Richet would suggest, the risks associated with these avenues of investigation were apparently worth it. The appeal of psychical research was in this sense similar to the appeal that animal magnetism had had in the eighteenth century for young men of science seeking ways of making revolutionary contributions to the scientific understanding of nature. Although the censure encountered by animal magnetism from the time of its introduction to France presents a stark illustration of the efforts of "normal science" to police its boundaries and defend prevailing paradigms, science remained in the nineteenth century what it had been since its development in the sixteenth century, a speculative enterprise with the ability to introduce earth-shaking novelties into the field of human knowledge. This was particularly true in France in the last decades of the century, when changes in the political climate opened up the possibility for the creation of a new "scientific psychology" just as discoveries in the physical sciences were breaking apart the scientific foundations that Newton had laid two hundred years earlier. Psychical research would stake its claim on the appropriately Cartesian threshold between the new psychology and the new physics.

2

The Development
of Psychical Research
in France, 1882–1900

In 1886 Pierre Janet, a young *lycée* professor in the northern town of Le Havre, addressed a report to the Parisian Société de Psychologie Physiologique that described a series of experiments in which he had placed an illiterate rural woman called Léonie B. into a state of somnambulism by, it seemed, mental suggestion alone. Instead of the usual "passes" that the magnetist performed in the presence of his subject, the young experimenter found that he only had to form in his mind a suggestion that Léonie slip into her sleeplike state in order for her to actually do so. This was done without any obvious outward signs or visible cues and, indeed, proved effective even at significant distances at which Janet was not visible to his subject. The same effect could be produced with Janet forming his suggestion from an adjoining room six or seven meters distant from Léonie, from another house five hundred meters away, or from the town of Graville, over two kilometers away.[1] The experiments that Janet and Joseph Gibert, a local physician, conducted with Léonie in the fall of 1885 suggested, on repeated occasions, the existence of a correspondence between Léonie's somnambulant state and the formation of a mental suggestion in the thoughts of her magnetizer.[2] Janet also discovered that Léonie could be compelled by mental suggestion to perform specific actions. At predetermined times she found herself serving unsolicited refreshments, closing and locking doors, and lighting lamps in the middle of the day. While she complained that the actions she was compelled to undertake were ridiculous, she performed them nevertheless, often in a state of emotional agitation.[3] In another experiment Janet's brother Jules magnetized Léonie and, removing himself to an adjacent room, held his arm over a lamp until his skin began to burn. Seemingly ignorant of what was taking place in the other room, Léonie responded sympathetically by clutching her arm in pain and indicating a place on her arm analogous to the site of the injury sustained by Jules. Pierre Janet noted that Léonie's arm reddened the following day and that she continued to complain of intense pain.[4]

The phenomenon of "provoked somnambulism at a distance," while well known in the annals of the early magnetists, was quite extraordinary from the perspective of the distinguished members of the society, all the more so given that the report was read before them by the author's uncle, the Sorbonne philosopher Paul Janet.[5] Published in *La Revue Philosophique,* Janet's reports, "so new and so interesting" in the eyes of a young Henri Bergson, were reinforced by similar accounts of mental suggestion by Charles Richet, Henri Beaunis, and Jules Hericourt.[6] While the indications of these experiments were extraordinary, Janet's approach to the "delicate subject" of *suggestion mentale* and *somnambulisme provoqué à distance* was conscientiously "prudent and skeptical."[7] In a consistently neutral tone his reports offered only the facts of his observation, without interpretation. Indeed, he admitted, his accounts detailed events that did not readily give way to theorization.

Pierre Janet's youthful efforts in somnambulism and the career in psychology that it helped to launch mark the measure by which the fascinating appeal of somnambulism was mobilized to the cause of scientific psychology. In the 1880s this cause was by no means certain to succeed in an intellectual climate split between the traditions of an academic philosophy that faced obsolescence in an era enthused by positive science and the medical community of the asylums, which was preoccupied with administrative functions and otherwise devoted to an experimentally underdeveloped organicism in which qualities of mind were simplistically tied to "cerebral localizations." In neither system were there both the available resources (i.e., the interesting psychological *sujets,* laboratories, and clinical space) and the inclination to study the "mind" on its own terms. The most effective means to break the dual monopolies represented by these competing systems was to produce facts that neither could easily assimilate. In its effort to discredit "normal" practices, the new science pointed emphatically to "supranormal" facts, attested to by men of good standing but well beyond the explanatory powers of either philosophy or medicine. In this effort Charcot's rehabilitation of magnetism as hypnosis was only a first step, remarkable in its own right for demonstrating an experimental means for inducing specific mental states but moderated by its recourse to physiological explanations and a politically opportune rendering of hypnosis as a form of mental pathology. Janet's efforts to revive as objects of study not just the physiological and behavioral effects witnessed by the ancient magnetists but also the quasi-mystical capacities of "clairvoyance" so frequently discussed in their texts presented a more ambitious challenge. "What a godsend," he would remark in retrospect, "for a young psychologist, twenty-two years of age [sic], curious as to all psychological phenomena, and drawn by the mysterious side of these occult faculties!"[8] The fact that Janet's report offered only observations and no explanations only served to highlight the methodological failings of the current psychology and would, at the same time, draw the newly respectable investigation of hypnosis into association with a variety of previously neglected phenomena associated with magnetism and its popular inheritor, spiritism.

Janet's personal intellectual lineage was a critical element in this challenge, offering as it did a measure of influence to the old academic philosophers even as they conceded the need to adapt the study of the mind to scientific methods. The young Janet's ties to Paul Janet offered assurances that the new science would not deteriorate into a crude materialism. A student and close disciple of Victor Cousin, Janet's uncle continued to be recognized to the end of his career as one of the last great philosophers of Cousin's tradition of eclectic spiritualism.[9] The term did not imply, as the Anglo-American term Modern Spiritualism did, a specific belief in the survival of the soul after bodily death but did promote the related postulate that the human spirit was a real, autonomous object and not simply, as the eighteenth-century psychology spawned by Condillac had proposed, an effect of sensible matter. Cousin's spiritualism reaffirmed the Cartesian faculty of self-consciousness by linking it to the exercise of volition, indicating a unitary self or *moi*. The eclectic aspect of this tradition came from its instrumental or, as some suggested, opportunistic willingness to embrace what was best in all schools of philosophy insofar as they served to cultivate the Good, the True, and the Beautiful. Eclectic spiritualism thus represented a form of intellectual compromise—an academic equivalent of the *juste milieu* by which the liberal monarchy of Louis-Philippe hoped to restore political stability after the revolution of 1830.[10]

Cousin's doctrine of the self was particularly appealing to a bourgeoisie seeking to justify its newfound social position as the product of a disciplined exercise of will. Appointed director of the École Normale Supérieure in 1830 and in 1840 named minister of public instruction in the government of François Guizot, Cousin institutionalized a philosophical curriculum that made the psychology of consciousness a central feature. Cousin's method, one that would draw much criticism from the philosopher of positivism, Auguste Comte, was entirely introspective. Access to the facts of consciousness came to the "psychologist" by turning his attention inward in order that the self might act as observer of its own inner faculties. While Cousin and his followers defended the objective quality of this self-observation, the method of introspection could hardly meet the criteria for objectivity that positivism celebrated in the natural sciences. While positivism would gather a significant following in the second half of the nineteenth century among those who wished to continue in the basic intellectual traditions of the Enlightenment, Cousin's *programme* in philosophy would, through its control of secondary teacher training at the École Normale, continue to exercise its influence over French thought well into the 1870s.[11]

For many positivists, Paul Janet's presence at the Sorbonne was a conspicuous sign of the entrenched nature of Cousin's philosophy of the self, whose adepts still held powerful positions in institutions like the Collège de France and the Faculté des Lettres. The faculties continued to see their role as the preservation of established forms of knowledge and were generally conservative in their attitudes toward new avenues of research. For example, as a member of the jury for Alfred Espinas's 1877 thesis "Des sociétés animaux," Paul Janet was said to have suppressed its historical introduction because Espinas refused to erase the name of Comte from the genesis of sociology.[12] Janet would earn the scorn of the pioneering sociologist, who would continue to accuse the adherents of moral philosophy of a *machiavélisme* designed to dissimulate "incoherent ideas."[13] Espinas's specific and repeated references to Janet's actions regarding his *soutenance de thèse* would tend to suggest that this encounter between sociology and philosophy indeed "lacked cordiality," as one author would later argue.[14]

While faithful to the principles of academic philosophy, the elder Janet was actually more open-minded in his attitude toward the experimental methods of the natural science than many believed. For Janet, the enormous successes of the positive approach to knowledge in the work of men like Claude Bernard, Marcellin Berthelot, T. H. Huxley, Hermann Ludwig von Helmholtz, and Wilhelm Wundt confirmed the tenuous position of a philosophy that had isolated itself from science.[15] By the late 1870s Janet was openly acknowledging the need to find a method of combining experimental and introspective approaches to man. For nearly three decades the partisans of positive science had succeeded in advancing their cause by contributing to useful scientific knowledge, while advocates of the old philosophy became embattled in theirs. For Paul Janet, the effect of the polemic that had broken out between the two camps after 1848 only served as a means to avoid the greater challenge of bringing the world of matter and spirit together into a single system of thought:

> On the one hand, some believed that the moment had come to substitute the reign of matter for that of the spirit. . . . On the other side, we were put right away on the defensive; we began by repelling attacks; we returned fire; and to those arguments drawn from the material world we responded with those drawn from the contemplation of the mind. But soon we came to see together that, instead of endlessly opposing the two worlds, the wisest thing would perhaps be to unify them and to challenge the facts of nature to explain the laws of thought. But in order to achieve this type of reconciliation every detail would have to be resolved; everything is, on the contrary, still yet to be done, and the fight continues as before: for in what proportion and in what order will one achieve the concordance of the two elements?[16]

Paul Janet's promotion of his talented nephew Pierre into a leading position in the emerging psychology presented one element of the philosopher's response to this question. While Paul Janet conceded that the new psychology would have to recognize as legitimate the criticisms that had been directed at the methodology of the old philosophical psychology (Charcot had referred to introspection as "rosewater psychology"), he also clearly worried that the materialistic tendencies of the experimental method would leave no place for an ethical conception of the self.[17] For his part, Pierre Janet would, near the end of his career, admit the profound influence of his uncle, whom he characterized as open-minded to the possibilities of science. If he remained faithful to Cousin's principles, he nevertheless "understood the importance of medical and anatomical studies to the moral intelligence of man."[18]

Guided by his uncle's influence, Pierre Janet's career would thus come to embrace a critical combination of philosophical, scientific, and medical approaches to understanding the human mind. As Jacqueline Carroy and Régine Plas have argued, it was Pierre Janet who would achieve the *voisinage* between scientific and philosophical psychology that his uncle had viewed as the salvation of philosophy.[19] It was the elder Janet who encouraged his nephew to combine his studies in philosophy at the École Normale with practical work in experimental science and introduced him to the physiologist Albert Dastre, who subsequently employed the young student in his laboratory at the Sorbonne. It was also the uncle who encouraged Pierre Janet to enroll in the Faculté de Médecine in order to obtain, among other things, the credentials needed to gain access to psychiatric patients for the purposes of psychological research.[20] Pierre Janet's intellectual formation also drew on the influence provided by his contemporary Henri Bergson, who had entered the École Normale one year ahead of Janet and would remain a supporter in, among other things, Janet's 1902 candidacy to a chair at the Collège de France. Émile Boutroux would, along with Paul Janet, sit on the jury that approved Pierre Janet's degree in philosophy in 1889, while Charcot and Richet would compose part of the committee that authorized his medical thesis on hysteria four years later.[21]

Although Richet was almost ten years older than Janet, Richet's career would parallel Janet's in ways that would eventually lead the two men to become closely associated in the promotion of both scientific psychology and psychical research in France. Richet would not only open the way to Charcot's legitimation of hypnosis with the publication of research on provoked somnambulism in 1875, he would also set the stage both ideologically and institutionally for Janet's research in Le Havre.[22] His 1884 article in *La Revue Philosophique* on the application of statistical probabilities to the study of mental suggestion would provide the precedent for Janet's work in Le Havre a year later.[23] It was notably Richet's theories of mental disaggregation, along with those of Frederic William Henry Myers, that would provide the basis for Janet's research in somnambulism and mediumism, giving him a basis by which to argue that the medium and the somnambule were identical.[24] While physical scientists had slighted the claims of spiritism for their discordance with natural law, psychologists saw in the capriciousness of the turning tables the signs of unconscious intelligent activity accessible to their concepts and their methods of investigation.[25] In the doctoral thesis that would provide the basis for *L'Automatisme psychologique* (1889) Janet turned his attention from mental suggestion to somnambulism in general and to the forgotten literature on table turning.

Rediscovered Precedents:
The Involuntarism of Michel Eugène Chevreul

Prior to the 1880s serious scientific work in France on the subject of spiritism had been sparse. Besides the poorly considered reply of Arago to Seguin's 1853 report to the Académie des Sciences, the phenomenon had received only isolated responses from academic scientists. While Catholic critics saw demonic influence and skeptics simple fraud, those who maintained a critical but open attitude toward spirit phenomena regretted the lack of a formal scientific investigation. While contemporaries of Mesmer could celebrate the Franklin commission's repudiation of animal magnetism at the end of the eighteenth century, mid-nineteenth-century opponents of spiritism found no such satisfaction from the institutions of official science. The tables were largely ignored.

One of the noteworthy exceptions to this general lack of interest by French academics was Michel Eugène Chevreul's 1854 study *De la baguette divinatoire du pendule dit explorateur et des tables tournantes.* The text revisits experiments that Chevreul had made public in 1833 in an open letter to André Marie Ampère "on a particular class of muscular movements."[26] In an 1854 communication to the Académie des Sciences, Chevreul offered an explanation of the turning tables related to one that he had developed in his earlier work on the dowser's rod and diviner's pendulum. These devices, he had discovered, moved without any noted muscular activity and, more importantly, without any volition on the part of the subject holding them. In his earlier work Chevreul found that he had only to put himself into a "disposition" amenable to the movement of the pendulum and it would begin to oscillate back and forth without his actually willing the muscular activity to achieve this result. The pendulum moved when held over metal, water, or living animals, as it was supposed to by folk practitioners, and ceased to move when any other material was interposed. The muscular movements produced were so slight that in order to stop the pendulum Chevreul only had to consider in his own thoughts that it was possible to do so. He concluded from this that there was "an intimate connection established between the execution of certain movements and the act of thinking that is relative to them even if the thought itself has not yet become the will to command the muscular organs."[27] Most significant to Chevreul was the fact that he could no longer reproduce the effect once he had discovered its source in involuntary muscular activity. In other words, once he had developed in his own mind a theory of cause not dependent on some actual physical relationship between the pendulum and the material beneath it, he could no longer put himself into the necessary disposition to achieve the movement. This led him to believe that the muscular activity was the effect of "exactly what the magnetizers called *faith.* The existence of this state is perfectly demonstrated by the account of my experiences. In short, as long as I believed that the movement of the pendulum in my hand was *possible,* it moved; but, after having discovered the cause of this effect, I was no longer able to reproduce it."[28]

Described variably as faith, intention, and desire, the disposition that Chevreul identified was not, he insisted, equivalent to will because he had not directed his muscles to undertake any action. Chevreul's only "wish was the execution of an experiment good enough to end the uncertainty in my mind on the question of whether the pendulum would be moved or whether it would remain at rest."[29] On the basis of his earlier experiments with the *pendule explorateur,* Chevreul would argue in response to the practice of table turning that the displacement of larger objects through involuntary muscular activity was simply the collective effect of a shared belief among séance goers that the tables might in fact move.

For Chevreul, the discovery held enormous implications for the practice of a science based on the capacities of human sensibility: "The principle of the *pendule explorateur* thus demonstrates to the experimenter the necessity of studying the influence of his thoughts on his own organs, since these serve as the intermediary between the exterior world and his understanding in the study of phenomena issuing from natural philosophy."[30] His experiments, in other words, "prove how easy it is to mistake illusions for reality" and showed "how men of good faith, and very enlightened for that matter, are sometimes led to resort to ideas that are altogether chimerical in order to explain phenomena that do not really issue from the physical world as we know it."[31] If in the late eighteenth century the attribution of cause to the imagination and imitation resulted in the official censure of animal magnetism, in Chevreul's 1833 account the discovery of the influence of thought on perception indicated future avenues of research.[32] The "disposition" that he had identified in himself could, he felt, be subjected to scientific investigation if, for instance, some relationship to the animal faculty of imitation could be established. The "faith" that had made possible the involuntary action of his muscles seemed to Chevreul to manifest itself in relations among individuals, especially among animals living in groups subject to "the influence of the leaders on subordinated individuals."[33] A study of the "fascination" that one animal in nature could provoke in another pointed the way to a more fully developed understanding of the faculties of imitation and imagination in human beings, faculties that were apparent, for example, in the correspondence between the involuntary gestures witnessed in the theatrical performance of an actor and the emotional qualities of the text that he or she recites.[34] In these recommendations Chevreul's discovery of a belieflike "disposition" through a subjective inquiry into his own mental state indicated not further self-reflexive experimentation but an objective study of human and animal comportment. Chevreul argued in solidarity with Ampère that "the path to follow in psychology is the one taken by the men to whom the natural sciences owe their progress and who share our conviction that there is no positive metaphysics for those who ignore the grand truths of mathematics and physics."[35] The collection of facts should, he argued, precede the development of any general system of philosophy. The idea of an objective *psychologie* in the 1833 letter contradicted the institutionalization of introspective psychology in Cousin's syllabus of 1832. Indeed, the very notion of involuntarism was antithetical to a Cousinian self that was defined by its unity, its volition, and its self-consciousness.

It was on Chevreul's 1853 work on the *baguette divinatoire, pendule divinatoire,* and *tables tournantes* that Richet would focus in his 1886 contribution to the Festschrift celebrating the centenary of Chevreul's birth. For Richet, Chevreul's study of involuntary movement was "epoch making in psychology in that it demonstrated in an irrefutable manner the fundamental fact that among the various muscular movements there are a great many that are neither recognized nor willed by those who execute them."[36] Not only did his discovery enable the researcher to refute the supernatural explanations attributed to involuntary muscular activity, it also provided a basis for what psychology had to that point lacked—namely, a means of studying thought objectively. By revealing that every thought or every emotion is accompanied by a movement of the body, Chevreul's discovery offered a method that combined the introspective method with a physiological technique that allowed the measurement of movement as the involuntary effect of thought.[37] Richet argued that "the involuntary movements that we execute and have no direct consciousness of seem to us the result of a force that is foreign to ourselves" and as such would appear "absolutely supernatural" had not Chevreul discovered the secret of involuntary action.[38]

By the time Pierre Janet revisited Chevreul's explanation of table turning to develop a theory of psychological automatism in his 1889 doctoral thesis, a psychology of mental disaggregation was redefining the activity that for Chevreul had remained "involuntary" and "machinelike."[39] The idea of a division of mental functions was not novel. Franz Joseph Gall had divided the brain into independent, localized functions in his studies of the physiognomy of the skull, and Comte had asserted, in reference to phrenology, that different divisions of the brain could be designated as the source of intelligence and of personal, as opposed to sympathetic, impulses.[40] These theories could only resolve the unitary aspect of the subject who speaks "I" by allotting this function its own cerebral location.[41] Janet argued, however, that, unlike the reflexive blinking of an eye or scratching of an itch, the physical activity that Chevreul had described revealed itself as willed and intelligent even if the mental activity that lay behind it remained unacknowledged.[42]

The disaggregation of the self proposed by the physiological theories of a cerebral unconscious were, for Janet, insufficient to explain the intelligence evident in the events of the spiritists' séances.[43] "In the presence of such facts, which are innumerable," he argued, "one cannot help but find that the physiologists, with their [theory of] unconscious cerebration, have stalled at the threshold of the question."[44] Janet was more inclined to agree with the epigraph of Kardec's *La Revue Spirite*: "Tout effet a une cause, tout effet intelligent a une cause intelligente" (Every effect has a cause, and every intelligent effect has an intelligent cause).[45] The form of mental disaggregation that Janet proposed provided unconscious activity with its own volition, independent of that exhibited in conscious processes. Will, a primary characteristic of the unified self of Cousin's philosophical psychology, was thus preserved by Janet within a subject divided into multiple selves, conscious and unconscious.

While Chevreul's account of the 1830s had promoted an objective psychology in opposition to the prevailing paradigm of psychological introspection, Janet saw in the 1880s that an overly narrow physiological approach had blinded itself to the intelligence and willfulness of unconscious activity and had thus opened the door to the application of retrograde superstitions to the explanation of psychological facts. Janet recognized that the reason Catholic accounts of table turning, such as Jules-Eudes de Mirville's *Des esprits et de leurs manifestations diverses* (1863), were more convincing, if ultimately objectionable, was that they emphasized deliberate and intelligent action in their attribution of cause to demonic agents. Janet reluctantly found himself in agreement with one aspect of Mirville's explanation, which observed that "there is in these tables the phenomenon of thought, of intelligence, of reason, of will, even of liberty when they refuse to respond, and such causes have always been called minds or souls by philosophers."[46] In response, Janet would argue, from a carefully maintained perspective,[47] the absolute necessity of the notion of subconscious activity to secular knowledge of the mind: "We must speak of thoughts without consciousness or beyond our consciousness if we want to rid ourselves of the innumerable little devils of M. de Mirville."[48] Janet would later express the need of finding a suitable rapport between objective psychology and metaphysics in order to give the soul the status of a secular, scientific object, displacing the "childish superstitions of the old spiritists."[49]

However, in the mid-1880s the notion of unconscious thought was still poorly understood, and Janet complained that it was often confused in the case of mediums with willful acts of dissimulation: "This [unconscious] nature does not seem to have been understood by the authors who discuss spiritism, for one sees them speaking straightaway of tricks and deception as soon as the unconscious of the medium is at issue."[50] Without a theory of genuinely intelligent unconscious mental activity, one was obliged either to ignore spiritism altogether (as had academic scientists), reject spiritism as a fraud (as did so many skeptics, often with disregard for or ignorance of the evidence), identify spiritism as a product of demonic influence (as had Catholic critics), or side in favor of the spirit hypothesis (and become a spiritist oneself). The misconception that understood subconscious acts exclusively in terms of fraud was, for Janet, a sign of the danger that the theory of mental disaggregation posed to the naive realism at work in lay skepticism. As an a priori dismissal, the charge of fraud obviated a consideration of mental disaggregation in a phenomenon such as automatic writing.

Janet looked to the special states evinced in spiritism as an opportunity for an experimental inquiry into pathological mental states, somnambulism, automatism, the psychology and physiology of perception, and the nature of unconscious activity. His study of the history of spiritism also served as a point of departure for general reflection on the increasingly prominent role of science in society and on the consequences of a popular interest in metaphysics that was largely neglected by professional philosophers.[51] In an era in which science was contributing enormously to human beings' understanding of their physical environment, the contributions of the same methods to an understanding of their own being were paltry and few. He argued that the great interest of psychology resulted from the hopeful application of science to the inquiries that human beings had so long posed to their own nature. "More than any other science," Janet would argue, "psychology approaches the concerns of philosophy and religion. This is without doubt what makes such a study so difficult, although it is also what makes it so interesting."[52]

In the account of spiritist writings that he published in *La Revue Philosophique* in 1892 Janet traced the path of a community that had in essence been abandoned by scientists, philosophers, and theologians who preferred to ignore the facts of spiritism rather than take on the difficult questions that they presented. Left to their own devices, spiritists gradually turned away from their early empirical efforts. The detailed reports of the early séances, if naive in their interpretations but rigorous in their observations, had, Janet regretted, given way to amateur metaphysical speculation of the most fantastical sort.[53] "For a long time mediumistic phenomena . . . were denied, ridiculed, and above all ignored. The pathological type of the medium, so intriguing and in reality so well described by the spiritists, was absolutely disregarded by doctors and psychologists. Instead of analyzing the facts, of discussing them, of comparing them to analogous nervous manifestations, one refused to see them, and the spiritists, left to their own devices without any prior learning and with insufficient means of study, naturally gave themselves over to reveries and the most naive superstitions."[54] Janet clearly hoped to rectify this situation by providing the science of psychology with a means of addressing these amateur reveries and of offering some corrective. This effort demanded, above all, that the states of dissociation found in mediumism and somnambulism be recognized as psychological realities so that psychology might find some means of redeeming the integrative faculties of the self.

The Question of "Psychology" in France

While significant progress had been made toward the experimental investigation of somnambulism and mediumism in the 1880s, the development of psychical research in France was largely contingent on a psychology that remained poor in its resources and uncertain in its methodology. Due to the shortage of laboratory space and the relative immaturity of the field, the methods of psychical research in the 1880s remained predominantly those of natural history. For French psychical researchers, the model study remained *Phantasms of the Living* (1886) by Myers and two of his compatriots in the Society for Psychical Research, Edmund Gurney and Frank Podmore.[55] The work represented a major landmark in psychical research in its comprehensive survey of incidents of possible thought transference or "veridical hallucinations," and Janet was prompted to cite it as well as the *Proceedings of the Society for Psychical Research* repeatedly in his *L'Automatisme psychologique*.

Throughout the 1880s and 1890s French psychical researchers remained without the desired laboratory facilities in the study of phenomena that were difficult to adapt to the requirements of experimental control. The immature state of psychical research was highlighted by Charles Richet in 1891 during the first year of *Les Annales des Sciences Psychiques* when he advised the editor, Xavier Dariex, to seek the assistance of his readers in communicating observations of interest to psychical researchers.[56] Richet jested that experiments in psychical research were so rare that the journal was liable to become a booklet of blank sheets of paper if it was to insist on reporting only experimental facts. Richet saw that psychical research had not yet entered into an "experimental stage in which everything becomes so precise and so complete that discussion and disputation are impossible."[57] While he recognized that experimentation was the only adequate basis for the establishment of scientific facts, Richet noted that psychical research was still in its empirical phase and that it should content itself for the time being with the methods of Gurney, Myers, and Podmore by collecting observations of the best possible quality from the best possible witnesses.[58]

Usually dated to the official foundation of Wilhelm Wundt's Leipzig laboratory in 1879, experimental psychology in the 1880s was still perceived as a young science and was only just gaining a presence in its own right within the official institutions that organized, funded, and legitimized scientific research and instruction. Psychology in France was still very much entangled, in both a conceptual and institutional sense, with physiology and clinical medicine, on the one hand, and philosophy, on the other. Hospitals like the Salpêtrière offered vast treasure houses of interesting research subjects who had long been controlled by a medical profession more interested in practical therapies than in abstractions and general theories of the human mind.[59] Generally true for much of this period, these prejudices were being worn away in the 1880s by prominent physicians eager to link their practice more intimately with a science in its ascendancy. However, the interpenetration of psychology and medicine in the form of a *psychologie générale* uniting clinical and experimental research continued to be thwarted by institutional pressures.

In the 1880s the most significant landmark for the study of scientific psychology in the faculties was the creation of a position for Théodule Ribot in physiological psychology at the Sorbonne in 1885. Ribot had argued in the preface to his work *La Psychologie allemande contemporaine* that physiology's growing understanding of the workings of the nervous system and of the relationship of events in the cerebrospinal system to psychical states made the old psychology of introspection seem insular and unworthy of the name of science. Rather than pursuing knowledge of the mind through interior observation and reason, psychology should emulate the biologist who "adds new engines to his arsenal each day, equipping himself with every weapon, multiplying his instruments and his means of measurement, substituting the passive and mechanical recording of phenomena in place of a subjective apperception, forever vacillating and fallible."[60] In fact, Ribot's relationship to the old subjective psychology was more complex than his writing sometimes indicates. Ribot upheld, in principle, the value of the subjective method but argued that this alone could not provide the basis of psychology. In the scientific status that he ascribed to the new psychology Ribot argued for a form of inquiry that dealt specifically with mental phenomena and not with the "self," the Cousinian concept in which critics recognized the outlines of what had been previously named the "soul." But if Ribot promoted a psychology based on the physiological methods that had made biology into an experimental science on par with chemistry and physics, his ascension in the academy hardly provided an occasion for transforming French psychology into an experimental science. Throughout the 1880s and 1890s access to French laboratories remained extremely limited. In the fifteen years since the foundation of Wundt's first lab, sixteen similar facilities had been established in the United States, four in Germany, two in England, and only one in France.[61] In 1894 control of Beaunis' Laboratoire de Psychologie Physiologique, located in four rooms on the third floor of the Sorbonne, was passed on to Alfred Binet, Janet's principal rival for a number of academic positions. Binet's presence in the poorly equipped lab was reputed to be infrequent.[62]

Ribot's *cours complémentaire* did not provide instruction in experimental methods but only offered an introduction to the latest psychological research to students of the Faculté des Lettres preparing for careers as teachers in philosophy. Ribot was not himself a laboratory scientist. His previous publications, which presented English and German psychology to French readers, were based on the presentation of the research of others. While Ribot insisted that experimental psychology was akin to the science of biology, he lacked the medical and scientific training that would have qualified him for the research he advocated.[63] In the final analysis, Ribot's methods remained heavily influenced by his literary and philosophical training,[64] and it was largely the eclecticism of his approach to, if not his conception of, psychological questions that allowed him to secure a newly designated chair in experimental and comparative psychology (*chaire de psychologie expérimentale et comparée*) at the Collège de France in 1888.[65]

As president of the Fourth International Congress of Psychology in 1900, Ribot again demonstrated his understanding that a viable science of psychology required a variety of approaches. A broadened definition of psychology had in his experience proven to be the condition for drawing adherents to the new field. Ribot maintained, however, that an understanding of the relationship between physiological processes and psychological states was to provide the true foundation for the field. In his opening remarks to the congress Ribot acknowledged the efforts of his predecessor, Carl Stumpf, who had altered the title of the Third International Congress of Psychology (1896) in Munich by removing "two apparently restrictive epithets, physiological and experimental," in an effort to liberalize the field.[66] While the modification did not, as Ribot mused, obviate the prominence of physiology, it did entail a broader scope for the general field that permitted in the general category of psychology an increasing degree of specialization. The third international congress consisted of contributions from four subfields. The fourth congress further divided the general field into seven specialties.

While specialization was hailed as a hallmark of success, in Ribot's mind the most important specialties remained those embodied in the sections touching on *psychologie cérébrale* and "psychologie dans les rapports avec l'anatomie et la physiologie." Ribot argued that physiological phenomena were the necessary condition of experimental psychology. But he maintained that psychology studied both aspects of the mind and that the field was not reducible to physiology in spite of its importance.[67] In his review of works published in the field in the four years since the third congress, Ribot foregrounded those on the study of anatomy and physiology by emphasizing the critical need to apply their findings to the study of consciousness: "First, [published works on] the anatomy and the physiology of the nervous system retain the place of honor by their importance and by their number. I will not insist on this point because one must admit that, if they offer the necessary and indispensable terms of psychological research, they will definitively remain auxiliary sciences and that as long as nervous phenomena remain uninterpreted and untranslated into terms drawn from [the study of] consciousness, one cannot yet speak of psychology."[68]

In spite of his insistence on the physiological, Ribot could not, in his rebellion against the institutions responsible for his own intellectual formation, dispense with metaphysical concepts. As John I. Brooks has argued, Ribot's status between science and philosophy was indeterminate, allowing him to be seen as a philosopher and as a scientist and often as both at the same time.[69] While he carried with him the legacy of his early instruction in philosophy, Ribot clearly intended that his efforts prepare the way for the triumph of science over the regime of the literary philosophers. Philosophy would, he argued, be restricted to questions of metaphysics, while psychology would undertake the development of positive knowledge of the mind.

While Ribot's advocacy of experimental approaches to the human mind gained substantial support throughout the 1880s, French researchers continued to struggle against the institutional resistance to the development of a full-fledged experimental program in psychology.[70] The difficulties of producing institutional alliances within a field still so divided between philosophical, physiological, and medical approaches are most evident in the fortunes of the Société de Psychologie Physiologique. Founded in 1885, the society provided an independent organizational basis for a general psychology by representing experimental, clinical, and philosophical approaches to psychology in the diversity of its membership, which included Ribot, Charcot, Richet, and Paul Janet, among others.[71] The society would also, as a result of Richet's efforts, make significant progress in situating French psychology in an international context by sponsoring the First International Congress of Physiological Psychology in Paris in 1889. The society, which was to provide a forum for Pierre Janet's earliest research on somnambulism and mental suggestion, gave considerable attention to the question of clairvoyance and the transmission of thought. It seems that these preoccupations ultimately alienated Charcot, on whom the organization depended for its moral weight and its legitimacy.[72] Charcot's interest in the society waned in his later years. He did not, for instance, appear at the 1889 congress in Paris, which foregrounded discussions touching on psychical research.[73] Three years before Charcot's death in 1893, the Société de Psychologie Physiologique foundered, leaving France with no independent association for the scientific study of psychology for the next six years. In the meantime, work on somnambulism and mediumism continued to appear in *La Revue Philosophique* and in the newly established *Les Annales des Sciences Psychiques,* which Richet founded in 1890 with the Parisian physician Xavier Dariex. The *Annales,* edited by Dariex and later by César de Vesme, counted frequent contributions from Richet and provided a general forum for contributors of various professional persuasions.

If the Société de Psychologie Physiologique failed primarily as a result of the lack of commitment from Charcot, it was also divided in principle by tensions between Paul Janet and Théodule Ribot. While the elder Janet had publicly supported Ribot's academic appointments based on the conviction that scientific psychology made up an important auxiliary to philosophical understanding,[74] as a representative of the legacy of Cousin, Janet opposed a physiologically dominated approach to scientific psychology. He agreed with Ribot's argument that psychology was a study of objective phenomena, but he emphasized in a way that Ribot did not that an "objective" study of the mind should not be dominated by biological conceptions. It was in the context of a philosophical reaction to Ribot that Pierre Janet entered into the field of psychology. While his research was far from faithful to Cousin's philosophy of the unitary self, the younger Janet was nevertheless conciliatory in his application of psychology to philosophy.[75] He would continue to echo the position of his uncle on the objective (rather than strictly physiological) nature of experimentation, and it seems that the younger Janet's election to Ribot's vacated chair at the Collège de France in 1902 was intended as a nod of recognition to the broader understanding of the term *experimental* as it applied to psychology.[76] In 1904, however, Pierre Janet would still find himself complaining that psychological concepts were dominated by an anatomical language that, while hypothetical, had managed to become prerequisite to the public's acceptance of otherwise difficult psychological theories.[77] A simplistic application of anatomical explanations to psychological facts was, from Janet's perspective, dishonest and antiscientific.[78] To the physiologist who would explain the association of ideas by pointing to the fibrous connections between brain cells, he asked, "By what right do you employ a terminology that would lead us to believe that you have made use of the scalpel and the microscope to resolve a colossal problem of histology and cerebral psychology?"[79]

Just as Paul Janet had promoted scientific psychology in the philosophy curriculum, so too did Ribot demonstrate his editorial ecumenicalism toward philosophy and psychology. His journal became a forum for the major philosophical figures of the time and was open to articles representing different approaches to the science of psychology. Although he was to continue in his own work advocating a physiologically based science of the mind, as editor of *La Revue Philosophique* Ribot would prove his openness to a variety of philosophical schools and scientific approaches. Like its English contemporary, *Mind, La Revue Philosophique* was an innovation in nineteenth-century philosophical publications because of its nonsectarian approach. Paul Janet, who contributed regularly to the journal and supported it from its first issue, saw *La Revue* as an indication of the necessary rapprochement between philosophy and science that would enable the practice of free thought that both the partisans of science and the partisans of philosophy held dear.[80] Janet argued that "only proximity can calm the fire of their divisions and their discord, and, in leaving aside all that unfortunately and uselessly insinuates itself, only the essential will subsist."[81] For Ribot, however, the strategy of putting these two approaches in proximity to one another was clearly intended to challenge the hegemony of academic philosophy by providing a forum in which eclecticism would be forced to defend its position vis-à-vis native positivism and the scientific psychology of the English and Germans.[82] Janet seems to have understood Ribot's intent in his warning to his younger colleague not to let his positivist leanings destroy the spirit of good faith necessary if *La Revue* was to thrive as a genuine forum for productive exchange.[83] This spirit was, in fact, largely sustained, making *La Revue* one of the most important publications in the emerging field of psychology. Articles focused on a variety of issues concerning perception, consciousness, intelligence, ideation, imagination, and volition. *La Revue* published proceedings of the Société de Psychologie Physiologique, including Janet's first reports from Le Havre. It also published research from the laboratory in experimental psychology that was established by Ribot and Jules Soury at the École Pratique des Hautes Études in January 1889. *La Revue* also dignified articles that took the phenomenon of spiritism as a matter of serious scientific inquiry and thus laid important groundwork for the research on mediumism that was to follow. Wilhelm Wundt would note the seriousness with which *La Revue Philosophique* presented research on spiritism and magnetism, remarking that "there one deals with these matters not as if they were simple curiosities."[84]

In the absence of a French organization comparable to the British Society for Psychical Research, *La Revue Philosophique* gave discussion to mediumism and somnambulism in a context that allowed contributors to reinforce claims of its relevance to scientific study. As a young science, the scientific psychology of Ribot and Pierre Janet turned, sometimes boldly, sometimes more cautiously, to the facts of somnambulism and mediumism in its effort to substantiate the claim that the mind could be studied through objective means. While these phenomena promised direct access to the facts of perception, memory, and cognition, they also held out in more spectacular forms like "mental suggestion at a distance" and "materialization" the possibility that the mind had a material nature that exceeded that of the brain and that could be observed in the influence that it exerted on the material world around it. The proposition, seductive to those concerned about the moral paucity of "materialism" in all of its forms, effectively reversed the hierarchy of causes proposed elsewhere in the natural sciences on the relationship between the moral reality of human beings and their environment. In contrast to the prevailing discourse of "degeneration," the revalidation of the spirit suggested by the facts of mediumism held great appeal both to those tied to the older spiritualist philosophy of the self and to a great many eager to find firm scientific footing for what had previously passed as religious beliefs. The notion that the mind exerted a direct influence on its material environment was, however, also of interest to those who viewed the facts of mediumism and somnambulism from the side of the physical sciences and who were eager to amend their understanding of these facts to the *fin de siècle*'s rapidly changing understanding of the physical world.

3

The Measure of Uncertainty

The Institut Général Psychologique, 1900–1908

As much as the debate about mediumism focused on the reality or absence of reality in mediumistic phenomena, it also raised the question of what reality exactly the study of mediumism should commit itself to testing. In France this question was in large part a product of the institutional and methodological divisions that had shaped the study of psychology up to the end of the nineteenth century. Whether the facts of mediumism were primarily physical or psychological in nature depended mostly on the position within the disciplines from which one approached the question. For those who understood the call for a rapprochement between philosophy and medicine as an opportunity to frame the emerging psychology in positivist terms, mediumism and somnambulism were interesting primarily for the physical and physiological facts they presented. This was true even in respect to the more mysterious phenomena associated with these two practices, which in the minds of many were to be either proved outright frauds or taken as evidence of marvelous properties yet unknown in the physical world. Even Pierre Janet would respond in his early writings to the allure of the marvelous that had surrounded these practices since their origins. His later, more mature study of psychological automatism in mediums and somnambules subsequently placed him at the center of a movement to establish an institutional basis for psychical research in France. When it became clear that any such study would be dominated by the parallel preoccupations of spiritualists, on the one hand, and the physical sciences, on the other, Janet departed. In a gesture that would help to establish an independent institutional basis for psychology in France, Janet would reaffirm the distinct nature of the object of psychology and leave the physical sciences mired in what proved to be a persistent uncertainty about the facts of mediumism.

The historical sketch of spiritism that Janet had provided in *L'Automatisme psychologique* ended around 1882, the year that marked a major transition in science's approach to the facts of somnambulism and mediumism. For Janet, this was the moment when the spiritists retreated from their nearly scientific descriptions of the physical and moral conditions of the séance found in the earlier literature into arguments over esoteric doctrine.[1] This was also the moment when scientific elites began taking the facts of spiritism more seriously. Indeed, by 1882 many of the institutional and ideological conditions for a systematic investigation of spiritist phenomena by scientific elites had taken shape.

The leading part in this development was played not by a French institution but by the British Society for Psychical Research (SPR), which had been founded in 1882 by a group of Cambridge scholars and associates of the moral philosopher Henry Sidgwick. Sidgwick's interest in spirit phenomena stemmed primarily from his doubts about the truth of miracles in the Christian tradition and from concerns about the implications that utilitarian philosophy and evolutionary science had on an ethical system that could no longer rely on the divine doctrine of Duty (a noninstrumental idea of conscience).[2] In general, the interest of Sidgwick and many of his associates developed in response to the challenges that secular thought posed to traditional doctrines of morality and can be seen as an effort to counter the spiritual emptiness that they perceived in scientific materialism.[3] Perhaps most important were the nagging facts of the séances themselves, which had already drawn the interest of certain members of Britain's scientific elite. Encouraged by the adherence of the physicist William Crookes and the naturalist Alfred Russel Wallace to Modern Spiritualism, the prestigious London Dialectical Society performed a survey in 1869 of individuals who had witnessed spirit phenomena and concluded by arguing that the facts warranted serious investigation by research scientists.[4] As an undergraduate at Cambridge, Sidgwick had helped to found the Ghost Society, which collected accounts of paranormal happenings, and by the 1880s Sidgwick's followers were proposing that he take a leading role in a new society to be devoted to systematically studying such events. The core of the organization was to be made up of Sidgwick's wife, Eleanor Balfour Sidgwick, her brothers Arthur and Gerald, Edmund Gurney, Walter Leaf, and Frederic William Henry Myers.[5] With one brother-in-law recently named archbishop of Canterbury and another a member of Parliament who would eventually become prime minister, Sidgwick and the other members of the group were in a position to attract a reputable audience for psychical research, people who, as Sidgwick put it in his first address to the SPR, had a "fair stock of credit to draw upon."[6]

In its first decades the SPR was endorsed by the most eminent members of British society, including the then current prime minister (William Gladstone), eight fellows of the Royal Society (including Wallace, Oliver Lodge, Lord Rayleigh, and John Venn), two bishops, and literary celebrities such as Arthur Conan Doyle, John Ruskin, Charles Lutwidge Dodgson (Lewis Carroll), and Alfred, Lord Tennyson.[7] Indeed, under the influential leadership of respected and innovative scholars the SPR grew into an organization of international reach, setting a standard for all psychical research in the nineteenth century. The list of members and corresponding members to the society would comprise the major figures in European and American psychiatry, psychology, medicine, philosophy, and literature: Eduard von Hartmann, Hippolyte Taine, Hippolyte Bernheim, Ambroise Liébault, Pierre Janet, Charles Richet, Théodore Flournoy, Cesare Lombroso, Albert von Schrenck-Notzing, G. Stanley Hall, William James, William McDougal, and Elizabeth Blackwell. William James would serve as one of the society's first vice presidents and would contribute articles to the society's *Proceedings,* as would eventually Freud, Carl Jung, and Théodore Flournoy.[8] Among notable French figures, the greatest levels of participation would be seen from Charles Richet and Henri Bergson, each of whom would serve a term as the organization's president.

From Psychical to Psychological:
The Institutionalization of Psychical Research in France

The success of the Society for Psychical Research in organizing and funding major research projects was clearly appealing to both Janet and Richet. With the dissolution of the Société de Psychologie Physiologique after Charcot's death in 1893, France no longer had any independent association that might compile the resources adequate for an experimental study of mediumism. By the end of the century a replacement for the society began to be seen as necessary if a systematic investigation of psychical phenomena was to take place. Oswald Murray of the National Liberal Club of London and Serge Youriévitch, a sculptor and attaché to the Russian embassy in Paris, began canvassing for such an organization and in 1899 approached both Janet and Richet with the idea of an international institution devoted to psychical research.[9] The problem of funding was to be resolved by drawing on the significant popular enthusiasm for the study of spirit phenomena from believers, skeptics, and the simply curious. Youriévitch and Murray hoped, in other words, to capitalize on the request by the general public that the issues surrounding spiritism be definitively resolved by science. Youriévitch had foreseen a research organization based on private contributions similar to the extraordinary fashion in which American universities were so generously supported by private endowments. Membership was to be drawn from among scientists as well as educated nonscientists with an amateur interest in the field of psychology.[10] Critical to this effort of drawing widespread support was a journal publicizing the details of the research and of the proceedings of the organization. Indeed, the first issue of the *Bulletin de l'Institut Psychique International* included an appeal by Janet to readers of "good faith" who were "disturbed and impassioned" by questions of psychism and "who appreciate[d] the social value in studying them." In exchange for their support, members would have the satisfaction of finding themselves in the company of great scientific minds, "eminent minds [who], like you, have a specific goal: they seek to break with routine and all of its deeply entrenched prejudices."[11] Given Janet's reputation for open-mindedness, his support for a new science of psychology, and his connections to the academic establishment, his participation as the head of the organization was seen as critical to its success.

The organization was founded in the summer of 1900, when a group of scientists began meeting in the elegantly appointed apartment of the Russian noble and mining magnate Teodor Sabachnikoff in anticipation of the Fourth International Congress of Psychology and decided to formalize their association by collecting dues as the Institut Psychique International in June 1900. The group included Youriévitch, Murray, Janet, Bergson, Richet, Émile Duclaux, Étienne-Jules Marey, Jean Mascart, Albert de Rochas, Hippolyte Baraduc, and Xavier Dariex.[12] When the international congress convened in August, Ribot announced the foundation of the nascent organization to be devoted to the "investigation of what the London Society has proposed to call 'supra-normal' phenomena," a research agenda that Ribot characterized as "the most cutting edge and adventurous part of psychology and not the least seductive."[13] Ribot's description of the institute in his plenary speech before the assembled congress showed interest without expressing any great personal commitment. His references to the institute suggest that, for him, the benefits of psychical research lay primarily in a better understanding of hypnosis and its therapeutic application.[14]

It was, in fact, through its association with somnambulism and hypnotism that research on spiritism claimed a presence in the 1900 congress. In the session devoted to the psychology of hypnosis, of suggestion, and of *questions connexes,* the congress opened its proceedings to participants with clear affiliations to spiritism.[15] Papers from Léon Denis, Gabriel Delanne, Gérard Encausse, Baraduc, and Dariex discussed a variety of supranormal phenomena, including the exteriorization of sensibility, measurement of the *force vitale,* clairvoyance, mental suggestion, the movement of objects without physical contact, and telepathy. The precedent for these presentations had already been set at the first such congress of psychology. Organized in 1889 mostly by Richet, the earlier Parisian congress had offered a section devoted to "hypnotism and phenomena cognate to those of hypnotism," which tended to "slope off," as William James had put it, into "those shady horizons with which the name of 'psychical research' is now associated."[16] Not in attendance at the 1900 congress due to poor health, James would hear in a letter from his friend Flournoy that the spiritualists' presentations on hypnotism and *questions connexes* were the highlight of the otherwise lackluster gathering.[17]

The excitement over these papers was sparked by the German neurologist Oskar Vogt, whose presentation "Against Spiritism" repudiated the "uninvited presentations" of the spiritists.[18] He regretted that, just as hypnotism and suggestion were being recognized as scientific and given useful therapeutic applications, the "spiritists invade our section and compromise it with their antiscientific presentations."[19] Vogt carefully qualified his complaint, arguing that he did not reject a priori the spiritists' claim that there exists a personality apart from its embodiment but insisted that such a claim could only be based on "precise facts, observed with all the scientific rigor possible."[20] As a physician, Vogt had personally observed that spiritists were neuropaths predisposed to hallucinations, and for this reason their observations lacked credibility. He also suggested that the study of spiritism was misguided by its inclination to seek objective evidence in the hypnosis-like states of the medium rather than using hypnosis as a technique by which the medium could be called upon to pay witness to her own subjective states. Vogt's comments, which introduced (perhaps naively) the specter of introspection into the proceedings, caused a riot among a group of French scientists whom Flournoy would refer to in his report to James as the "narrow-minded anatomophysiological group."[21] For these scientists, the allusion to introspection brought surging to the surface the bitter academic struggles over the meanings of "psychology" in France. At the head of the so-called anatomophysiological group, Paul Valentin took the occasion of Vogt's comments to reiterate the only term upon which in his view a "scientific psychology" could be based: "If we do not accept psychology as the study of the functions of the brain, our sciences of nature are nothing but a vain term. [Psychology] is a branch of biology whose only place is between physiology and sociology. Spiritists study the exteriorization of a soul whose existence *in us* is still to be demonstrated. Psychologists study the functioning mechanism of the cortical neurons, the seat of the manifestation of consciousness in cerebral life."[22]

In other words, only a psychology that studied the brain could claim the legitimacy of science. Other approaches, whether these took as their object the mind, the self, or the soul, were by implication to be compared to spiritism as a result of their mutual lack of scientific legitimacy. The participant most scandalized by the discussion of spiritism was Parisian physician Paul Hartenberg, who identified in the spiritists' presentations the Cartesian legacy preserved in Victor Cousin's eclectic spiritualism, that is, the "old illusory dualism."[23] For Hartenberg, the best response to the spiritist interlopers was to recall the legacy of Pierre Cabanis and Franz Joseph Gall by "accept[ing] the rigorous scientific conclusions of positive psychology, which sees in thought only a certain function of a material organ, the brain."[24] In spite of his distinctions between the "psychological organ" and the other organs of the body, Hartenberg observed that "the brain exercises an influence on the rest of the organism that is not the same thing as talking about the power of the mind over matter."[25] Hartenberg's reply effectively reversed Vogt's association between introspection and good scientific psychology by holding Cousin's *philosophie spiritualiste* responsible for *spiritisme*:

> It seems to me that Theosophists, spiritists, ecclesiastics, [and] mystics of all types have joined together here, consciously or not, in combat against what they still call "materialism" under the influence of a kind of neospiritualist urge. But there is a misunderstanding. . . . Our particular psychology is not concerned with the sources of psychological phenomena or with the spiritual force they are or are not the result of. Nor does it concern itself with the ends to which these phenomena lead: it studies only the facts as they present themselves, and this is all.[26]

Hartenberg concluded by demanding, along with Ebbinghaus, that the *questions connexes* be excluded from the section on hypnosis in subsequent congresses. Hippolyte Bernheim, who presided over the session, agreed that the discussion of these issues should be cordoned into their own subsection.[27]

In this atmosphere Ribot's announcement of a new organization devoted to the study of supranormal phenomena was bound to meet with apprehension. Its most eloquent defender at the congress was Julian Ochorowicz, a former philosophy professor from the University of Lemberg and newly named librarian for the Institut Psychique International. Ochorowicz's address hailed the institute as "a permanent international center for all brands of psychological research, including those that had not yet entered into the official domain of psychology."[28] Ochorowicz anticipated the complaint of the anatomophysiological group by tying the research of the institute to the positive science of Auguste Comte and assured the congress participants that the methods of the new organization were to be marked by their absolute independence from the metaphysical tradition that had "eschewed experience" and "ignored shared scientific method."[29] The institute was to be equipped with a conference room, a library, a museum, a clinic, a journal, and, most important, a laboratory.

In spite of Ochorowicz's assurances, the behind-the-scenes endorsement of Richet, and the sumptuous reception given by Sabachnikoff, the newborn institute was, in Flournoy's estimation, about "as glamorous as a soap bubble that was about to burst."[30] By August many of the principal figures were beginning to recognize the professional liability that the institute presented. Ribot and Binet remained distant from Janet and Richet during the 1900 congress in view of the latter's role in the new institute.[31] William James would publicly object to the fact that his name had been listed among the members of the organization without his authorization.[32] Janet also seemed to chill at the prospect of being associated with the stigmatized institute and would soon beat a strategic retreat.[33]

One indication that the original research agenda of the Institut Psychique International had failed to secure support was the immediate change in its name proposed during an organizational meeting open to all participants of the international congress. In the aftermath of the "stormy" session of the section on hypnosis and *questions connexes,* several participants had grown concerned that "behind the word *psychique* there was the dreaded phantom of *études psychiques* [psychical studies]!"[34] As a concession, the name was changed to Institut Psychologique International just before the congress convened. In spite of the name change, most of the principal organizers of the institute remained privately committed to its initial research agenda.[35] The broadened scope of interest implied in the word *psychologique* would, however, open the organization to a variety of competing views. In his presentation to the international delegations Flournoy joined Ochorowicz by figuratively waving his "little censer" at its tumultuous christening and insisting that the institute pursue its intended mission:

> Several members of this Congress seem to fear that the epithet *psychiques* betrays some secret and guilty inclination of the future institute for the types of investigations that our friends across the Channel and across the Atlantic designate by the term *psychical research*—investigations so compromising, as everyone knows, that one does not speak of them openly but only in whispers and that in a congress as respectable as ours are prudently dissembled under the ingenious rubric *questions connexes*. No one more than me admires the delicate art of keeping up appearances. But since we are here, speaking only among us, you will pardon me for calling a spade a spade and admitting that behind these *questions connexes* there is in reality spiritism, occultism, and the other *bêtes noires* of contemporary scientific psychology. . . . We understand that many are liable to shudder in seeing that the Institut International will take into consideration all of these horrible things and engage in what they consider to be the path to perdition. Yet I do not blush to say it: I am of the completely opposite opinion. Far from dreading that the institute will occupy itself with spiritism and occultism, I propose that it is exactly this domain, adored by some and reviled by others, that must constitute the object *par excellence* of [the institute's] impartial investigations and the principal purpose of all of its efforts.[36]

While the institute would survive until 1933, for those present at the international congress in 1900, such longevity seemed unlikely. In the organizational meeting that immediately followed the congress, the executive committee of the institute decided that their efforts would have to be postponed until half a million francs could be raised, which to Flournoy indicated that the whole thing was to be postponed indefinitely.[37] He reported to James that "the Institute could live only on misapprehension; it was dead as soon as people began to suspect it a little."[38] The organization whose original name had echoed that of the Society for Psychical Research would, in the spring of 1902, find a definitive title as the Institut Général Psychologique (IGP).[39]

As originally conceived, the institute's mission was to respond to a public call for a scientific study of spiritism and to vulgarize the results of its research for the benefit of interested laymen. In his initial program to the patrons of the institute, Janet had drawn attention to the great wealth of privately endowed American universities as a model.[40] He argued that while, in the second half of the century, psychical sciences like neurology and psychometry had benefited from the experimental method and inductive reasoning, they had, in general, suffered from a lack of resources, especially in the form of fixed laboratories.[41] The ambitions that Janet had laid out for the institute in 1900 were proving difficult to achieve by the beginning of 1901. By the spring of that year the IGP had enrolled four hundred members but had only marshaled enough pecuniary support to make small and ultimately meaningless contributions to laboratories already in existence.[42] The organization's library was growing as a result of the volumes contributed by its members, but the institute was still far from organizing its own permanent laboratory or museum.

As the head of the institute's executive committee, Janet was initially optimistic about its prospects. An independent research organization patterned after the existing institutions of philosophical, physiological, and medical instruction could, he argued, achieve what an official institution could not, "to put the utmost priority on the study of human thought in all of its physical manifestations as well as its moral ones, in its superior functions as well as its most basic, in its normal aspects as well as its pathological ones."[43] In the best spirit of his uncle, Janet promoted the institute as a means of transcending the ideological disputes that had stunted the development of psychology in France. The institute's library would, he proposed, juxtapose works on the histology of neurons with those offering more daring speculation on supranormal faculties such as lucidity and action at a distance. Such an organization would, he argued, avoid the worst excesses of the tendencies represented by both areas of research. "Isn't this the best way," he asked, "to regulate these various studies one alongside the other, to advance positive study of this unknown domain, to give solidity to ideas that are still only hypotheses, to eliminate these poorly grounded reveries that, all by themselves, will fade in their proximity to these other ideas?"[44] His program for the organization of the institute's laboratories was similarly characteristic of this inclusive approach. Resources for psychological, physiological, and physical laboratories were to be equally allocated, and while each specialty would undoubtedly pursue independent areas of research, in the investigation of mediumistic phenomena, such as the displacement of objects or automatic writing, each specialty would ultimately contribute, "collaborating to develop an understanding of the relation of the physical and the moral, each playing a preponderant role in the development of the psychical sciences and in the understanding of human nature."[45] In essence, the institute promised to be an organization that could be all things to all people.

Behind this generous ecumenicalism, however, Janet was deeply concerned about the influences that the organizational realities of the institute would have on its research agenda. On the one hand, he was happy to draw upon the financial support made available through widespread membership. Financial independence from the official state institutions would effectively free psychology from political concerns that had historically sustained a philosophical psychology long past its point of relevance. On the other hand, open membership and private contributions threatened in their own right to compromise both the goals of the proposed research and its credibility. Janet's open attitude implied, in other words, only the free exchange of ideas among intellectual elites and not a dialogue between these elites and a public that was, he felt, little disposed to understand the complexities of psychology. Indeed, Janet quietly cringed over the populist nature of the organization, especially in regard to the study of certain types of phenomena that so fascinated the public. Could a genuinely nonprejudicial attitude be maintained by a public so unversed in the tentative ways of science? "Wouldn't," he speculated, "these sponsors demand in return for their support the most immediately seductive types of inquiry [and] adventurous solutions in regard to these occult questions?"[46] The experimental nature of the research to be performed by the institute also precluded popular participation. Of the facilities of the institute, Janet cautioned, "These laboratories cannot be open to all researchers. This would quickly result in the greatest disorder."[47]

The situation constituted a kind of double bind in which either strategy would constitute a losing proposition for psychology. It was, of course, the institute's promise to resolve these "occult" questions by scientific means that had drawn public support in the first place. This was clearly understood by Flournoy, who agreed with Janet to the extent that "the general public will never bring its offerings to an institution whose aim is not to satisfy the public curiosity on psychic, occult facts."[48] For Janet, the problems ensuing from the institute's populism highlighted the contradictory benchmarks of scientific success and legitimacy at the turn of the century:

> The Institut Psychologique will, in my opinion, find itself faced with a dilemma. Either it will neglect the truly scientific work with long-term payoffs in order to satisfy the public and draw financial contributions, throwing itself into passionate and irresolvable issues and immediately losing its good reputation among scientists, or it will favor serious physiological, psychological, or clinical studies in order to please men of science and incite the great displeasure of the public, quickly alienating its discouraged subscribers. It will be honorable but poor, and since there is significance only by virtue of fortune, it will be once again completely useless.[49]

Janet's solution to this dilemma was to transform the institute into a public facade for another research organization with a more solidly scientific reputation. While the membership of the larger institute was to remain open to nonscientists with wide-ranging opinions on the subject of psychology and psychical research, the newly formed Société de Psychologie (progenitor of the Société Française de Psychologie) was to be made up only of scientists and academics whose credentials and motives in the scientific study of psychology were above suspicion.[50] On the one hand, Janet explained, there was the "Institut Psychologique, a gathering of quite diverse individuals, men of the world interested in a wide range of questions relative to the mind, a gathering having as its goal to encourage and materially support a great diversity of works in psychology."[51] On the other hand, there was the "Société Psychologique, a much more homogeneous gathering of scientists seeking only to verify and to discuss theories."[52] These were, he argued, "two quite different things that must be kept independent of one another."[53] Membership in the much smaller society was to be limited to forty, and presentations to the group were subject to the prior approval of the officers, which included Janet (president), Binet (vice president), Ribot (honorary president), and Georges Dumas (general secretary).[54] Notably absent from the roster of members was Charles Richet, a sign perhaps that Janet was consciously distancing himself from his older colleague.[55] Janet's leadership role in the institute had been the condition upon which other prominent scientists agreed to participate, and many of these individuals defected with Janet to the more insular society while nominally maintaining their membership in the larger organization.[56]

For some members of the more populous Institut Psychologique, Janet's organizational revisions represented a betrayal of the first order. César de Vesme, editor of the popular *Revue des Études Psychiques,* expressed his sense of exasperation when he discovered that his status within the organization had been downgraded from "titulary member" to "adherent."[57] When he asked for a definition of this unfamiliar designation at the administrative offices of the Institut Psychologique he discovered that it, in fact, had no precise definition, since the institute had not yet passed any bylaws governing the activities of its members.[58] Nor, Vesme discovered, was there any definitive membership at all, at least not any list of members that he might be permitted to consult. Compounding his frustration was the fact that none of the early activities of the institute touched on the questions that it had been organized to answer. Echoing Flournoy's cautions about the public's motives in supporting the organization, Vesme mused, "Are we to be told that the public has opened its pocketbooks so that it can be instructed in [the] method of measuring tactile sensibility, shown the sensory paths leading to the medulla, or taught why certain optical illusions are produced by moving a paper with a few circles drawn on it around a table?"[59] Instead of the great work anticipated by the public, hoping to see the question of mediumism resolved, the institute focused instead on esoteric neurological phenomena of interest only to specialists in that field. For Vesme, the motives for these bait-and-switch tactics were clearly pecuniary. Michel Sage, the author of a résumé of the SPR's investigation of the American medium Mrs. Piper, caricatured Janet's motives for creating the Société de Psychologie in similar terms: "The moment is propitious, he says, since we are offered what we have lacked until today, money."[60] Indeed, Janet did welcome the "room and board" offered by the popular organization, and his society did appropriate the lion's share of the institute's *Bulletin* to publicize its proceedings.[61] For Vesme, the inaugural lecture before the society by Alfred Binet was like the stone slab that "falls heavily over the opening of a grave . . . after the priest has pronounced *Requiem aeternam.*"[62] Janet's first presentation to the society, which addressed the mental pathologies exhibited in religious ecstasies, established his opposition to all mystifications by applying a method familiar from Charcot's *Les Démoniaques dans l'art.* The presence of the society in the *Bulletin* of the institute would gradually diminish after the winter of 1901, and by 1904 Janet and Dumas would found a separate publication: the *Journal de Psychologie Normale et Pathologique.*

Janet's defection from the institute was sparked primarily by his desire to make of mediumism an object of psychological study and not a set of facts to be proven or disproven. One can also not discount the influence that careerism had on his decisions.[63] No longer the young *agrégé* seeking to make a name for himself, Janet was, during the time of the 1900 congress, acting as *suppléant* to Ribot's vacated chair in experimental and comparative psychology at the Collège de France. Janet's appointment to the chair would represent the culmination of the strategy that Paul Janet had put into play decades earlier in an effort to preserve within the new psychology crucial features of the old philosophical doctrine of self. Janet could hardly risk damaging his candidacy by tying his name to the dubious field of psychical research. The misappropriation of the account of his early experiments in Le Havre had made him cautious about committing his reputation to the study of controversial phenomena when he could not personally control the meanings attributed to his research. He had learned shortly after the publication of these experiments that his purely descriptive accounts could be readily exaggerated into supporting conclusions that he had carefully avoided making.[64] His caution with regard to the study of mediumism is evident in his *L'Automatisme psychologique* and in his later writings on spiritism, in that his interest had clearly narrowed in these works to the practice of automatic writing. Among the many phenomena exhibited in the context of spiritism, it was only automatic writing that he would personally continue to view as fertile terrain for the experimental elaboration of the forms of unconscious mental activity.

Rayonnements and the Physics of the Social

With Janet's effective departure, the institute was legally reconstituted in 1902 as the Institut Général Psychologique (IGP), with new leadership provided by men highly placed in the administration of the state.[65] The organization acquired as its president of honor Léon Bourgeois, whose role in the institute was actually fulfilled by his friend Louis Herbette, a veteran state councilor and penal expert who had been brought to the organization by Youriévitch after working with him on the organization of the 1900 Exposition Universelle in Paris. Herbette addressed the general assembly of March 1902 by welcoming the participation of "individuals belonging to the army, the navy, the diplomatic service, the administration, the great legislative bodies, and the judiciary" for the real-world experiences they could bring to the study of "Man."[66] The advantage of this inclusiveness for Herbette was to introduce practical knowledge into a domain that had been dominated for more than half a century by the eclectic philosophers. The advantages of such a "general" institute were alluded to by Herbette: "Truly general is an Institut Psychologique that calls upon its adherents—even those foreign to philosophical works, even those less inclined toward abstract theories—to gather together the multiple resources of science. All the sciences must contribute to the constitution of psychology, that is, to the knowledge of man and to the ways in which he is governed."[67]

Under the influence of Herbette and Bourgeois, the mission of the institute would be yet again redefined. The original desire to investigate supranormal phenomena associated with hypnotism and mediumism was now displaced by an instrumentalization of the new science, which sought to recruit psychology to the study of the mechanisms by which men might be better "governed." This appropriation, tied to the need for funding, effectively compromised the independent status hoped for by Janet and others by providing a means for encouraging conformity between the interests of the organization and the interests of the state.

In 1901 these interests were most often expressed in connection with the neo-Jacobin doctrine of *solidarité*, or solidarism, which had developed in the last decade of the nineteenth century in response to the failures perceived in the contractual social model of liberalism and the concerns among republicans about the collectivist alternative proposed by socialism. Solidarism seemed to offer a solution to the failures of classical liberalism by deemphasizing individual autonomy and stressing in its place the individual's natural obligations to society. In the hands of its chief theorist, Alfred Fouillé, solidarism sought to reclaim the language of the natural sciences from the social Darwinists and apply it to a political doctrine in which principles of cooperation and integration would replace the conflict-based model of social relations.[68] Essential to this cooperative, organic model was the idea of a social division of labor studied in animal groups by Alfred Espinas and in human societies by his younger colleague at the Faculté des Lettres of Bordeaux, Émile Durkheim.[69] Solidarism argued that within this social division of labor individuals benefited in a measure disproportionate to their own contributions. These benefits and the debts they imposed on individuals were to serve as the new basis of the social bond.

In the midst of the growing enthusiasm for these ideas, both philosophical and sociological, psychology would also be drawn upon to challenge conventional liberalism's notions of the individual. Fouillé was especially interested in the new psychology to the degree that it no longer emphasized the given unity of the *moi* but, rather, saw the self as a composite joined by a process of integration. This model of the self, which Pierre Janet had developed in his work on psychological disaggregation, complemented the social doctrine of solidarism by suggesting that the sense of self developed out of the aggregate faculties of the mind only as a result of an ongoing process of integration.[70] In this integrative psychology the individual represented a community unto itself that functioned only as a result of the contributions of its various parts. As Fouillé put it in his 1891 review of developments in the new psychology, "a living being is in reality a society of living beings pressed one against the other and in immediate communication."[71] Just as each cell could be considered a living organism that lives only to the extent that it coordinates its efforts with other cells, so too was each individual's survival and well-being dependent on the work of other individuals. Janet's ideas about the mind thus offered a powerful metaphor for the notion of a social division of labor and the integrative function of the state.

This analogy might have remained academic if the doctrine of solidarism had not played such an important role in the ideology of the French Republic at the turn of the century. It was the ubiquitous republican statesman Léon Bourgeois who popularized and refined Fouillé's ideas in his very successful 1897 book *Solidarité*.[72] It was also Bourgeois who, along with Charles Seigno-bos, Ferdinand Buisson, and Émile Durkheim, would promote solidarism as the guiding doctrine of French education at the Congrès International de l'Éducation Social, which gathered in Paris in September 1900, one month after the International Congress of Psychology, which saw the foundation of the Institut Psychique International.[73] The participation of both Bourgeois and Fouillé in the Institut Général Psychologique after 1902 suggests what sort of ambitions these republican ideologues might have had for the new organization.

As it was reconstituted in 1902, the new mission of the IGP was to be ful-filled through four new research sections. The relative importance of these sections indicated a movement toward areas other than psychical research. The most prominent of the sections in the *Bulletin* was clearly the group de-voted to the study of zoological psychology (chaired by Eugène-Louis Bouvier and Edmond Perrier, whose work on insect colonies supported the postulates of solidarism).[74] This was followed by a section for the study of collective psychology and a group for the study of moral psychology and criminality. Collectively, these fields fulfilled the criteria that Herbette had articulated for a successful psychology. Ever attentive to developments in the IGP, Flournoy would note sarcastically the compromise represented by a reorganization that gave prominence to the three sections devoted to "truly serious work."[75]

The fourth group, which Flournoy described as "tiny relative to the oth-ers," was left to carry out the original intent of the institute's founders by dedicating itself to the study of *phénomènes psychiques*.[76] The members of the Groupe d'Étude des Phénomènes Psychiques (GEPP) included Jacques-Arsène d'Arsonval, Édouard Branly, Édouard Brissaud, Émile Duclaux, André Weiss, and Étienne-Jules Marey—men who represented the combined ideological and institutional legacies of Claude Bernard, Louis Pasteur, and Charcot.[77] A notable exception to the predominance of physiologists, physicists, neurolo-gists, and chemists in the psychical research group was Henri Bergson.[78]

Conspicuously absent from the roster was Pierre Janet, who in Febru-ary 1902 was named to Ribot's chair at the Collège de France. One can only speculate that, given the composition of the group, Janet saw little oppor-tunity to exploit mediumistic phenomena for the benefit of psychology as he understood it. Indeed, when the group publicized its principal goals and concerns in February 1902, it did so in a language suggesting a research agenda more concerned with testing the objective reality of mediumistic phenomena than its indication of psychological facts: "What is the proportion of objective reality and what is the proportion of subjective interpretation in the facts described under the names of mental suggestion, telepathy, mediumism, levitation, etc.?"[79] Such a question could, they argued, only be addressed "through the application of precise methods of observation and rigorous experimentation such as those that are in use in laboratories."[80] This desire to mobilize the experimental techniques of the physical sciences was inspired not only by concerns about the role that the medium's subjective motivations played in the phenomena but also by a fair amount of hope that some genuine physical force might be discovered. In the context of an ongoing scientific revolution epitomized by wireless telegraphy, X-rays, radioactivity, and the special theory of relativity, the physical world in the period from roughly 1894 to 1905 was indeed open to such marvelous possibilities. Fast-fixed notions of space, time, and matter were readily giving way to daring reconsiderations that GEPP research hoped might substantiate the various phenomena of mediumism.

In the context of this shift in the paradigm of modern physics, something like Mesmer's universal fluid seemed to many less laughable than it had been in the past. The mechanical model of nature, which tended to conceptualize cause as a material relation between substantial and consistent objects, was giving way to a language of physics filled with metaphors of amorphous fluids and the indirect action of *rayonnements* (rays).[81] The validation of this language would mark the beginning of a rivalry within the study of mediums between causes rooted in the *physique* and those tied to the *morale*. The psychical researchers of the GEPP would not, for instance, take as their point of reference the Romantic appropriation of animal magnetism by Puységur with its emphasis on interpersonal rapport. Rather, their approach would more closely parallel Mesmer's original teachings, with their indications of an etheric fluid that surrounded bodies in nature and acted as the medium by which the mechanical action of one body might influence another removed from it in space and, perhaps, time. In the context of this emerging paradigm, the original desire of Janet, Ribot, and others to bring objective methods to the study of psychology readily gave way to a desire to use the study of mediums as a means of better understanding physical reality.

Many members of the IGP were extremely optimistic about the possibility that unknown physical mechanisms had a role to play in mediumistic phenomena. As the physiologist d'Arsonval noted, "In our era, in spite of the remarkable progress made by science, it would be dangerous and inexact to say that we know absolutely all the forms of energy that surround us. There are perhaps certain forms of this energy that originate in living beings and are totally unknown to us."[82] The world was, after all, viscerally alive with invisible forces, as the recent discoveries of radio, X-rays, and radioactivity had demonstrated.

The same enthusiasm that surrounded the discoveries of Oliver Lodge, Wilhelm Roentgen, and Pierre and Marie Curie also helped to sustain one of the more notorious scientific follies of the twentieth century—Réné Blondot's 1903 "discovery" of N-rays. Named after the city of Nancy, in which Blondot worked, N-rays were thought to be a property of both sunlight and the human body, and their presence was indicated by their effects on electrical sparks or phosphorescent substances. In 1903 d'Arsonval, upon presenting Blondot's findings to the GEPP, suggested that instruments be used in their research to measure whether the visual hyperacuity of hysterics might be attributable to their perception of N-rays or whether or not mediums and hysterical subjects might themselves emit any special form of electromagnetism.[83] In his reflections on the possibility of telepathy, Alfred Fouillé would consider N-rays only one of an infinite series of forces to be discovered by science, which, in naming them, would use up "every letter of the human alphabet."[84]

Such hopes for the GEPP were briefly thwarted in 1904, when the group was struck by the death of its principal member and president, the biologist Émile Duclaux. For several years the pages of the IGP's *Bulletin* fell silent on the subject of psychical phenomena. Behind the scenes, however, the group was making preparations for and undertaking an extensive series of investigations. The great problem facing the GEPP was apparently in finding individuals capable of producing, in a controlled laboratory setting, the phenomena that had been so frequently observed elsewhere. A general appeal was made to the main body of the IGP with the hope that information about people in possession of such abilities would be forthcoming, but the response was minimal. The reasons for this were puzzling: "Is it because they fear that phenomena produced in an intimate circle will not be capable of manifesting themselves under different circumstances? Is it because they think that mediums risk being intimidated by men of science? Is it because they suspect the methods of laboratory experimentation will not be as welcoming and nice as elsewhere? Is it because mediums fear losing their reputation if they cannot, under certain conditions of control, produce manifestations?"[85] The answer to the problem came in 1905, when, through the intervention of Charles Richet, the group was able to procure an especially exceptional subject able to produce phenomena with the regularity demanded by laboratory research.

Bad Subject: The Experiments with Eusapia Palladino at the Institut Général Psychologique

The choice of Eusapia Palladino would in many ways help to reinforce the direction that the nature of the research conducted by the GEPP was to take. Unlike other mediums who specialized in phenomena that suggested subjective processes (like automatic writing or trance lectures), Eusapia specialized mostly in physical phenomena of a very impressive character.[86] A woman of very modest origins, she had by 1905 already established a reputation for herself as the greatest physical medium since Daniel Dunglas Home had thrilled European audiences in the mid-nineteenth century. By the end of her life Eusapia had performed for many of the most eminent members of the European and American scientific communities.

Born to a peasant family in 1854 in the mountainous region of Abruzzi, Eusapia was orphaned as a child and received no formal education. At the age of thirteen or fourteen she began having visions and discovered her ability to move objects without touching them. A laundress by profession, she gave occasional séances until she was engaged in the household of the professor Ercole Chiaia as a companion for his daughters. Chiaia brought Eusapia's powers to the attention of Cesare Lombroso, who subsequently introduced her to leading psychical researchers like Charles Richet, Alexander Aksakof, and Albert von Schrenck-Notzing.[87] Thus, Eusapia was launched into an international career as the "Sarah Bernhardt of the mediums" and would subsequently become the subject of hundreds of scholarly works devoted to the phenomena she produced.[88]

Eusapia's reputation as a medium was, however, far from spotless. Having been introduced to Frederic Myers at Richet's country estate near the Mediterranean town of Carqueiranne, she would be brought to London in 1895 for what proved to be a disastrous series of séances with the members of the SPR.[89] It was Richard Hodgson, then secretary of the American SPR, who recognized during the London experiments that Eusapia cheated in order to free herself from the physical controls of the experiments.[90] In the more chaotic moments of the séance Eusapia liberated her hands by placing the hand of the controller on her left on top of the hand of the controller on her right. Instead of maintaining contact with Eusapia's hands, the observers on either side were left holding each other's hands. As a result of this discovery of fraud, Myers came to doubt his earlier observations. Sidgwick and Podmore considered that Eusapia's credibility was permanently compromised, and she was barred from any further experiments with the SPR.

Others adopted a different response to the incident by arguing that although it was recognized that Eusapia cheated in some instances, this did not explain the phenomena produced when no cheating was detected. Sympathetic observers noted that Eusapia's ability to perform admittedly varied based on the circumstances she found herself in and suggested that she cheated only when she was fatigued or in a particularly demanding environment (480). Because her livelihood depended on the payments she received for her services as a medium, she sometimes, it was argued, resorted to desperate measures. For her part, Eusapia represented herself as someone who did not welcome or understand the origins of her powers. She claimed that she possessed no control over the phenomena produced and that afterward she retained little memory of what had occurred.[91]

The changing status of Eusapia's reputation among psychical researchers is instructive as to the doubts and vacillations that characterized their field as a whole. After her exposure before the SPR Eusapia returned to France in 1898 to undergo a series of experiments with Richet, Flournoy, Myers, and Émile Boirac.[92] Participants noted that these séances occurred under much better circumstances than those with the SPR. Eusapia allowed the lights in the séance room to remain lit and notified the observers just prior to each new manifestation so that they could direct their attention and better scrutinize each phenomenon as it occurred. While many of the more spectacular phenomena (such as the levitation or breaking of the table) did not take place, the phenomena that Eusapia did manage (particularly the sounds coming from an untouched violin and the billowing of the curtain behind the medium's chair) did not seem to have been produced through fraudulent means. Myers returned to England in December 1898 and announced publicly his belief that the phenomena were genuine.[93] It was in the wake of this partial rehabilitation that Eusapia would be presented to the members of the IGP in 1905.

Charged with a preliminary investigation of Eusapia in Naples, GEPP representatives Serge Yourievitch and Jules Courtier would return with their medium to Paris, where the IGP would launch a cycle of experiments lasting three years (417). Thirteen séances were held at the IGP offices on the rue Condé during the first year of investigations, followed by five more in 1906. The séances of 1907 were held at the home of Yourievitch, where Eusapia lived during her stay in Paris.[94] Forty-three séances in total were organized for the members of the GEPP and included the frequent participation of Richet and Pierre Curie. Occasionally accompanied by Marie Skłodowska, Curie would remain active in the group until his accidental death in 1906. Members of the GEPP regretted that Curie's wisdom, the quality of his methods, and his perseverance could never be put to use to "discover in these paths still so obscure the explanations and the causes of phenomena."[95]

At the end of 1908, after three years of research, the IGP published its long-awaited findings. The drafting of the report was entrusted to Courtier, a close associate of Alfred Binet at the Laboratoire de Psychologie Physiologique at the Sorbonne.[96] Courtier's report detailed the course of the investigations from the adoption of experimental protocols to the summary of the group's findings. It was clear from Courtier's account that the experiments with Eusapia were costly. By 1908 the GEPP figured as the most important of the IGP's research groups, which now numbered five, with the addition of a section combining *psychologie artistique, psychologie morale et criminelle,* and *psychologie individuelle.* In his budget proposal of 1908 Youriévitch (who had taken on the office of vice president) allotted 3,000 francs for the psychical research group and only 500 francs for the other four.[97] This allocation was necessary to pay the more than 2,300 francs owed to Eusapia in honoraria.[98] The total cost of the Eusapia experiments conducted in 1905 alone had been 5,910 francs, an expense that was met by the implementation of a fund-raising lottery authorized by the minister of the interior on 26 January 1905.[99] The remaining cost was due no doubt to the adoption of mechanical devices needed to record and corroborate the effects most often witnessed (changes in temperature, the movement of objects, sounds, apparitions) as well as to identify phenomena beyond the range of human perception (X-rays, electrical fields, magnetic fields, radioactivity, sonic vibrations). The equipment was also intended to eliminate the possibility that the phenomena as observed were influenced by errors in perception resulting from fatigue and inattention in the observers as well as from the poor conditions of the séance room. Courtier maintained in his report the effectiveness of these techniques: "The recordings did not permit us to cast doubt on the displacement and complete levitation of heavy objects with simple contact or even with no evident contact; any hypothesis of collective hallucination must on this basis be discounted" (514). In cases where it was buttressed by mechanical inscription, the reliability of observers' perception was placed beyond doubt. The indeterminacy of the group's conclusions regarding physical phenomena would thus stem not from the facticity of the events themselves but rather from the uncertainty surrounding their causes.

In the three years that the group studied Eusapia, equipment and procedures continued to be introduced and adapted to the difficult experimental conditions. Members hoped that the mundane objects—the tables and chairs that had for decades served as the principal "instruments" of spiritists' séances—would be replaced by more specialized recording devices to measure the action of the force produced by the medium (416). Some of these means were relatively simple: modeling clay and smoked paper to record the contact of spirit hands and fingers. The more elaborate instrumentation, drawn directly from the experimental apparatus developed by Marey in his studies of human and animal physiology, was designed to measure the muscular contractions of the medium and the corresponding movement of objects (416–17). A stenographer was employed to register the observations of the scientists and record at each passing moment the level of their control over the subject (520). True to the method of Marey, a great deal of attention was devoted to synchronizing the various forms of data to a time scale so that an accurate comparison could be made between the instrumental readings and the stenographer's notes. Eventually, a device was incorporated into the system that indicated the relationship of the events in time by marking the passing minutes.

As well as monitoring the more familiar events of the mediumistic séance, the scientists in the group hoped to record as yet undiscovered physical phenomena beyond the range of human perception. Tests were devised, for instance, to measure whether or not the air surrounding the medium was ionized or exhibited an unusual chemical composition (510). In 1905 two séances were conducted at Charles Henry's Laboratoire de Physiologie des Sensations at the Sorbonne to determine whether or not the subject produced any unusual thermal phenomena or a magnetic field—which she did not (510). The committee also explored means for directly measuring the forces exerted on the objects and instruments of the séance room. Édouard Branly reported to the group on his experiments with Hippolyte Baraduc's *biomètre,* a simple device from the realm of animal magnetism (essentially a free-moving spindle inside a glass enclosure) designed to measure directly the force of the *rayonnement vital.* While Branly's study of the device was inconclusive, he conceded that "nothing . . . would be more natural than to see a *rayonnement* issue from a living organism that was limited in its effect to influences exerted on other living organisms."[100] Conversely, as a way of investigating the influence of naturally occurring environmental conditions on the production of phenomena, the group proposed to determine the effect of sonic vibrations, electromagnetism, radiated heat, light, X-rays, and radioactivity on the events of the séance (417).

Fulfilling the interests of the physiologists Marey and Richet, the group also gave special attention to the physiological status of the medium. The examination of Eusapia was to be continual throughout the séance, with equipment and observers in place to note her circulation, blood pressure, respiration, secretions, temperature, electrical potential, electrical resistance of her tissues, autonomic reflexes, visual acuity and field, muscular capacity, reaction time, cutaneous sensibility, and mental processes (479–80). The rates of her pulse and respirations were to be taken fifteen minutes after the séance had concluded, and her urine was to be examined every forty-eight hours (490–94). In December 1907 the name of the group was changed to Section des Recherches Psychiques et Physiologiques "in order to indicate that, in this research, we mean primarily to employ the methods of physiology."[101]

The lighting in the room was, of course, of prime importance to visual controls and observations. The room, illuminated with gas, was equipped with an optometrist's chart so that at any moment participants could gauge their visual acuity. Errors in depth perception, sense of direction, and the localization of phenomena increased noticeably in proportion to the level of darkness. The principal concern was the effect of light on the retina and the ability of the human eye to adapt to changes in its intensity (419). Observers had noted the inverse correlation between the amount of light in the séance room and the intensity of the phenomena produced by the medium. In a well-lighted room the observers noted sounds "as one might expect from the articulation of a single finger or a fingernail" (433). In near-total darkness the witnesses observed the movement of large objects and the apparition of "spirit hands" emerging from the *cabinet noir*. Eusapia maintained that, due to the sensitivity to light brought on by her trance state, she could only produce phenomena when the lights were dimmed, and it was shown that changes in the amount of light did in fact produce physiological changes in the medium. When the lights were brought up, Eusapia's respiration, blood pressure, and pulse increased. On one occasion the stenographer's lamp flared, and the sudden increase of light sent Eusapia into a *crise* lasting several minutes during which it was noted that her pulse was very elevated (490–92). The group, eager to record the apparitions of black or luminous forms photographically, persisted in their efforts in spite of Eusapia's complaints about the use of flash lamps. They conceded to Eusapia's request to forewarn her of their intent to take a photograph in order that she might prepare herself against the sudden increase in the amount of light. The procedure, it was determined, made photography an unreliable record of events, and its use was discontinued (525). Of the dozen or so photographs taken, none was conclusive that the levitations occurred through supranormal means.

Given the need to adjust to the changing disposition of the medium and the shifting concerns of the observers, the methods of control involved a great deal of improvisation and adjustment. Control by touch remained the most reliable but far from perfect method of monitoring Eusapia's activities. Eusapia often complained of hyperesthesia, an extreme sensitivity in her wrists, forearms, and backs of her hands, making it difficult for controllers to maintain a confident grip. Often the séance would have to be called off until the condition had subsided (489–90). As a solution, Eusapia allowed the controllers to sew two ribbons, twenty centimeters in length, between her sleeves and the sleeves of her controllers on either side. The method was intended to eliminate the need for touching her hands while restricting their movement. Eusapia objected that the procedure reminded her of the methods that asylums used to restrain the mentally ill, and they decided to abandon it (518). "As much as possible," the two observers sitting on either side of Eusapia controlled her feet by keeping them in contact with their own (420). Her legs were monitored either by a controller placing a hand on her lower thigh with his fingers interposed between her knees or visually by an observer under the table equipped with a candle (552, 435).[102] Among those who served most frequently in this capacity, Courtier notes specifically Pierre Curie, Marie Curie, Charles Richet, and Henri Bergson (435). On other occasions Eusapia's feet were simply bound to her chair (543).

The group took great precautions to prevent Eusapia from cheating in her effort to elevate the table. The levitation of the table was recorded by spring-loaded electrical switches placed in a cavity in the lower portion of each leg. Each switch activated when the leg was no longer in contact with the floor, sending a signal to a recording device. The table legs were eventually encased in long wooden sleeves attached to the floorboards designed to prevent Eusapia from lifting the table with a toe slipped underneath a leg or by exerting lateral pressure with her thighs or knees. When the table levitated even higher from the floor, it was determined that the sleeves might actually provide a higher point of leverage, and they were removed. The researchers then applied a similar control to Eusapia herself by encasing her feet and legs in a wooden box attached to the floorboards (445–46). The top of the table was unscrewed from its supporting frame, eliminating the undersurface as a point of leverage. Both the top and detached frame were successfully lifted from the floor (447).

The observing scientists often marveled at these events. The movement of a smaller three-legged gueridon, fifty centimeters to the right of Eusapia's chair, became cause for consideration when it was seen to be drawn to and pushed away from Eusapia's position without any perceived contact. On one occasion this small side table levitated from the floor entirely, slowly rotated upside-down, and came to a rest on the main séance table. Pierre Curie's observation of this phenomenon would become a point of reference on many occasions during the discussion following the presentation of Courtier's report: "What is astonishing is the precision with which the gueridon moved without touching anyone. It made a nice curve and did not touch me at all" (543). In another instance the smaller table resisted the efforts of the observers to physically lift it. "One would have thought it nailed to the floor," d'Arsonval exclaimed (473). For his part, d'Arsonval was inclined to see in the displacement of objects the effect of natural forces. In one instance he was reputed to have seized the gueridon in midflight and "cried out in the idiom of the physicist: 'It is absolutely the resistance of the magnetic field!'"[103]

Under the best conditions the participants witnessed partial and total levitation of the larger table weighing seven kilograms and bearing an additional weight of ten kilograms (435, 510). With her chair placed on a Marey scale, Eusapia achieved total levitation of the table with both her hands and legs controlled (435). The scale, which consisted of a coiled rubber tube between two boards, indicated downward pressure on Eusapia's body, causing observers to conclude that the force used to lift the table originated there. In one instance, after Eusapia expressed her annoyance with the device, the rubber tube of the scale was ruptured at a place where it passed inside the *cabinet noir* (470).

This feature of the séance room naturally drew a considerable amount of attention. The curtained enclosure, which had been in regular use by mediums at least as early as Crookes's séances with Florence Cook in the 1870s, was supposed by mediums to provide a means of collecting the fluidic energy produced by the circle. Mediums usually sat in front of these enclosures but could draw the curtains around them as needed. Eusapia, who usually remained visible, produced a phenomenon that caused the curtain of the *cabinet* to billow on alternating sides even when her hands and feet were well controlled. When observers applied pressure to the billowing cloth, a resistance was felt "much like what one might encounter from a hand or a fist" (447–48). The same billowing was witnessed with the fabric of her dress even when her ankles were tied to the legs of her chair. Pierre Curie was particularly struck by this phenomenon and proposed that the force be directed under a strip of woolen fabric that he held on the floor near Eusapia's feet. The fabric undulated from the floor along with the leg of a small table located nearby. In a subsequent séance Curie brought with him an apparatus consisting of a sewn tube of fabric attached to two wooden frames and asked that Eusapia direct this force through the tube (468–69). Eusapia complained that the opposite end of the tube was too far from her and that the fabric was stretched too tightly. The frame nearest her was suddenly knocked about and violently broken to pieces without any contact perceived by her controllers—Pierre Curie on her left hand, Richet on her right, and Youriévitch at her feet.

These physical forces were accompanied by a variety of visual phenomena. Simple points of luminescence were frequently observed, often accompanied by the smell of phosphorus. More complex "materializations" in the form of hands and arms were most frequently noted by the controllers closest to Eusapia. During the tenth séance in 1905 Courtier's report recounts the appearance of a "black arm": "M. Curie and Youriévitch saw it quite clearly. We saw again that a black arm from the left side of the curtain approached several times and forcefully touched M. Komyakoff on the shoulder. It was seen by M. Curie, Bergson, Gramont, Komyakoff, and Youriévitch (controllers M. Komyakoff to the left; to the right, M. Curie)" (479).

Instances of sometimes brusque physical contact contributed to the often chaotic atmosphere of the séances. Observers reported being tapped on the shoulder, poked in the back, and pinched. They felt their hair being pulled, and their chairs were sometimes suddenly jerked from underneath them and overturned (473–75). These moments were often preceded by long periods of waiting in a somber room for events that might or might not occur. When phenomena did occur, they were often instantaneous and so varied in nature that the participants were generally unprepared to observe each event in its particularity. Courtier recognized that the "sensorially precarious conditions" of the séance produced mental and emotional changes in the observers. In these circumstances the observers' mental condition was characterized by a division of attention, a state of anticipation, feelings of astonishment, and general fatigue (519–20). Courtier noted that the unavoidable emotional response to the phenomena put the mind into an "overly excited state" that tended to undermine "healthy judgment" (520). Observers were reminded to guard themselves against the possibility of suggestion and were asked to admit the possible contributions of their own desire to the production of phenomena. Courtier would, for instance, consider the impact of the collective desire to produce phenomena by citing Ampère's famous *coup de pouce* (nudge) as an illustration of the involuntary assistance that even the best scientific observer might provide to an anticipated event (564–65). Observers were cautioned not to add anything to their statements beyond what was actually observed and to avoid engaging a memory of previous events in completing their current observations (520).

The problem of the observer's subjective perception persisted in spite of the use of mechanical recording devices. While outright hallucination could, Courtier argue, be discounted, the conditions of observation continued to frustrate the realization of subjective certainty. In the final analysis, the technical apparatus employed in the experiments fell far short of the assurances sought by the men of the group. Courtier lamented, "How far we are from the patient experiments of the laboratory, where the conditions of the phenomena are regulated and calculated in advance, where one can observe a single fact at a time, in a tranquil and quiet state of attention!" (520). Courtier noted, however, that even events witnessed in the best possible circumstances could produce confusion and doubt (556). One such occasion, immediately following a séance, found Branly and Courtier observing in full light as Eusapia, by placing her hands a few centimeters to either side of a glass, caused the object to vibrate and break without touching it. "We believed that we had really seen the phenomenon. That evening we were convinced; but two days later we began to doubt ourselves and would have liked to have had the test repeated" (556). Initially convinced that this action had been realized by nonnormal means, their attitude changed as passing time allowed them to doubt their perceptions.

Maintaining a productive working relationship with Eusapia was a constant process of negotiation. A cordial rapport between the medium and the members of the research group was not only necessary to preserve her cooperation, it was also recognized as a contributing factor in the production of the phenomena themselves. Eusapia explained the importance of amicable relations in terms of her sensitivity to the disposition of the fluid of her controllers. When phenomena failed to occur, Eusapia would often ask for her controllers to be replaced by other members of the circle (435). Courtier explained the importance of the social atmosphere of the séances in terms of securing Eusapia's confidence. Along with the lighting and the methods of control, "the moral disposition of the participants [was] from her perspective just as important for the success of the séances. As long as she feels herself in friendly company and, moreover, in the company of people who she knows have confidence in her, we have noted that the phenomena produce themselves rapidly and that the séances were much stronger" (448).

The need to maintain an atmosphere conducive to the production of phenomena meant that the scientists were often obliged to yield to Eusapia's refusals concerning their methods of control and observation. Eusapia would not, for instance, allow a nonparticipating observer to sit near her during the séance for the purpose of observing the visual phenomena that could only be seen in close proximity to her (518–19). Such a person, she argued, would disrupt the fluid produced by the circle. Eusapia also rejected the group's proposal to have her admitted to a clinic for the purposes of submitting her to a thorough medical examination. In the group's discussion of this refusal d'Arsonval grudgingly conceded, to the amusement of his colleagues, that "Eusapia is a subject but a very bad subject (laughs). We are obliged to take her as she is" (561).

During the séance of 27 June 1906 Eusapia was suspected of having freed one of her hands for the purpose of cheating and was deeply vexed by the accusation. Eager to regain the group's confidence, she asked that the lights be turned up and that she be brought a glass. Placing her hands about three centimeters to each side, she pulled the glass toward her without any apparent contact. She then vibrated her hands in the air, and the glass emitted a sound as if a wet finger had been rubbed around its rim. She then gestured abruptly, and the glass fell to the floor and broke, again without any apparent contact (511). Courtier concluded from her efforts to prove herself that, while Eusapia's amnesia suggested a second state in which conscious "will" played no role, she could nevertheless invoke and direct her powers when motivated to do so (545).

That Eusapia cheated was certain. In the GEPP experiments she was caught on one occasion using a hair to move the leaves of a plant. On another she palmed a small finishing nail and used it to depress the platform of a scale whose surface had been covered in smoked paper (521). While acknowledging these undisputed acts of deception, the researchers still questioned whether or not they were justified in dismissing all of the phenomena she produced as the effect of fraud. When pressed in the discussion following the presentation of his report, Courtier remained uncertain whether the known instances of fraud automatically discredited everything the group had witnessed. The problem, it seems, lay with the motivations for cheating, which could be of either a conscious or an unconscious nature. While Courtier was willing to recognize that mediums were not normal psychological subjects, that they exhibited abnormal or even hysterical temperaments, he could not ultimately distinguish between consciously motivated fraud and the dissimulations of unconscious mental activity. He acknowledged that mediums "lose control of themselves in their second states [and] are suggestible toward the realization of the phenomena anticipated by the audience. In these moments of hyperexcitability and fatigue they will undoubtedly allow themselves to cheat rather than produce nothing at all" (539). At the same time, however, he was nevertheless inclined to acknowledge that the source of fraud could lie in a medium's very rational interests. He noted that Eusapia had feared for some time that the powers that had earned her such great renown were diminishing as she entered old age and suggested, with Youriévitch, that she needed regular financial support that was not contingent on her continued ability to produce phenomena (510, 565, 571).[104] Courtier and Youriévitch argued that, as well as eliminating a major source of fraud, the group would also fulfill its responsibility to treat Eusapia humanely by offering her a yearly stipend of 1,200 francs. According to the logic of this philanthropic gesture, fraud was not an innate characteristic of a subject divided into multiple selves; rather, it extended quite simply from a rational concern for material well-being.

Doubts about motivation in the subject also gave researchers cause to doubt their own subjective relation to the events witnessed. In one remarkable exchange Joseph Maxwell, a doctor and jurist from Bordeaux whose own research had led him to a greater degree of certainty than that professed by Courtier, proposed that the question of fraud be framed differently:

> M. MAXWELL—Here is how we must pose the question: Is there a general suspicion of all of the phenomena, or are there a certain number of phenomena that seem to you to remain above any suspicion of fraud?
>
> M. COURTIER—I can form convictions but not, strictly speaking, certainties grounded in objective proofs that would be valid for all.
>
> M. MAXWELL—In the report that you have presented it cannot be a question of convictions. Conviction is a personal thing that one cannot hope to transmit. You present the facts: it remains to be seen whether or not you present them in the spirit of certainty. (563)

Intervening on Courtier's behalf and as president of the research group, d'Arsonval noted that in spite of belief to the contrary, the possibility of fraud could not yet be eliminated: "There are some phenomena that have been well observed in a number of facts in which we could not discover fraud, but we cannot affirm that it did not take place. We have observed phenomena: we believed that they were protected against fraud, but we cannot be scientifically certain" (563).

This final rhetorical formula—"scientifically certain"—would become the focal point of Théodore Flournoy's response to the Courtier report and the indecisive outcome of the Eusapia experiments. Out of a professed lack of competence, Flournoy generally avoided an approach to mediumism that emphasized physical phenomena.[105] In his own celebrated work with Hélène Smith, Flournoy had emphasized instead the functions of imagination and ideation in shaping the medium's productions. Rather than the astonishing materializations and movement of objects achieved by Eusapia, Hélène Smith had based her mediumship on demonstrations of clairvoyance (e.g., she revealed to Flournoy knowledge of his private family history) and on a series of spectacular romanesque accounts of her past lives and extraterrestrial travels.

Observing the proceedings in Paris from his position at the University of Geneva, Flournoy complained that Courtier's report and the position taken by most of his colleagues simply perpetuated the uncertainty surrounding the séances. Recounting the story of one of his compatriots in Geneva who had earned the nickname "M. Noui" for casting an ambivalent vote in a popular referendum, Flournoy argued that, with the formula "scientifically certain," the scientists of the GEPP had answered the question "Oui ou non?" with a firm "Noui." Indeed, Flournoy argued that the effect of the report and the manner of its presentation were to "confuse the reader and to plunge him into complete uncertainty." Presented with an "avalanche of facts" in the initial chapter, the reader was then led through a series of physical and physiological experiments unaccompanied by any evaluation from the author. Courtier then returns tellingly to the instances of fraud in the final chapter "in such a fashion as to leave in the mind of the reader, as a final impression, a suspicion that the marvels of Eusapia could have well been only a deception from beginning to end." For Flournoy, the discussion following the presentation of the report was similarly designed to "prevent at all cost the formation of a precise opinion in the reader as to the reality or nonreality of Palladien phenomena."[106] The forum would give d'Arsonval the opportunity to acknowledge that he had "formally seen the levitation of objects without being able to perceive the mechanism by which these levitations were produced and without having my attention drawn to any fraud." At the same time, d'Arsonval would continue to reiterate that "none of these experiments can provide me with scientific certainty regarding the phenomena" (567).

For the members of the group, the lingering uncertainty surrounding their experiences remained a product of the subjective nature of their observations. In the final analysis the techniques of objectively recording events as well as the methods of control were insufficient to establish the "certainty, that is, a scientific demonstration of the reality of phenomena" that the group had sought (567). Branly concurred: "I have seen, but I do not have enough confidence in myself to be sure. My sight is not sufficient. I would like a more effective means of control, one that is not subjective" (567).[107] Certainty could only be achieved by procuring more pliable research subjects willing to submit to more severe methods of control and by eliminating subjective errors of observation through the introduction of more sophisticated equipment. According to Courtier's description, the ideal subject in this case was one who proved to be "very honest, [and] who accepts the means of control and the guarantees that will provide us with certainty—subjects who will not make us waste our time on deplorable simulations and render our efforts sterile" (546). As for the observers themselves, their role was to be relinquished to nonsubjective means of inscription. As d'Arsonval would put it, "We would like to implement controls of a purely physical nature in which subjective sensations will intervene less and less. This will be an occasion to undertake a thorough battery of new experiments where, in the place of the senses of the observers, we will substitute material means of inscription" (566).

Spiritism had developed as a result of techniques based on the use of very ordinary and readily available objects. In the effort to build an exclusive practice as the basis of a socially privileged production of knowledge, psychical researchers had, in essence, undermined their own capacity to act as authoritative witnesses. In d'Arsonval's prescription the capital of the scientist was no longer to reside in his intellectual autonomy and social independence. Rather, the production of value was to come to rest more and more on the material means by which the scientist could realize an objective knowledge of the world without leaving traces of his own, ultimately unreliable subjectivity. In the ideal passivity of the medium the scientists found the mirror image of the ideal subjectlessness of science. But where this absence of subjectivity could not be fully realized, where the continued operation of desire was suspected, the accounts of the séances continued to be framed by a frustrating uncertainty.

The Master and His Double

Charles Richet and the Literary Unconscious

In 1889, in one of the many accounts he presented over the course of his career on the subject of somnambulism, the eminent physiologist Charles Richet wrote of a Parisian doctor named Laurent Verdine. Verdine had discovered a young woman in the provincial town of Plancheuille who appeared receptive to what Richet's friend and colleague Pierre Janet had publicized three years earlier as "mental suggestion at a distance."[1] The woman of Richet's account, referred to as "Marthe" and described as a novice attached to the local parish, had been consulting Verdine about a chronic lung infection when she spontaneously fell into a somnambulant state. In her trance Marthe revealed to Verdine an alternate personality calling herself Angèle, which was, Verdine discovered from the local priest, the nun's given name. Upon further investigation Verdine learned that Marthe had grown up in the care of a Parisian orphanage and was known to be the daughter of an impoverished peasant woman but that nothing was known of the identity of her father. He soon discovered, however, that Marthe's second personality possessed knowledge of the obscure details of her past, specifically, the name of her father and the location of a hidden testament bequeathing to her this man's enormous wealth.

Keeping his knowledge of her somnambulism from the other residents of the village, Verdine experimented with Marthe in secret over the course of several days, during which he discovered her responsiveness to his purely mental (i.e., not verbalized) suggestions. The relationship between the young doctor and the somnambule soon developed into a matter of great concern when, upon returning to his room one evening, Verdine was astonished to find Marthe as Angèle waiting for him. Dressed in a white frock and with her long blond hair uncovered, Angèle appeared to Verdine to be responding to the charged emotional attitude that the physician had unwittingly developed for his lovely young subject. She made a scandalous proposition, vowing her obedience to the doctor and proposing that they leave Plancheuille together: "I will be your slave, your thing."[2] In light of the sensational accounts in the popular press associating rape and hypnosis, Verdine was understandably anxious that the whole affair would be construed by the authorities as an illicit seduction.[3] The young doctor, bewildered by the passions that stirred in him, came to doubt the motives of his research, acknowledging that in this instance "it was not the sacred fire of science that made his heart beat and that burdened his breast. To love Marthe, to love Angèle . . . What was the source of this madness?"[4] As Angèle embraced him Verdine "renounced his role of master," asking only that she cooperate with him in his efforts to cure Marthe of her underlying physical ailments.[5]

Richet's account of Laurent Verdine and Angèle de Mirande was, of course, entirely fictional. Published under the pseudonym Charles Épheyre as the short novel *Soeur Marthe,* the work's treatment of somnambulism and mental suggestion mixed what was for Richet a matter of serious scientific inquiry with the familiar forms of the nineteenth-century *roman de moeurs*. If the relation (of the "young doctor in love") described in Richet's novella had become a convention in French literature, its recognition was all but prohibited in the real scientific milieu inhabited by its author. This was especially true given the terms by which republican social doctrine sought to reframe individual desires as social duties by, for instance, drawing upon the natural affinities that linked the procreative drives of the individual to the integrative functions of the family.[6] If male sexual desire could, within the family, be seen as a guarantee of social order, outside of this contractual framework it suggested an unregulated nature that served only to particularize interests and compromise interpersonal guarantees of good faith. As leading contributors to the transparency of the public sphere, male scientists could hardly afford to compromise their objectivity by acknowledging that the excessive libidinal attachments they pathologized in their (often feminine) subjects were also operative by degrees in their own field of activity. If as a novelist Richet had recognized the role played by the passions in the pursuit of knowledge, this was only to place them at the limits of intelligibility (i.e., to equate them with madness). In this regard his gesture was typical of the one by which science affirmed its impartiality and objectivity by refuting the subjective experience of desire and displacing it to the field of literature.[7]

Richet's *Soeur Marthe* and the place it occupied in his career provide a telling point of coincidence in which a transgressive sexuality is linked to the would-be transgressive practice of literature. If in 1889 Richet the novelist could contain the danger that the passions posed to science within the charmed circle of his fictional account, in 1905 Richet the physiologist would find himself utterly disarmed by a manifestation of this same specter in his real-world work as an experimental scientist. Such a manifestation could only take the form of a scandal in which the scientist's otherwise objective contributions to public knowledge were transformed by public suspicion into expressions of pure self-interest.

A scion of a French medical dynasty that has endured to this day, Richet was often hailed by contemporaries as one of the more eminent scientific figures of his generation.[8] A disciple of Marcellin Berthelot and Étienne-Jules Marey, Richet became a professor of physiology at the Faculté de Médecine in Paris at the age of thirty-seven and would go on to reign as a mandarin of the Parisian scientific community, serving as a member of the Académie Nationale de Médecine and editor of the influential *Revue Scientifique*.[9] In 1914 he would secure a seat at the Académie des Sciences (and serve as its president in 1933) after having won the Nobel Prize in 1913 for his work on anaphylaxis. Upon his death in 1935 Richet's peers would look back on his career and proclaim him France's heir to the scientific legacy of Claude Bernard.[10]

If Richet's achievements speak of a great man of French science, they also belie his ambivalent relation to the scientific legacy that he had inherited from his father. A prominent Parisian physician, Alfred Richet was widely esteemed in the medical community in France and exercised his influence over generations of interns making their way through his surgery at the Hôtel-Dieu. Charles Richet also enjoyed important connections to the world of publishing through his maternal grandfather, Antoine-Auguste Renouard, and, eventually, through his brother-in-law Charles Buloz, editor of *La Revue des Deux Mondes,* which published Richet's *Soeur Marthe*.[11] Drawn to the study of philosophy as a young man, the wayward Richet would adopt a course of study in medicine out of pragmatism more than due to the desires of his family.[12] Even as he built a distinguished career in science on his own merits and energies, Richet's youthful enthusiasm for literature continued to find expression in his long career as a poet, novelist, and dramatist. In most of his early literary efforts the patronymic that still graces the corridors of the Faculté de Médecine in Paris would give way to the phonetic union of Richet's final initial with that of an early friend, Paul Fournier (i.e., F.R., or "Éphèyre"), with whom he coauthored his first book of poems at the age of twenty-five.[13]

Figure 4.1. Seventy-seven-year-old Charles Richet in the courtyard of the Sorbonne during the Third International Congress for Psychical Research, 1927.

Richet's dual career as scientist and poet was often a matter of confusion and concern for many of his peers and admirers. For the botanist Gaston Bonnier, Richet embodied an "impossible alliance," combining in one person the perspicacity of the experimental scientists and the dreamy introspection of the poet.[14] The German psychologist Max Dessoir, author of the 1890 study *Das Dopple-Ich*, called Richet a "strange mixture of scientific rigor and poetic indulgence."[15] The novelist and occultist Jules Bois would likewise note that "this rigorous and prudent analyst is also a dreamer, as sincere and as honest as ever, but inclined toward lofty ambitions" in which "dreams and fantasies play a preponderant role."[16] Jean-Louis Faure of the Académie Nationale de Médecine would argue that it was impossible in the case of a man like Richet to separate in his work "that which is due to his qualities as a scientist and that which was born of his poetic imagination."[17] More than simply a source of confusion, Richet's romantic orientation seemed, to his friend the poet René

Sully-Prudhomme, a moral peril: "Professional rumors," he noted, "are rarely generous to the poetic aspirations of men of science, which are presented as flagrant negligence toward a work bound by its commerce with reality. . . . I know too well from experience the ravages that an impetuous love of poetry can cause to an honest existence. . . . I feared for you and for physiology."[18]

The Language of Reality

Though often exaggerated as a real feature of the intellectual life of late nineteenth-century France, the theme of the "two cultures" embedded in the concerns of Richet's contemporaries nevertheless played an important rhetorical role in the political developments of the early Third Republic.[19] In its enthusiasm for scientific forms of knowledge the republic tended to privilege what Théodule Ribot called "facts, thorough study, and scientific culture" over "verbiage and eloquence."[20] This demarcation served as a point of attack not only against religious and romantic thought but also against the legacy of Victor Cousin in the field of psychology.

For critics of this legacy, the "literary" quality of exposition that characterized works of introspective psychology was often the main focus of criticism. Tacitly associated with the dandy's obsession with aesthetics, the quality of "eloquence" was also cited as an objectionable quality of the Cousinian style.[21] Critics argued that the emphasis on aesthetics in scholarly discourse meant that knowledgeable erudition was sacrificed to an appealing form of presentation that tended to confuse the critical capacities of mind. As early as 1867 Felix Ravaisson would note a sense of betrayal among those scholars who had been drawn to Cousin's approach as young men only to discover later that they had unwittingly "yielded to the seduction . . . of words or of style."[22] By the early decades of the Third Republic this characterization of philosophical language would serve to challenge the authority of an intellectual elite whose identity was rooted in the kinds of literary fluency afforded by the study of classical languages. The derogation of style thus had a social as well as an ideological component. This was apparent in the debates that in the last years of the nineteenth century surrounded the efforts to modernize the university curriculum in a way that would facilitate the movement of students from an emergent middle class into the disciplines and professions.[23] The artful formulations that had served as the distinguishing mark of a cultivated intellect were to be replaced by a language accessible to all by virtue of the fact that it looked to words as representations of objective reality. By 1903 Alfred Croiset, the director of the Faculté des Lettres at the University of Paris, could argue that to "really know is not to fashion beautiful logical or verbal constructions, it is to penetrate straight to the real, and to model one's ideas upon the real."[24]

In the field of psychology it was Ribot who would propose to institutionalize this critique of language in *La Revue Philosophique* by welcoming philosophical works of all stripes and refusing only those that simply rejuvenated old philosophical doctrine "by a talent for literary exposition" indicative of "an eclecticism that would have no value and nothing in common with the spirit of our *Revue*."[25] Otherwise a supporter of Ribot's efforts to modernize psychology, Paul Janet would denounce his attempts to marginalize followers of Cousin's eclecticism. Janet argued that language was the essential foundation of all thought and explained that "the talent for exposition is what was rarest in philosophy and constituted philosophy as such."[26] He maintained that only by giving thought a variety of forms in language could one arrive at the realization of new ideas. For his part, Ribot continued to insist on satisfying the "strong desire for information" evident among a new generation of scholars.[27] Contributors to *La Revue Philosophique* were warned that they would be expected to produce facts and not the "imaginary creation or mystical effusions" that resulted from the philosopher's *sens intime*.[28] Without such facts the practice of psychology was reduced to an empty verbalism by which "one ends up by being able to act only on signs, all reality having disappeared."[29] The psychologist was "in this circumstance a novelist or a poet of a particular type . . . and psychology becomes a form of probing and well-reasoned literary critique, nothing more."[30]

These efforts to foster more objective forms of knowledge by purging psychology of its literary qualities were paralleled by concurrent efforts in the field of literature to lay claim to the descriptive language of the sciences. While many would dispute whether Émile Zola's naturalism ever realized the agenda he set out for it in his essay *Le Roman expérimental* (1880), the potential of a scientific literature was at least great enough for someone like Richet to imagine a successful integration of the two fields.[31] Richet's 1880 article on hysteria would, for example, argue that literary accounts could offer a great deal of insight into a disease that was otherwise notoriously difficult to define. Moving without hesitation from a discussion of real-world clinical observations performed in Charcot's clinic to a series of references to novels, Richet celebrated the "descriptive style" of literature capable of "mix[ing] art and pathology" and that seemed to him to surpass the best clinical accounts of the day.[32] Thus, in Octave Feuillet's novels "the symptoms are so clear that there can be no doubt" that what they represented was, in fact, a "well-performed observation . . . a veritable *human document*."[33] The heroine of Jules and Edmond Goncourt's *Germinie Lacerteux* was "certainly a hysteric," as was that of Albert Delpit's *Le Mariage d'Odette*.[34] Passages from the work of Anatole France indicated "precise scientific gestures" in a description of his heroine's diet, her taste in novels, and her excessive sentimentality. The preeminent example—indeed, the archetype—was, of course, Emma Bovary, who was for Richet "the most vivid, the truest, most passionate of hysterics."[35]

The effect of such an approach was to suggest that literary art was more or less compatible with the work of science as long as the author resisted the introspective gestures of the romantic artist and spiritualist philosopher and instead adopted a descriptive style that modeled its representations on observed reality. In other words, while subjective descriptions of the psychological states of the author were discounted as conceits of style, art and literature that employed an objective point of view to describe the outward manifestations of these same states were becoming increasingly serviceable to science.[36]

One advantage of the descriptive style was that it served to reinforce a notion of the author as freestanding observer, removed from the world he or she so accurately described. Those authors who had produced the vividly descriptive characterizations to which Richet turned for their objective value did not, however, always understand their creations in these terms. This was clearly true in the case of Flaubert in that the psychopathology that Richet's article attributes to his most famous heroine also had an acknowledged subjective status in the life of her creator.[37] To the Parisian physician who diagnosed Flaubert in 1874 as "a hysterical woman," the novelist famously acknowledged, "Doctor, you are absolutely right."[38] Richet would, nevertheless, firmly deny that subjective accounts of hysteria had any diagnostic value. Indeed, he cautioned his fellow doctors not to mistake their patients' "personal novels" for reality. Hysterics are, he argued, those who "tell absolutely false stories" and "enumerate all that they have not done, all that they have done, with an incredible luxury of false details."[39] To the doctor who encountered such subjects in his practice, Richet warned that their principal wish was only "to trick him, to hide the truth from him, and to show him things that don't exist just as much as to dissimulate those that do."[40] The possibility that the practitioner of the descriptive style might also suffer from such pathologies seems not to have occurred to Richet, who saw in such accounts only true-to-life facts.

The Man of Genius

As a writer himself, well versed in the psychological theories of his age, Richet was not completely ignorant of the possibility that the mental processes that characterized certain forms of mental disease might also play a role in the creative efforts of both writers and scientists.[41] His preface to Cesare Lombroso's 1889 book *L'Homme de genie*, for instance, concurred with the work's thesis that genius and insanity shared the same psychological characteristics and that the language of insanity was "extremely proximate to poetry."[42] This did not mean, as so many critics of Lombroso's book had assumed, that Richet's friend had rendered genius indistinguishable from madness.[43] Rather, what Richet emphasized in Lombroso's work was the importance of the inhibitive faculty by which the man of genius makes discriminating use of the involuntary mental processes that incapacitate the madman. The similarities between the novelist's experience of the creative process as a dictation of spontaneously occurring narratives and the automatic discourses of the somnambule were well recognized by Richet's contemporaries.[44] But, Richet argued, in order to transform the "association of audacious and unpredictable ideas" into art, the man of genius must exercise that critical faculty of will that "tempers and corrects these strange associations" and brings them into accordance with reality.[45] Genius was, by this account, a product of the encounter between involuntary processes and the inhibitive faculties of will.

Richet clearly had a personal interest in both defending the sanity of the poet and showing the innovative effects of involuntary inspiration in areas other than poetry. Indeed, he concluded that the imagination, tempered by critical judgment, was just as important to scientific discovery as it was to poetry.[46] Citing Pasteur as his example, Richet proclaimed that "the scientist has the right to an [intensity of] imagination bordering on delirium if he knows how to temper it with the weight of his knowledge and the penetration of a serious and unyielding critical spirit."[47] Thus, in Richet's analogy, while Don Quixote's surprising association of ideas reveals his noble genius, his lack of a critical faculty makes him "like a somnambule, incapable of distinguishing that which is from that which is not."[48] This dreamer finds his natural counterpart in Sancho, whose common sense protects him from the delirium of his master at the cost of limiting his perception of the world to the superficial appearances of things.

This opposition of active inhibition and passive inspiration would have been quite familiar to Richet's contemporaries, since it was exactly this formulation that Cousin had used to adapt the sensationalist psychologies of Locke and Condillac (which represented the mind as passively receptive) to a philosophy of an active, willful self. Richet's rendering of this duality, however, performs a curious inversion of the class and gender hierarchies that Jan Goldstein has identified in the Cousinian concept of the self. In Goldstein's view the terms of activity and passivity employed by Cousin not only reproduced a set of social relations derived from the "mechanics of human sexual reproduction" but also tended to privilege the reflectivity of the bourgeois male philosopher over the "aggregated, inarticulate, and 'spontaneous' condition" of mind lived by the great mass of humanity.[49] In Richet's rendering these hierarchies are inverted through an analogy in which the ennobled term is to be found not in the willful activity of the self but in a passivity akin to somnambulism.[50] In his references to *Don Quixote* and the practice of animal magnetism Richet transforms the internal tension of the creative mind into an externalized relation between the magnetizer and his somnambule. The relation of power within this pairing was hardly stable, as the overwhelmed Laurent Verdine of Richet's *Soeur Marthe* would observe. In Verdine those rational, realist, and inhibitive qualities of mind that Richet thought essential to the man of genius are ultimately undermined by passions that appear quite unexpectedly. Angèle's erotic attachment to Verdine thus marks the limits of self-mastery in a scene that Jacqueline Carroy-Thirard describes as one of the clearest early accounts of what Freud would later dub "countertransference."[51]

If in this fashion Richet the novelist anticipates the clinical insights of Freud, in his refusal to consider the meaning presented in the content of hysterical discourses as something more than just lies, Richet the scientist leaves the subjective experience of seduction unanalyzed. For the physiologist Richet, the analysis of love was best left to that other domain that the rhetoric of the two cultures had so firmly opposed to science. Indeed, while Richet's 1891 article "L'Amour, étude de psychologie générale" begins by defining love as a phenomenon fully of the order of nature, Richet curiously cuts short his scientific observations on the subject. "Why insist?" he exclaims. "So many writers, poets, novelists have spoken of love that it would be folly to want to give here, for the hundred millionth time, a shapeless and poorly conceived psychological description."[52] Even the poet would, however, be rendered speechless in the face of an irreducible form of love that Richet dubs *l'amour brutal*—that force that "every man, young and ardent, feels when he is next to a beautiful girl who offers herself to him."[53] Such love was not the "noble sentiment that the poets sing about. It is a brutal physical desire. It is love, if you will, but a love in the most animal and material of forms."[54] Love in this form casts a shadow of obscenity from which neither poetry nor science could redeem the edifying bonds of friendship and family that republican ideology considered so essential to the social order. The man who found himself under the influence of such passions no longer possessed that inhibitive function of will by which he exercised mastery over his representations. Where there was *l'amour brutal* there could be no impartiality, no guarantees of sincerity, and no assurances of good faith.

The Villa Carmen Affair

When situated within the field of science, the specter of male sexual desire would prove catastrophic to the authority that science had claimed on the basis of its ability to represent reality objectively. In those circumstances in which desire was felt to be operative, one could no longer look to the scientist as a guarantor of the transparency and objectivity that were supposed to provide for consensus within the public sphere. Nowhere in the course of Richet's career was this clearer than in the 1905 *affaire* that surrounded his affirmation of the spirit apparitions he observed while participating in a series of séances at the notorious Algerian villa of a retired French army officer and his wife. Named after the matron of the household, the Villa Carmen became the scene of astonishing events in which spirits took on physical form, breathed, walked, talked, touched observers, posed for photographs, and then vanished like vapor. Richet's testimony, which appeared alongside photos of a phantom in *Les Annales des Sciences Psychiques* and, in an abbreviated version, in *Le Figaro*, detailed these experiences and confirmed that the phenomena had not been produced by fraudulent means. The claim was stupefying both for Richet's peers in the scientific circles of Paris and for those enlightened members of the French reading public who were inclined to look to science as a means of dispelling the ancient sources of superstition.[55]

Overlooking the Bay of Algiers, the Villa Carmen was the home of Gen. Elie Noël and his wife, Cécile Chatard (called Carmen or Carmencita), who had been initiated into the practices of spiritism some fifteen years earlier and had held regular séances ever since.[56] The most notable spirit appearing at these gatherings was that of a three-hundred-year-old "Hindustani priest" named Bien-Boa, who, over the course of the years, revealed that Carmencita Noël was the reincarnation of an Indian princess who had been his lover three centuries earlier.[57] It was in a small pavilion on the grounds of the Villa Carmen that Bien-Boa first materialized into his humanlike form. Walking among the séance participants, he lavished attention on Mme Noël, frequently touching and kissing her in an affectionate manner. Although Carmencita was identified by Bien-Boa as the key participant and true medium of the séances, he made it known that his materialization depended on others whose bodies provided the fluidic substance from which his material form was composed. It was Marthe Béraud who performed this service in the materializations witnessed by Richet. This nineteen-year-old girl, who was to have been the Noëls' daughter-in-law prior to their son's death in 1904, gave issue to strange progeny.[58] Magnetized in a curtained corner of the room, Béraud remained visible during the materializations through an

Figure 4.2. Bien-Boa photographed by Richet at the Villa Carmen in 1905. Reproduced in Richet, *Traité de métapsychique,* 647.

opening in the fabric. At her feet formed what was described as a ball of tissue, a substance that gave Richet occasion to coin the term *ectoplasme,* a substance he suspected was physiological in origin. From this ball developed the head of Bien-Boa, which lifted vertically from the floor to achieve full stature, complete with cloak, helmet, and beard.

The extraordinary physical manifestations at the Villa Carmen, which had first received notice in the British spiritualist journal *Light* (1895), would compel Gabriel Delanne of *La Revue Scientifique et Morale du Spiritisme* to publish more complete accounts beginning in 1902. In July 1905 Delanne traveled to Algiers, determined to witness the materializations firsthand, and was joined in the middle of August by Richet. Together the spiritist and the physiologist scrutinized the coach house for all possible signs of deception. Richet concluded to his satisfaction that, in spite of the manner of Bien-Boa's emergence, the room's flagstone floor had no trapdoor. Richet also dismissed the suggestion that some duplicitous role had been played by two other women who frequented the séances (the *négresse* Aïssa and a palmist called Ninon) on the basis that the collusion of the socially respectable Marthe with such persons was unthinkable, given her "purity" and the "simplicity of [her] soul."[59]

Richet argued that unconscious deception on the part of the medium and hallucination on the part of the spectators were likewise impossible. The former was ruled out by the elaborate nature of the manifestations, which would have required conscientious planning and conspiracy among a number of participants, including Béraud, her two younger sisters, the coachman Areski, as well as Aïssa and Ninon.[60] The stereo photographs taken during the séances showed the ghost and medium on the same plate and indicated that the apparition was not simply the medium in disguise. The empty appearance of the sleeve of Marthe's dress in one photo was, Richet argued, only an indication of the disaggregation of the medium's body into the ectoplasm that constituted the material substance of the apparition. For Richet, these images were also the primary proof that Bien-Boa was not the product of a collective hallucination. This was further confirmed by a test in which Bien-Boa blew through a rubber tube into a bottle of barite, the results of which confirmed respiration. The physiologist concluded from this that "B.-B." (as Richet dubbed him) "possessed all the attributes of life" and was not, as some had speculated, a mannequin or some hastily assembled puppet.[61] "I have seen it emerge from the cabinet, walk, go, and come into the room," he professed to *Le Figaro*. "I have heard the sound of its footsteps, its breathing, and its voice. I have touched its hand on several occasions."[62] Far from confirming the existence of spirits of the dead, these observations indicated for Richet only the presence of matter in a living state. The representational form given to the materialization suggested only the effects of the medium's imagination on the ectoplasmic extrusion. Prefaced by a statement of reticence about the dangers of rendering these observations public, Richet's account conveyed his belief that the phenomena witnessed were not the product of deception.

While Richet's testimony stopped short of affirming the existence of spirits of the dead (indeed, he never endorsed what psychical researchers referred to as the "spirit hypothesis"), it nevertheless placed into evidence facts that seemed to support some of the most unbelievable claims of the spiritists. A reporter for *Le Matin* expressed the puzzlement prompted by Richet's claims:

How does one not take seriously the testimony of a man of this worth, whose scientific authority is only equal to his moral authority? If you insinuate that in such a matter authority has nothing to do with it, I invite you to read *Les Annales des Sciences Psychiques,* and you will note as the illustrious scientist does that it is impossible to take any further precautions in the prevention of fraud. Yes, after this single reading the most exacting mind must consider itself satisfied. . . . And yet . . . yet, there are in this account of the experiments in Algiers so many extraordinary "abracadabra" details![63]

Richet's most esteemed colleagues, including Théodule Ribot, Pierre Janet, and Théodore Flournoy, would tend to echo this sentiment by reaffirming his reputation as a perspicacious man of science.[64] More skeptical readers were, however, less inclined to give Richet the benefit of the doubt and wasted no time constructing an alternative version of events. The clinical psychologist Paul Valentin, for instance, complained that Richet was inadequately trained to study spiritism.[65] The phenomenon, he argued, clearly belonged to the domain of mental pathology and was not subject to the experimental methods of the physiologist. Valentin argued that, had Richet studied Béraud more cautiously from the perspective of a clinician, he might not have been afflicted by the hysterical contagion of the séance.[66]

In raising the issue of hysteria, Valentin exposed Richet to the insinuations of lesser figures who argued that the account of the apparitions in *Le Figaro* suggested nothing of the moral authority and intelligence of a great man of science. In a tale not unlike Richet's own *Soeur Marthe* the skeptical account of the Villa Carmen séances would invoke sexual desire in order to disqualify Richet's statement as a disinterested contribution to public knowledge. This version of events would originate with Hippolyte Rouby, a relatively obscure director of a private asylum in Algiers who performed his own investigation of the Noëls and their entourage and presented his findings publicly at the Université Populaire d'Alger in March 1906. The apparitions, he asserted, were nothing more than the product of an elaborate hoax.[67] He explained that he had in his possession confessions from both Marthe Béraud and the "Arab coachman Areski" to support his claims. It was Areski who appeared with Rouby and obliged his audience with a theatrical demonstration of the means by which he had played the role of Bien-Boa.[68]

Rouby would repeat his case before the distinguished gathering at the International Congress of Medicine in Lisbon in April 1906, conjuring up an image of a household in which spiritist séances were merely occasions for wild, late-night burlesques hosted by a charming if neurasthenic and self-credulous Mme Noël and her myopic and obligingly naive husband.[69] Rouby assigned the greatest degree of malice to the young Marthe, who apparently delighted in abetting Mme Noël in her otherwise harmless delusions. By Rouby's account, the deception was a characteristically Oriental and feminine one in which the perpetrators "served to carry under their skirts or their dresses, under their jackets or in their knickers utensils, *haïcks,* false beards, and other accessories for the comedy that these frauds prepared to enact."[70] The concealing garments were often removed during the course of the séance as the spirits of Bien-Boa's sisters, "dramatically *décolletées*" and with "thighs worthy of the chisel of Praxiteles," appeared and performed barebreasted "warrior dances" for the audience in attendance. In other words, Rouby concluded, "they weren't bored at the Villa Carmen."[71]

Drawing from insinuations made against the character of the young medium by Mme Noël herself, Rouby suggested that the deceptions engineered by Marthe had a particular effect on the illustrious Richet, one that eroded his better judgment and completely compromised his authority on the subject of spirits. Mme Noël, eager perhaps to draw others into the titillating scenarios recounted and pantomimed in the course of the séances, observed a number of improprieties in the relationship between Marthe and her esteemed visitors from Paris.[72] Her acceptance of gifts of jewelry from both Gabriel Delanne and Richet was deemed inappropriate by the matronly Noël, as was the physical contact between them occasioned by the séances.[73] The most serious accusation by Mme Noël involved Richet's relationship with a spirit newly arrived at the Villa Carmen—that of Phygia, an ancient Egyptian priestess of the Temple of Heliopolis who presented the "perfect and complete materialization of a young woman, twenty years old, blond, attractive, of the Greek type."[74] From behind the curtain of the *cabinet noir,* Phygia offered Richet a thick clump of her long blond tresses, from which he cut a small sample for inspection. She then emerged from behind the curtain wearing a white "Oriental" costume recalling those worn in ancient civilizations. She kissed Richet "warmly" and, in turn, allowed the gentlemen of the séance to kiss her hand. The next day Mme Noël was surprised when Phygia appeared to her in her bedroom and, sitting on the edge of the bed, joined the lady of the house in "endless small talk," all the while exposing her handsome bare feet.[75] Perhaps most amazing of all, Mme Noël claimed that Phygia had left the Villa Carmen to dine at the Palace Hotel with Richet and Marthe, the public appearance of the apparition being less remarkable to Mme Noël than the fact that Marthe departed the household in the company of an older man without an appropriate chaperone.[76]

Richet's version of the appearance of the Egyptian princess differs only in detail from that which Mme Noël presented to an Italian journal. In his 1922 *Traité de métapsychique* Richet recounted how the promise was made to him that he would "see what [he] desire[d]" if he postponed his departure from Algiers and how, during the séance of the following day, there appeared from behind the curtain of the *cabinet noir* the "face of a young woman, extremely pretty, one could say beautiful, with a sort of golden band of a diadem covering her blond hair."[77] The next day Richet found himself in the bedroom of Mme Noël, who had been taken ill, and thought he saw a vaporous form in the adjacent water closet. When he approached, the form seemed to dissolve, but Richet admitted in his account that "my memory concerning this instance is rather confused."[78]

Repeating Mme Noël's claims before the doctors gathered at the Lisbon congress, Rouby asserted that he was "making nothing up," exclaiming that "this concerns Ch. Richet, professor of physiology at the Faculty of Paris and member of the Academy of Medicine."[79] Rouby's implications are quite apparent in the question he put to Richet: "Did you write your article in the *Annales* [*des Sciences Psychiques*] to conceal a vulgar escapade?"[80] In contrast to the claim by Delanne that Richet's affirmation had confirmed the hypothesis of spiritism, Rouby concluded that the physiologist's authority in the matter of spirits was void. In the final analysis Rouby noted that "reasons of sentiment, and not those of rigorous verification, served as the basis for Professor Richet."[81] Thus, Rouby's effort to determine what really happened in the encounter between Marthe and Richet concludes, inevitably it seems, with a scene of seduction.

For those who embraced the theory that Richet had been duped, the question of how was still not entirely clear. In the discussion immediately following Rouby's presentation the psychiatrist Ernest Dupré would propose that Marthe Béraud and Richet presented a form of group psychopathology in the union of the *mythomane* and the *thaumatomane,* a pairing of "liars and of intentional simulators who take pleasure in tricking the credulous, the naive, and those with minds inclined to cultivate the marvelous."[82] What Dupré dubbed the "personal novels" of the pathological liar were, he noted, the product of normal conscious activity in children but revealed a constitutional tendency for regression in women and a rarer sign of infantilism or feminization in men.[83]

In the psychological literature produced in the wake of the Villa Carmen affair, Richet would continue to serve as a kind of prototype for the ways in which even the most skilled men of science could stray from reason into the errors of belief. Gustave Le Bon clearly had Richet in mind when, in his 1911 treatise on the psychology of belief, he turned to the question of the scientist's belief. "How is it," he asks, "that a scientist is led to leave the cycle of rationality, to penetrate into that of belief?"[84] "In order to understand how first-rate scientists, accustomed to rigorous scientific experimentation, can come to admit certain miraculous phenomena such as materializations, one must never lose sight of the fact that rational logic and mystical logic often subsist in the same mind, as positivistic as it might be. The spheres of the rational, of the mystic, and of the affective are, I will repeat, independent, and the sources of our conviction change according to our passage from one to the other."[85]

Taking the hypothetical case of the "very skeptical" scientist who decides to undertake an experimental study of phenomena produced by "occultists," Le Bon traces the process by which rationality is overturned by belief. Entering into a circle of true believers, the only place where such phenomena are produced, the scientist finds himself waiting attentively in a darkened room for noises, moving furniture, luminescence, and materializations.[86] Leaving unsatisfied, he comes back again and again, and by the action of this expectant attention "the unconscious of the skeptic becomes more and more disposed to suggestion, and his critical spirit fades."[87] Consciously persisting in his rationalism, he conceives of experiments and makes use of the most delicate recording instruments of physics. He lays this "trap" for the spirits, but they prove capricious, and the experiments fail.[88] In the hope of success he lets his guard down, at which point the worst fraudulence goes unnoticed. Convinced that the phenomena that he has finally observed are authentic and that his conviction has been arrived at by rational means, he makes his beliefs public. Thus, according to Le Bon, the scientist who enters into the cycle of belief "will admit without difficulty that a helmeted warrior can emerge from the body of a medium and walk around the room having the participants check his pulse in order to prove that he is more than a simple phantom, an impalpable vapor."[89] This was not a fault of character, Le Bon stressed, but a universal capacity for belief possessed by the scientist and the ignorant man alike. By Le Bon's account, the predilection for belief could exist in the same person alongside the most developed critical faculties of the scientist. While Dupré's theory of mythomania characterized dissimulation as a conscious activity indicative of mental pathology, Le Bon argued that belief was unconscious and universal.

This is why the most promising intervention in the debate surrounding Richet's assertion was to come out of an approach that suspended the question of whether or not the spirits of the Villa Carmen were real. Addressing the Institut Général Psychologique in 1908 in the wake of its four-year-long investigation of the Italian medium Eusapia Palladino, Flournoy argued that while physiological and physical approaches to mediumism had reached an impasse in the question of experimental controls, psychology was fully prepared to move forward on the subject of the mediums' representations, what he called, in reference to his own study with Hélène Smith, their "personal novels."[90] Though perhaps "wonderfully naive" in retrospect, the account Flournoy presented in *From India to the Planet Mars* (1900) had an advantage over other approaches to psychical research in that it emphasized the affective dimensions of the medium's representations as opposed to the objectivity that was so often at issue in the field.[91] While some, like Valentin and Richet, tended to see the confabulations apparent in mediumistic and hysterical discourses as cause to dismiss them from scientific consideration, Flournoy would make their similarity to works of fiction the basis of a psychological analysis by invoking a capacity of mind that the British psychical researcher Frederic Myers had described as "mythopoetic."[92]

While Flournoy was occasionally subject to the lure of reality embedded in Hélène Smith's remarkable "hindoo" language (referring it, for instance, to his colleague the linguist Ferdinand de Saussure to measure its similarity to ancient Sanskrit), his principal approach was to see the "novels" of mediums as merely imaginative efforts by which their authors worked creatively to subvert the limits imposed on these women's expression of sexual desire.[93] While both Hélène Smith's preferred spirit guide, Leopold, and Carmen Noël's Bien-Boa were regarded for their high moral character and paternal affection, they simultaneously revealed through "the most incendiary declarations" that a more passionate and carnal relationship had existed between them in past lives.[94] Rather than seeing this twofold relationship as a symptom of the ambivalences that structured human desire generally, Flournoy was inclined to look for corrupting influences in the mediums' immediate environment by, for instance, conjecturing that the mediums' representations were a response to the crude influences that these otherwise virtuous women were submitted to in their daily lives.[95] At the Villa Carmen the bad influences of garrison life to which Carmen Noël had been exposed most of her life were personified in the spirit of the crass commander Brauhauban, "a joker, a prankster of bad taste, especially concerning women."[96] Flournoy concluded that the phantoms of the Villa Carmen were a mechanism of "feminine defense," an "imaginative elaboration" of the medium herself, and a "product of her creative fantasy."[97] Flournoy thus effectively turned the question momentarily from the widespread preoccupation with the reality of spirits to the psychology of the mediums themselves.

As innovative as they were in the discussion surrounding the Villa Carmen affair, Flournoy's theories would nonetheless fall short of a much more comprehensive analysis of mediumism. In his own work with Hélène Smith, Flournoy diligently chronicled Smith's past lives and travels to Mars. What is left out of these accounts is any consideration of his relationship to them. His reluctance to take into account the intersubjective dimensions of the séances would be understood by his grandson Olivier Flournoy as the product of his grandfather's inability to openly espouse what was, in fact, the central insight of his work. If, in Flournoy's work, the scientist affirms that "he must be rigorously objective . . . he knows perfectly well that he cannot be." What the work of the elder Flournoy discovered "but doesn't manage to say is that the subjectivity of the observer is also part of the scientific domain."[98]

For his part, Richet would continue to affirm the disinterested nature of his claims about the apparitions of the Villa Carmen. More than redeemed by his 1913 Nobel Prize, Richet would argue in 1922 that, "with sixteen years of distance, it seems that the objections issued against me were quite worthless and merit all of my disdain."[99] Evidence of materializations would intensify in the years to come, corroborating Richet's claims that he had not been deceived and that he had sincerely represented his findings. While the objective reality of such phenomena and the certainty of the experimental controls under which they were produced inevitably remained open to doubt, objective certainty nevertheless continued to remain the aim of both psychical researchers and their critics. As for the question of the author's subjectivity, this could only serve to compromise the field of science and was safer left to poets and dreamers.

5

In the Wake of War

The Institut Métapsychique International

The years between 1918 and 1923 were marked by several important events in the development of psychical research. Interest in spiritism was dramatically renewed in this period among the millions seeking messages of redemption and rehabilitation in the aftermath of the great catastrophe of the First World War. Psychical research was a clear beneficiary of this abundant popular sympathy, gathering moral and financial support that had been lacking in earlier decades. Principal among the various developments in the field was the foundation in 1919 of the Institut Métapsychique International (IMI), which in the interwar period was to take up where the Institut Général Psychologique had left off a decade earlier. Efforts among psychical researchers to establish their field among the disciplines and organize themselves along professional lines intensified with the foundation of the IMI. The first of several International Congresses of Psychical Research was held in Copenhagen in 1921, and the following year saw the publication of Charles Richet's *Traité de la métapsychique,* which was to have served the field as a standard text. The year 1922 also paid witness to a well-publicized investigation of the phenomena of mediumistic materializations at the Sorbonne, which intensified public debate surrounding the field, its findings, and its methodology.

If psychical research in France benefited from the upsurge in the popular appeal of spiritism, it would also suffer as a result of those associations that linked the would-be science to what many saw as popular superstition. The founders of the IMI willingly encouraged this popular support, arguing that psychical research would achieve moral redemption in the wake of the great catastrophe. The message was utopian in its appeal, promising as it did to establish the means by which, in the legitimizing terms of science, the living and dead might establish communion with one another and establish a lasting, universal peace. For those scientists who were actually to put their reputations at stake, such claims were seen as damaging to the credibility of the enterprise. As Pierre Janet had recognized many years earlier, psychical research could not succeed in both the realm of science and the realm of popular opinion. It could be popular and prosperous or it could be scientific, but it could not be both.

The Immortal Dead

In 1899 the American medium Leonora Piper delivered a message in a trance state that was dutifully recorded by Richard Hodgson of the Society for Psychical Research. Piper spoke of the difficulties that many had in coming to terms with the reality of spirit communication and foretold of a transformation of consciousness in which man, purified and cleansed by a terrible future war, would open his eyes and see beyond his mortal life to a pure existence beyond death. Recalled in the preface to Arthur Conan Doyle's 1918 work *New Revelations*, Piper's prescience was, for many, confirmed by the experience of the First World War. Spiritism, which in the nineteenth century had focused on personal losses associated with the intimacies of the bourgeois family, now took on collective meanings in proportions unknown to other periods. While spiritist meanings were only one element in the narratives of mourning and redemption in postwar culture, they were an unusually prominent feature of such narratives, given the relative importance of spiritism in relation both to the secular myths of French nationalism and the myths of institutionalized Christianity. In interwar France spiritist practices of communication and ideals of the future life would combine with more conventional Christian concepts and would in some instances overshadow them. It is doubtful that the practice of mediumism would have been so revitalized in the popular imagination if it had not been for the tragedy of the First World War. Spiritism was, it seems, perfectly suited to the effort to transform great suffering and loss into an occasion for national redemption by permitting the souls of the dead to remain in communion with the soul of the living France. Spiritism had the additional advantage over conventional forms of mourning in that it presented a means of transcending the nationalist ways of thinking that had since 1914 served to justify hateful actions between men. Spiritism in the interwar period drew upon an image of the spirit world in which humanity in general, joined in spirit with the dead, would progress toward a future life in which suffering and loss would play no part.

The renewed interest in spiritism was aided in no small part by the public conversion of scientific and literary celebrities during the years of the war. Although Conan Doyle's interest in spiritism dated to the late 1880s, his full faith in spiritualist teachings would only come about after the death of his son Kingsley in 1917.[1] Among scientists, the most important figure to engage in the spiritualist cause in this period was Oliver Lodge. The famed British physicist had been involved with psychical research since the earliest days of the Society for Psychical Research and would in 1915 take a definitive position on the spirit hypothesis after a communication with the spirit of his son Raymond, killed near Ypres. The father, who had been made famous in 1894 as the first person to transmit and receive wireless radio signals, became convinced that communication with his dead son was possible after a medium described to him in detail a photograph of Raymond taken hours before his death and that only later arrived by mail. Lodge's book, *Raymond, or Life and Death* (1916), recounted in detail the series of events that had resulted in his conversion and that had compelled him to adopt an admittedly personal position on the question of survival from which "sentiment is not excluded."[2] This personal conviction would, of course, shape Lodge's professional commitment to psychical research and the scientific legitimacy of survival. Such professions of faith would help to refurbish what for many had become a laughable practice. Even Conan Doyle's friend, the skeptical if open-minded Harry Houdini, would consider that, for all the movement's follies and conceits, Doyle's contributions to the spiritualist cause had done much to transform it into a "beautiful faith."[3]

Serving as it did to unite the memory of the war dead with psychical research and spiritism, Lodge's *Raymond* would become immensely popular in England, and its message would resonate loudly in America and on the Continent. In the year that the English edition appeared, Lodge would issue an appeal entitled "To the Grieving of All Nations" (delivered to the French press by his friend Charles Richet), which argued against excessive mourning by reminding readers that death was not the worst fate man could endure. Indeed, those lost to the war could rest content that they had performed a service to their countries and could still help those who were waiting to join them. "They accomplished their task down here; they will accomplish it up there; and we can, with ample confidence, await the future reunion that will come in its own time. If only these truths could shine in the eyes of the multitude, there would be not only greater resolve but also greater hope."[4]

Appearing in a French edition in 1920, *Raymond* would become both a source of inspiration and a work of reference for those sympathetic to psychical research and to spiritism.

The nineteenth century has been characterized by historians as a period in which the affective relations within the family intensified in proportion to the economic and cultural meanings that this intimate sphere of life now assumed.[5] Accordingly, the earliest spirit communications of the 1850s had often served as a means of mourning the loss of a child, a parent, or a beloved companion. After 1918 spiritism facilitated practices of mourning that were both personal and collective. Longtime believers welcomed this renewed interest in spiritism as a sign of the increased willingness to accept a reality that had, for them, been in evidence since the middle of the previous century. In this context spiritism would even draw the interest of those who held traditional religious views. Prominent Christians openly welcomed the reconciliation between the living and dead, which the practice seemed to offer, and looked to science to provide the proof by which the practice might be integrated into their religious beliefs. In 1919 James Welldon, dean of Durham Cathedral, would advise his congregation that whether or not spirits existed in the form that the spiritualists proposed, the church must nevertheless prepare itself to embrace new truths—truths that were to be fashioned by men of science:

> Among the greatest consequences of the war, the most remarkable of all is the desire of so many pious souls to communicate with the dead. . . . We know that the dead are still alive. We know that they entered into a better, more expansive life, but can they tell us something of this life even if only to reassure us by personal communication, that they are still living? It is the silence that is so terrible; this long, persistent, inexorable silence. . . . The main thing now is that spirit phenomena must be scrupulously examined by men of science, that their discipline alone in the methods of exact science makes them competent to judge the evidence of new discoveries.[6]

Quoted at length in *La Revue Spirite,* Welldon's sermon stood as an argument for the grand fusion of spiritism, science, and Christianity that French spiritists had promoted since the 1860s. In France pious souls had already begun to look to the proofs of science to give certainty to their faith. The radiant forms that Hippolyte Baraduc would photograph above his son's deathbed at the moment of his passing would serve as evidence of a life independent of the body. That the death from tuberculosis took place in a hostel in Lourdes during the period of national pilgrimage only served to reinforce the link between psychical research and traditional forms of piety.[7]

Of course, in postwar France not everyone would be so convinced that a communion with the dead authorized by science was the recommended path to travel for those grieving their losses. Some French Catholics had very different opinions. The Parisian priest Joseph Bricout would regret that ideas drawn from spiritism had gained such influence: "A single book," he complained, "has been recognized by our doctors and pontiffs as giving us authentic revelations of our fallen heroes: *Raymond* by Sir Oliver Lodge. . . . 'Have you read *Raymond?*' an enthusiastic theosophist asked me. Yes, I have read it. But what a bunch of childish platitudes."[8] In a review of a 1923 book by Alice Vega entitled *Les Présences invisibles* the prominent Catholic writer and *académicien* Georges Goyau agreed that spiritism trivialized the moral imperative that asserted itself in the wake of the war. Direct communication with the dead only obviated the immensely difficult moral transformations pursued in a relation to God.[9] For Goyau, spiritism was the product of a faith distorted by science, a symptom of the recognition by science that its repudiation of the Unknowable could not withstand the anguish that the living suffered in relation to death. Psychical research exemplified the effort to compensate for this failure of science with a scientific theory of survival. "What strange adventure is that of scientism," Goyau remarked.

> After having confined itself to the domain of raw experience, after having built a wall between our thought and that which it treated disdainfully as the Unknowable, scientism feels itself one day silenced, lamentably voiceless, in the face of the anguished cry of souls. . . . So then scientism, troubled but not resipiscent, consents to organize experiments to expose in this Unknowable a few of its secrets. Without honorably making amends with the metaphysics of religion, [scientists] put themselves to the task of inventing "metapsychics." Since they do not want to renounce their positivism, they indiscreetly solicit so-called positive science to bring rays of light into the tombs of the dead and a ray of serenity into the hearts of the living. There is no mention of the divine revelation of God, who is refused any say in the matter. But with pretentious naïveté they listen to their mediums with great attentiveness.[10]

While attitudes among Catholic leaders in France were unlikely to be as liberal toward psychical research and spiritism as those evident in Welldon's address in Durham, some evidence suggests that in France as well the communications described by spiritism could be reconciled with more traditional forms of religiosity. Such was the case, for instance, in communications that were to provide the basis for the seven published volumes of *Lettres de Pierre*, in which for nearly twenty years Cécile Monnier dictated extensive treatises from her son, a French soldier who died in the Argonne in 1915. When first contacted by Pierre in August 1918, Mme Monnier was instructed to "think of nothing, take a pencil, and write!"[11] She wrote "without hesitation or reflection" and had no awareness of what she was writing. "I *annulled* myself, almost materially," she wrote in the preface of the published edition.[12] But because Pierre came to her through the intervention of God (she was devoutly Protestant), Monnier did not see any similarity between her writing and the automatic writings of mediums. On inspection of the letters the Monnier's family pastor agreed that the style and the points of inquiry were characteristic of what he had noted in Pierre over the course of the boy's religious instruction. While the communications would eventually develop into protracted meditations on theology, the initial exchanges were of an exceedingly intimate nature:

> The tenderness that always united us is so pure. . . . We cannot even fathom the extent to which it is *tight* . . . like a bond, a knot, that *nothing* can break. Life may have separated us . . . death will unite us more intimately than ever! . . . Thus, dear mother, be content to know that our trio has not been called upon to disappear. . . . [D]o not fear any separation resulting from death, we will be reunited, and we will rediscover the sweet intimacy of the past. Dear mother, when again we find one another here, it will be your little Pierre who will fall into your arms.[13]

In spite of a father who did not believe that the communications were real and attributed them to his wife's grief, the messages from Pierre to his mother obstinately literalized his continued presence in her life decades after his death. For the grieving mother, it was life and not death that had created such mournful loss. By negating the independent physical lives that had separated them, death became an occasion for intimate reunion in which mother and son became one by speaking with the same voice.

As historians have shown, elements of Christian myth played an important role in the commemorative practices that followed in the wake of the First World War.[14] Many of the themes of sacrifice and redemption evident in this postwar commemoration were in many ways simply an extension of the sacrificial myths of the war experience.

One place in which this fusion is particularly evident is in the storyline, common to the postwar period, involving soldiers rising from the dead to defend their position against an advancing enemy. As a variant of similar reports from the front in which saintly or angelic commanders on horseback appeared before troops to rally them to victory, accounts of *revenants* offered explicit images of heroism and literalized the patriotic myth of an undying nation. Offered in different versions either as fact or as fiction, the tales served to recount the reparations of moral debt that the nations of Europe felt they owed to the millions of young lives lost to the trenches. In one early study of the literature of the Great War, Jean Norton Cru suggested that the popular theme of the dead rising from the battlefields had its origins in an actual incident reported by Jacques Péricard in April 1915 in which a group of soldiers, badly wounded during a German offensive, rose to the call of "Debout les morts!" to drive back advancing German troops. The theme of an undead army rising to the defense of the fatherland stuck in the popular imagination and became the subject of a variety of subsequent accounts.[15] Roland Dorgelès's popular 1923 novel *Le Réveil des morts,* for example, tells the story of an engineer who, employed in the reconstruction of the "martyred villages" near the front, is plagued by a sense that he has profited from the deaths of millions of his countrymen. These feelings manifest themselves in a dream in which an army of dead soldiers rise from the battlefields to seek retribution from those who took undue advantage from their sacrifices.[16] Perhaps the most famous rendering of the tale takes place in Abel Gance's 1919 film *J'accuse,* which tells the story of a frontline soldier, Jean Diaz, who is driven insane by the death of his comrade and the rape of his girlfriend by marauding German soldiers. Diaz (played by the celebrated actor Séverin-Mars) wanders among the trenches and villages near the front prophesying that an army of the dead will return to the home front to pass judgment on the living.[17]

By representing his protagonist's war-induced insanity as an ecstatic religious state, Gance confirms the primacy of Christian meanings in the 1919 version of *J'accuse.* In his 1937 remake of the film, however, these religious elements would be displaced by references to scientific experimentation in which Jean Diaz, no longer a poet, is found experimenting with the optical properties of a newly developed glass in a makeshift laboratory near Douaumont. The experiment inadvertently resurrects the dead from the nearby cemetery, who, once again, march on the great cities of France. In Gance's personal journals, published in the 1930 book *Prisme,* the use of optical technology as a means of reanimating the dead is revealed to be more than a metaphor for cinema. Influenced by arguments prevalent in spiritism and psychical research, Gance speculates that death was simply another state of matter, and, just as X-rays revealed the inner secrets of opaque substance, other forms of electromagnetic radiation might penetrate the mysteries of death. In a 1922 note on the death of his wife, Ida Danis, Gance would affirm that "it is not possible that, when a cherished being dies, it disappears entirely."[18]

For psychical researchers, the war presented a windfall of the types of phenomena that they had endeavored to study for decades. Psychical researchers were quick to conjecture that, given the emotional intensities of the front experience, instances of psychical phenomena were likely to increase. In 1916 *Les Annales des Sciences Psychiques* would recount a number of incidents involving visions of ghost armies among frontline soldiers.[19] From the perspective of psychical research, however, this was not necessarily to claim that these visions had been simply hallucinations. Reflecting back on the war experience in 1922, the essayist Jacques Lourbet would note that "the cataclysm that brought human emotions to paroxysm must have, it seems, multiplied the phenomena of telepathy, of lucidity, of foresight, or premonitory dreams."[20] The idea that these phenomena were most pronounced in incidents involving death or some similarly charged life event was a long-held hypothesis of psychical researchers. It was on the basis of this that in 1916 Charles Richet issued an appeal to soldiers through the *Bulletin des Armées de la République* to report any premonitions or telepathic experiences they or their comrades might have experienced at the front.[21] Many reports of such instances were reproduced by Cesar de Vesme in the pages of *Les Annales des Sciences Psychiques*. From 1915 to 1918 the journal published hundreds of accounts of "veridical hallucination" reported by mothers who correctly sensed the distant deaths of their sons as well as accounts from soldiers whose impression of a death in the family was later proved true by the arrival of correspondence from home. De Vesme recognized that these phenomena had a clear relationship to pathological mental states brought on by fatigue and anxiety, but he noted that the striking similarity among the different accounts was nonetheless a matter of great interest for science.[22]

A Renaissance of Idealism

In July 1919 France officially celebrated its victory in the war and marked the occasion with a grand procession through the Arc de Triomphe and down the avenue des Champs-Élysées.[23] The following day, in the Chambre des Députés, the soon to be president of the republic, Paul Deschanel, would frame the procession as a moment of national communion between the living and dead: "The greatest hour of history passed by yesterday. All of France, the living, the dead—the dead who will live as long as a conscience drives the universe—all of France and all of humanity . . . have communed in the same glory and in the same religion."[24]

The theme of an immortal dead and of their communication with the living was, of course, quite familiar to spiritists, who were eager to claim the relevancy of their doctrine to the concerns of the nation in the years following the war. Invoking Deschanel's speech, *La Revue Spirite,* the official organ of Kardec's Société Spirite, would assert the priority of the spiritist movement in the work of restoring unity to the nation.

> According to the grand discourse of M. Deschanel in the Chambre, France, by the voice of the living and by the voice of the dead, compels us to work for the recovery that must give us a better humanity. And it is we, the spiritists, on whom falls the honor to be at the head of this movement. It is we who address ourselves specifically to the invisible world, it is we who receive their communications, it is we who hear their voices. It is thus we who must spread the good word. We will welcome, from these alleged "dead," all the assistance that they can give us. Their manifestations proliferate. All the while, on the side of the living, a man guided by the purest, the loftiest philosophy has come to us, giving service to our cause in the means of action required by the task to be accomplished.[25]

Spiritists had not only been granted a moral mandate, they also now had the financial means to put it into effect. The great patron of the spiritist cause alluded to in *La Revue Spirite* was Jean Meyer, a wealthy wine wholesaler from Beziers who would step forward with the funds necessary to rehabilitate the institutional bases of both spiritism and psychical research in the interwar period. By 1916 Meyer had already proven himself a great advocate of spiritism by assuming a leadership position in the Kardecist Société Parisienne des Études Spirites and by resurrecting *La Revue Spirite,* which had ceased publication in 1914. Collaborating with prominent spiritist leaders like Léon Denis and Gabriel Delanne, Meyer would revive the foundering Union Spirite Française in 1919 as a means of coordinating with smaller regional organizations in order to better diffuse Kardecist doctrine. In 1923 Meyer would also establish the Maison des Spirites in Paris, a complex of offices on the rue Copernic that was to serve as the headquarters of the Union Spirite, the Federation Spirite Internationale, *La Revue Spirite,* and Éditions Jean Meyer, which published many important works on spiritism and psychical research in the 1920s and 1930s.[26]

In 1919 Meyer would also provide the principal financial support for what was to become the major French institute in psychical research in the interwar period, the IMI. While there were no formal institutional ties between the IMI and the other beneficiaries of Meyer's largesse, the spiritist community was nonetheless inclined to identify the mission of the IMI as part of its own. In the 1920 article connecting the cause of spiritism to the moral reconstructions of the *après-guerre, La Revue Spirite* applauded the foundation of the IMI as the beginning of a new era in which "light was brought to bear on the shadows, and the terrible nightmare of the war was dissipated."[27] The moral crisis represented by the weariness and apathy left in the wake of the war would, in the work of the IMI, be averted by a science that was to give the dead a positive presence in the world of the living. From the spiritist perspective, the mission of the IMI was to silence those who had made spiritism the subject of endless ridicule by addressing the question of survival through the means of serious science. With the intervention of an organization of such prestigious membership, spiritists hoped that their doctrine would finally achieve the serious attention it deserved. No longer, they argued, would one be able to "affect complete indifference before such a serious question."[28]

At a 1919 conference members of the Union Spirite hypothesized that, with the reawakening of belief following the war, spiritist teachings would finally be recognized by official science. Gabriel Delanne, both the president of the Union Spirite and member of the directing committee of the IMI, opened the conference by announcing the foundation of the IMI as an event of "capital importance." He was followed by his deputy, Jules Gaillard, who explained:

> It is science alone that liberates [thought] from every prejudice and shows us, with exactitude, the laws of nature. But [science] must be free of preconceived ideas and study the soul objectively by the positive method, that is to say, by the means of observation and experimentation. Thus the certainty of the existence of the soul will quit the domains of philosophy and religion to enter into that of Science. Scientists of the avant-garde who have explored this new domain have concluded that the soul is not a metaphysical entity but, rather, that it possesses a real existence.[29]

Looking to the scientists of the IMI for confirmation of their doctrine, spiritists would take on the task of formulating a scientific basis for a new society along spiritist lines. Borrowing from the same set of themes that Deschanel had employed in his address to the Chambre des Députés, spiritists characterized their role in the postwar period as an essential part of the social regeneration that was to proceed from the sacrifices of the war. Those who had worked to defeat evil now "worked without rest in the edification of the peace, and, in a sanctified atmosphere, itself purified by the violence of the storm, we can once again take up our march toward the light and toward liberty."

Stand up then! Hail the new dawn. Courage, confidence, put us to the task without further delay. We have accomplished the first part of our task. Our dear *invisibles,* who stirred in our soldiers the heroism that made them victorious, are still near us. In the task of regeneration and of peace their aid, which never wavered, will not mean any less to our salvation. . . . Joyously we march, all with the same spirit, toward the conquest of the future by the best organization of the new world. This time victory will be definite.[30]

Such themes were not confined to political speeches or to popular religious discourse. Science also reaffirmed its moral agenda in this period. In the case of psychical research, the formal distinction with spiritism could hardly prevent scientists from defining the task of the postwar period in terms that reflected those invoked by politicians and spiritists. In October 1918, only weeks before the cessation of hostilities was formalized, an Italian doctor and state functionary named Rocco Santoliquido would initiate efforts to enlist support for a permanent, international institution of psychical research that was to become the IMI.[31] In his correspondence to Charles Richet, Santoliquido would frame the goals of the institution in terms identical to those that the spiritist leadership would employ two years later. "The moment has come," Santoliquido would announce, "to realize the grand project that psychical researchers have toyed with for so long now: to found an international institution that will centralize all that touches on our studies and permits us to take on all relevant questions." He continued: "To work, then, my friend; the time is right. The success of our armies, the triumph of those ideas that we hold dear, permits us to foresee the progression of thinking humanity into a newer, superior phase. At the same time that it brings definitive peace, victory must also give us something more; a light of hope to those who mourn their children, killed for an ideal; a ray of truth to those who seek in good faith."[32]

A medical doctor and specialist of public hygiene who had enjoyed a number of high administrative offices in the Italian state, Santoliquido had come to know Jean Meyer during the war, and together the two men hatched the idea of a laboratory for psychical research with the means to pursue investigations *à longue haleine.*[33] With the financial backing of Meyer and the commitment of another close associate, Gustave Geley, a director of clinical medicine at the hospital in Annency and former intern in the hospitals of Lyon, Santoliquido would press forward with his ambitions and address correspondence to Charles Richet, courting the esteemed physiologist's participation in the new organization. Just as Meyer provided the IMI with crucial economic capital, the esteemed Richet was to provide it with the cultural capital capable of establishing its reputation as a legitimate institution of scientific research. This was the necessary counterweight to IMI's financial dependence on the spiritist Meyer.

Not all those solicited would agree that the organization conceived by Santoliquido was the best means of forwarding the cause of psychical research. Indeed, many perceived the effort to establish an international institution under French leadership as a threat to the autonomy of other, long-lived, nationally oriented research institutions like the Society for Psychical Research. Oliver Lodge, responding to Santoliquido's October letter (forwarded by Richet), agreed with the notion that some sort of organization would be useful in cultivating popular opinion and fostering a commitment toward the field among a new generation of scholars, but he feared that the adverse publicity invited by such a cause might, in fact, "risk exaggerating and intensifying the centers of opposition." Considering these risks, Lodge argued that the best work was the sort of individual work that "one can pursue tranquilly without drawing hostile attention and without adopting an aggressive attitude." On the timeliness of Santoliquido's efforts, Lodge expressed his conviction that "hardships caused by the war will open hearts to the teachings of the facts" but emphasized that these facts ought not to be "shouted in the public square."[34] Lodge concluded that the best way to proceed was by means of the quiet efforts of the national research institutions.

In response, Santoliquido would insist to Richet that a substantial international organization was essential to the "primordial necessity" of maintaining, protecting, and training mediums who would otherwise be left to make their living through the commercial exercise of their talents—a proposition that Lodge also recognized as a serious danger to the field. "Mediums selected, educated, trained would," Santoliquido explained, "be extracted from the struggle for existence [and] put in circumstances in which they could consecrate themselves exclusively to their mediumship."[35] The international scope of such an undertaking was indicated by the fact that many of the best mediums came from regions where the funds available for psychical research were limited. Sponsoring and protecting these precious resources, the IMI could then make its mediums available for local societies and research groups. As for the researchers themselves, the emergence of a talented and enthusiastic group of young scientists (notably, Jean-Charles Roux, Stephan Chauvet, and Gustave Geley) indicated that the time to cultivate new talent in the field was now. The effort to fund mediums and researchers on an international scale was not, Santoliquido assured Richet, an incursion on the autonomy of the national organizations like the Society for Psychical Research. Rather, it was a means of coordinating efforts between them to the greatest utility of all. Santoliquido believed that the risk of inciting legal or administrative opposition was minimal, even though he recognized that the hostility of official science was quite real.

Such concerns did not ultimately dissuade Santoliquido from pursuing what he took to be the true cause of the new institution, "the propagandization of idealism" against the materialism that he saw as the principal threat to moral and scientific progress. "What we are contributing to," Santoliquido proclaimed in his reply to Richet, "is a veritable renaissance of idealism." He continued, citing the need to profit from the renewed enthusiasm for psychical research: "The stakes for the future are considerable. This means knowing whether or not humanity will have or will not have an 'ideal'—whether it will orient itself toward the great hopes based on science or whether it will darken under Bolshevism. This is the dilemma we are confronted with. It is urgent. It is not a matter of whether one succeeds or fails. This is an obligation to be met, a compelling obligation that one does not argue with."[36]

It was not only in the interests of privately persuading Richet that Santoliquido would characterize the IMI's purpose in these terms. In July 1919 the organization would officially publicize its mission in the popular press by issuing an appeal to "idealists of all nations and of all beliefs," asking for the support of those who recognized in the IMI's mission the makings of "the greatest of the sciences, called to transform the moral and social life of humanity." Such statements were unprecedented in the field. While earlier promotional efforts had looked to popular interest for support, they tended to preserve a sober, deliberative tone even in their most speculative moments. Clearly, the carefully measured language of science was no longer sufficient to match the enthusiasm of the public for the field. While taking no position on the survival hypothesis, the IMI's press release appealed directly to "those who mourn their war dead" and to "all those who believe that the renovation of humanity to be derived from such suffering can be neither sure nor complete if it is not accompanied by a rebirth of Idealism." This invocation of idealism was not simply rhetorical. In the context of the vitalistic theories that the IMI was to promote in the interwar period, "idealism" referred to a specific theory of cause, one that Santoliquido claimed would "henceforth be confirmed with and by science."[37]

The choice of Gustave Geley as the director of the IMI could not have been more appropriate to the mission Santoliquido had projected. Not only had Geley made a name for himself promoting an established institutional basis for the field, he also demonstrated an approach to psychical phenomena that one reviewer of his work called "profoundly idealist" in its conception of things.[38] Working from the basis of recognized phenomena like cryptomnesia, Geley promoted a conception of psychology that overturned the psychophysical parallelism dominant in scientific psychology throughout the first decades of the twentieth century. Indeed, Geley concluded from his study of mediumism that thought was not the effect of the physiological processes of the brain but that the existence of the brain was, like all matter, subject to an organization that was the outcome of the directive principle of thought. The *moi* or "self" was not, Geley argued, simply the sum of neurons but, rather, indicated the existence of a capacity to centralize and coordinate the organic complex identified within the smallest divisions of the brain. For Geley, self-consciousness provided evidence of a higher, directive agency that he called "dynamo-psychism." By his account, the cerebral psychism that many took as the seat of the self was just the greatest among the many effects of a superior psychism that had the capacity to objectivize itself in both intellectual and material representations. Dynamo-psychism produced its effect not only in the embodiment of individual consciousness but also in the material form of the universe as a whole. The principle of organization did not discriminate between organic and inorganic forms of matter, which were structured by a universal process evinced by the phenomenon of "ideoplasty" by which mediums imprinted specific ideational forms on their ectoplasmic materializations. Drawing from Arthur Schopenhauer's discussion of Will and Eduard von Hartmann's conception of the Unconscious, Geley's dynamo-psychism viewed consciousness as the evolutionary telos of this directive agency.[39]

René Sudre, who would become involved in the administration of the IMI in 1921, argued for the perfect feasibility of Geley's thesis in the survey of psychical research that Marcel Prévost had solicited from him for *La Revue de France*. "How does the mind act on matter?" Sudre asked rhetorically. "How does it transform an interior representation into an exterior form? The hypothesis of idealism, that is to say the identity of the subjective and the objective, raises no great difficulty. One must admit that every act of thought is ideoplastic. There is a reversibility of perception that constitutes the retinal image and projects it into space."[40] Sudre argued that psychic photography (*psychographie* or *skotographie*), in which the medium could inscribe a detailed image on a sealed photosensitive plate simply by touching it, constituted further experimental proof of idealism as conceived by Geley. "As with materialization," Sudre argued that in this phenomenon "thought was able to embody itself in space, erasing or rather *displacing* the Cartesian dualism of thought and extension [*étendu*]." The interior image of thought projects itself into external space as an image and "passes by every degree of materiality until it becomes visible."[41] For Sudre, the unknown forces at work in these visible manifestations of thought seemed to rest with the identity of matter and energy indicated by the ongoing revolution in the field of physics. His speculations that psychical projection constituted a form of energy, a *rayonnement humain*, was supported by the medium's ability to produce the effects of light, heat, electricity, and force by the occult power of her mind.[42]

Science, Not Spiritism

While Sudre acknowledged the merits of a causal theory in which idea and substance were identical, he rejected the rhetorical idealism in which Santoliquido and others promoted the field of psychical research. Sudre admitted that the appeal to persons who had endured losses in the war was an efficacious means of gathering popular sympathy and support for the IMI but argued that the exploitation of the ambiguity between psychical research and spiritism for short-term gains ultimately undermined efforts in the field to achieve scientific recognition and legitimacy. Clearly intent on marking the distinction between psychical research and the general resurgence of faith in the aftermath of the war, Sudre argued that the latter tendency suggested widespread mental pathology. Introducing the IMI to readers of *L'Avenir* in the summer of 1919, Sudre argued that a catastrophe like the war tended to "leave behind painful realities," prompting those who suffer "to escape into dreams" and into the assurances of "belief," tendencies that demonstrated the failing powers of adaptation and mental depression brought on by traumatic experiences. In other words, Sudre argued, the resurgence of religiosity in the postwar period was nothing more than a widespread symptom of neurosis. To suggest that the interest of scientists in psychical phenomena was the product of the same "innumerable losses" that were causing so many to embrace "the marvelous" or bringing so many to the doorstep of the church would simply be to discount both the rationality of psychical researchers and the validity of the phenomena they studied. "This is not," he argued in reference to the IMI, "a movement characterized by religion, not a call to faith." Sudre maintained that the research efforts proposed by the new institute had nothing to do with spiritism or, for that matter, with theosophy, magic, astrology, or the cabbalistic arts. None of those who made up the ranks of the IMI were beholden to anything but the interests of science. In contrast to

Santoliquido, Sudre outlined the goals of the scientists affiliated with the IMI in carefully delimited terms: "It would be a gross error to assume that these respectable men would put themselves to the task of verifying the pretensions of charlatans and chiromancers, of extralucid somnambules, and tellers of tall tales who have exploited public credulity for centuries. Above all, these men are scientists. They deny nothing in the results achieved by science. They only demand the right to review the hypotheses that are conceivable when these no longer encompass the facts that they would establish."[43] The IMI was, Sudre proclaimed, not an organization of spiritism. It was science that was to be practiced there and not religion.

This was undoubtedly the spirit in which Charles Richet ultimately agreed to join the new institution in 1919 as its president of honor. While Richet had himself lost his son Alfred to the war, he never spoke of this personal tragedy in any professional context in which the facts of psychical research were at issue.[44] Oliver Lodge, for all his hesitations about the practicalities of the IMI's approach, was sufficiently persuaded by its mission to join its directing committee three years later. With Santoliquido as president, Gabriel Delanne as vice president, and Gustave Geley as acting director, the administrative committee of the IMI was completed by the participation of Count Armand de Gramont (member of the Académie des Sciences), Jules Roche (deputy and former minister of commerce, industry, and the colonies), Émile Calmette (doctor inspector-general), Georges Teissier (professor of clinical medicine at the faculty of Lyon), and the astronomer Camille Flammarion, a longtime adept of *spiritisme.* Endowed with a substantial operating budget and a lavishly appointed mansion in an elegant district of northwest Paris, the IMI was, on 23 April 1919, officially classified by the Ministère de l'Intérieur as an association *reconnu d'utilité publique.*[45] To many, the foundation of the IMI signified that psychical research had finally attained the respected position it had long merited.

Delivered by Jean Meyer's generosity from the inconveniences of their orphaned science, the psychical researchers who joined the IMI found themselves in surroundings that were uncharacteristically luxurious for an independent *société savante.* The IMI's elegant headquarters, located at 89, avenue Niel, provided ample space for a dedicated laboratory with advanced lighting and photographic apparatus, a lecture hall, a conference room, archives, and a heavily frequented library.[46] Where the standing of earlier institutions in psychical research had depended primarily on the scientific reputations of their members, the location of the IMI added the allure and prestige of the *beau monde,* qualities that were a sign of respectability for some and cause for suspicion among others. The sumptuousness of the IMI's facilities was clearly a matter of interest for the correspondent of the popular pictorial magazine *J'ai Vu,* who noted the "tall coachway door opening onto a courtyard of hewn stone and marble, a large stairway, the banister of sculpted wood."[47] The walls of the interior were "hung profusely with tapestries, gold leaf and fine woodwork in the rooms . . . all giving this mansion the impression of wealth and space." For this journalist, the opulence seemed all too appropriate given the "grand new truths" that were to be discovered there—the "new certainty" that was to serve as "the point of departure for a new humanity."[48]

In promoting the IMI in the national and international press, Geley and the other members of the committee helped to foster this perception that the IMI was opening a new era in scientific discovery, one that would serve the interests of all humanity. Detailed notices of the IMI's inauguration appeared throughout the Parisian and provincial press and in the more specialized journals of spiritists, occultists, and theosophists.[49] The IMI also lived up to its proclaimed internationalism by drawing the attention of readers in Brussels, Barcelona, Geneva, Mexico City, and Cairo.[50] The tone of *L'Horizon* of Brussels was characteristic of the general opinion in the press, championing as it did the IMI's effort to undertake public investigations into an area where, previously, "only the rare initiate was admitted."[51]

While the publicity received by the new institute was generally sympathetic, not all were impressed by its elegant surroundings or convinced that the research to be conducted there was in the public interest. For Dr. Gustave Krafft, a laureate of the Académie Française and correspondent for *La Cooperation,* the fact that the great scientists like Crookes, Richet, and Flammarion were "partisans of spiritism" amounted to little in the way of convincing him of the merits of their work. "Even the most stable of brains," Krafft argued, "are capable of letting themselves be deceived," and it was, in fact, the elite nature of the IMI that gave Krafft his great cause for doubt. Describing the unspecified "institute of spiritism," which he was "permitted" to visit upon the intervention of "friends in the highest of places," Krafft marveled at the organization's facilities, suspecting that the grandeur of the séance room must have given the spirits vertigo. He was much less impressed with the actual evidence presented by the institute's director (presumably, Geley). Mocking the photographs of spirit materializations he was invited to examine, Krafft was disappointed to find that no actual mediums were present during his visit. The best ones, he jibed, were Polish, and "perhaps there was an embargo against their exportation." Asking the director whether he might be permitted to attend a future "séance of reincarnation," Krafft was informed that those who attended had to undergo a long process of initiation so that the mental harmony and good faith necessary for success would be abundant. "I fear," Krafft retorted, "that I will never fulfill all of these conditions."[52]

While indicating that he was not an "inflamed positivist" and doubting that any scientific law could ever "enchain Nature," Krafft nevertheless considered the spiritist movement as a whole a danger to society, particularly one so destabilized as was Europe after the war. "Cerebral equilibrium is fragile," Krafft explained. "To abolish the critical sense of the individual to make him see, hear, and touch things that don't exist is no longer a mere parlor game, it is a dangerous abuse of human weakness. The postwar period has brought us a resurgence of mysticism and of credulity, which is producing victims in every milieu."[53] Krafft concluded by offering his encouragement to those who publicly called spiritists to task by challenging them to make good on their espoused moral agenda. He was particularly sympathetic to the arguments of the former deputy Gustave Hubbard, who publicly chastised the prominent spiritist Marinette Benoît-Robin during a conference hosted by Les Amis du Faubourg Montmartre. "Leave us alone! Citoyenne! With your tables and your interviews with the dead!" Hubbard exclaimed. "It is not the dead but the living to whom one must talk! Walk down the boulevards; go into the slums and fight against tuberculosis, alcoholism, and debauchery. That would be better than to prattle away with the dead."[54]

In tying itself to traditional sources of prestige, the IMI sought to acquire a firm financial footing, which would allow it to pursue investigations with a regularity that had been beyond the means of earlier French efforts in the field. For some, the visible signs of the institute's financial well-being lent an air of social standing appropriate to the moral leadership that it sought to provide. This strategy also, however, left the organization exposed to social criticism that saw in its opulence the typical signs of the frivolous and puerile pursuits of the moneyed classes. This criticism was particularly damaging given the volatility of the political and social environment in France in this period. By 1920 the great national unity that Deschanel had foreseen in his 1919 speech commemorating France's victory was quickly exposed as a myth as the wartime consensus of the *union sacrée* deteriorated precipitously into a series of massive labor protests. The idealistic rhetoric upon which the IMI had come into being in 1919 would prove less appealing by 1921 as the domestic problems and international crises destroyed the hopes for national unity and international peace expressed by so many in the months immediately following the Armistice.

As the institute finally settled down in the last months of 1920 to begin conducting practical scientific work on the phenomena of mediumism, some of its members grew increasingly concerned that their autonomy would be compromised by the influence that Jean Meyer's largesse might have on their research efforts. By the mid-1920s those members most insistent about the organization's independence from spiritism gradually began disappearing from its ranks. Geley died in a plane crash in 1924 shortly after requesting that Meyer drop all references to the survival hypothesis from the written description of his office.[55] Réné Sudre, extremely critical of spiritism, was ostracized in 1926 by members of the directing committee who worried that his vocal opposition would compromise relations with Meyer.[56] Even Santoliquido, with whom Meyer had hatched his ideas for the IMI, would depart unexpectedly in 1929 over concerns about the direction the institute was taking.[57] The death of Jean Meyer in 1931 and the dispute among his heirs over his estate would further erode the stability of the organization, which would lose many of its most esteemed members by the middle of the 1930s.[58] The IMI continued to function as an organization devoted both to preserving the history of psychical research and to promoting new research in the field of parapsychology, which would by the 1930s replace the spectacular experiments of psychical research with more readily controlled statistical studies of unusual cognitive phenomena. The IMI's fortunes would never again reach the levels enjoyed in the decade following the First World War. Having long since broken any formal ties to spiritism, the members of the IMI continue today to labor in inauspicious circumstances with open-mindedness and a diligence that far surpasses the level of material support for their efforts.

In spite of the hopes invested in the field of psychical research in the years following the First World War, the IMI would suffer from the paradox that had plagued earlier efforts to institutionalize the field in France. Drawing its support from individuals with clear ties to the world of spiritism, the institute would enjoy financial stability and the social prestige that came with it. It would also, by this same strategy, compromise its independence and raise doubts about its ability to provide the transparency necessary if it was to uphold a democratic ideal of science. These doubts would plague the young institute as it set out in 1920 to provide conclusive evidence of the more extraordinary phenomena of mediumism. Following the field of psychology in its rejection of all things related to hypnotism, hysteria, and unconscious mental processes, the IMI would stake its legitimacy on the objective method of experimental science, which in this context meant that it would stake its efforts on the materiality of mediumistic phenomena.

The Limits of Method
The Question of Good Faith and the Decline of Psychical Research

In spite of the increased enthusiasm for psychical research in the years immediately following the end of the First World War, the field would fail to find acceptance within the realms of official science and skeptical popular opinion. This is not to say that psychical research was simply dismissed or ignored. Indeed, a great deal of interest, both skeptical and sympathetic, was shown, much more so, in fact, than was exhibited for that other heterodoxy within the field of modern psychology—psychoanalysis.

From the perspective of the French attitudes toward science, psychical research had an advantage over psychoanalysis in that, in spite of the questionable nature of the mediumistic phenomena themselves, psychical research professed the principle of determinacy by eschewing subjective phenomena. This was especially true in the years during and immediately following the war, when researchers focused almost exclusively on mediumistic materializations. Manifest in substantial physical effects that could readily be seen and measured, this capacity of mediums would become the focus of psychical researchers as they worked to gain the acceptance of the scientific community as a whole. As long as scientists and the general public marveled and despaired over mediumistic materializations and struggled with one another over their meaning, psychical research would continue to sustain doubt within the general field of scientific knowledge. If French scientific figures were willing at least to consider the claims of psychical researchers, this same generosity was not forthcoming when it came to claims of Freud and his followers, which were largely ignored until the late 1920s. While mediumism continued to fascinate the public and incite responses from the domain of "official science," psychoanalysis would generate little enthusiasm outside of a small group of clinical practitioners and a literary avant-garde that would seize upon Freud's views of the unconscious for what they took to be its liberatory potential.

If the materializations studied by psychical researchers in the years following the First World War had the benefit of lending themselves to objective methods of study, their great disadvantage lay in the fact that, because the mediums capable of producing such phenomena were so rare, the experiments were not widely reproducible. Psychical research thus found itself in a situation in which phenomena became increasingly tangible and increasingly visible at the same time that they became less accessible to the general public. Mediumism in this form was no longer open to the widespread public scrutiny it had enjoyed in the past, making public knowledge increasingly reliant on the accounts of elite researchers. In this situation the question of good faith that psychical researchers had so often raised about their mediums now became a feature of the relationship between the elite practice of science and the general public. Dependent on the press accounts that shaped their understanding of mediumism, the general public was also inclined to apply standards of truth completely alien to the methods of experimental science. It was in the gaps produced by the opposition of journalistic, historical, and juridical methods of investigation, on the one hand, and experimental methods, on the other, that the traditional doubts surrounding mediumistic phenomena intensified.

With the emphasis on material phenomena, the hypothetical substance that Richet in 1905 had dubbed ectoplasm came to play an increasingly important role in the experiments of psychical research. With many of the best physical mediums of the previous century disappearing (Eusapia Palladino died in 1918), a new generation of mediums was emerging with an impressive mastery over the production of the ectoplasmic forms of such great interest to scientists in this period. In the first years of its activities the most prominent efforts of the IMI were devoted to the study of materializations and, in particular, to the talents of three mediums: Franek Kluski and Jan Guzik (Guzyk), both Polish, and a Frenchwoman known as Eva Carrière.

Matter and Spirit

The IMI's bid for scientific recognition began in earnest late in 1920 with a series of experiments involving a banker from Warsaw named Franek Kluski (a.k.a. Teofil Modrzejewski) and a group of observers composed of Geley,

Richet, Armand de Gramont, and the Polish count Jules Potocki. With his hands and feet immobilized, Kluski proved himself able to produce ectoplasm from his nose, mouth, and especially the area below his waist. This ectoplasm circulated about the room, touching the various observers.[1] These partial and fully formed materializations, often produced by the dozen, were sometimes visible, sometimes not and were subject to a procedure of control that produced some of the most curious artifacts of psychical research in this period, a series of plaster castings made from wax molds of "spirit" hands, feet, and faces.[2]

To confirm that the "ideoplastic" forms seen and felt in the course of the séances were indeed composed of a material substance and not simply the

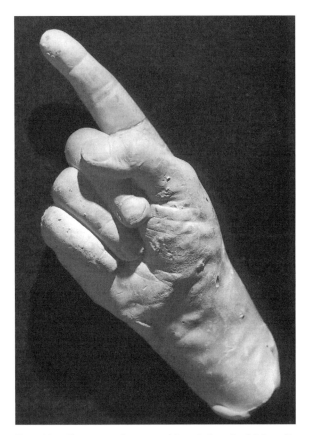

Figure 6.1. Plaster cast from a mold made by a "spirit hand" of the Polish medium Franek Kluski in 1920. IMI 22: 15.

product of collective hallucination, the scientists developed a procedure in which the medium was to direct these forms to a small tub of hot water in which floated a thin layer of melted paraffin. When the hands emerged from the tub, the wax "glove" was allowed to cool and harden. As the ectoplasm of the spirit hands dissipated, the thin and fragile wax molds were deposited, usually in the hands or lap of one of the observers. The castings produced from these molds rendered plaster facsimiles showing all the structural and surface signs of human appendages. From these, Geley discounted the possibility that the molds were produced by a rubber hand filled with air or water, since this would have resulted in obvious balloonlike deformations of the overall structure. Nor, he argued, were they produced by the medium's hands, since the observed creases, pores, fingernails, and even fingerprints were quite distinct. While some of the molds produced only partial impressions (the tips of the fingers or toes, the cheek and jaw of a face), in other cases they produced entire hands extending to the wrist and even sets of hands with the fingers intertwined. The topological impossibility of extracting real human hands from such molds without breaking them was confirmed by the opinion of experts in plaster casting. This, of course, left the possibility that the molds were produced by a more elaborate method prior to the experiment and secreted into the séance room without the knowledge of the observers. Geley eliminated this possibility by secretly adding a chemical to the paraffin that was later detected in the finished molds, indicating that they were indeed composed of the same wax that the scientists had provided in melted form.[3] Speaking of the Kluski experiments at the annual meeting of the directing committee, Geley noted that the molds of the materialized hands were "obtained under conditions of control that, for the investigator of good faith, leave no place for doubt concerning the authenticity of the phenomenon."[4] These were, Geley affirmed, "materialized organs" and not "vain simulacra or flat images": "They have three dimensions and allow us to recognize all the anatomical details that characterize living organs. They have a skeleton, muscles, tendons, a pulse, and nerves. The smallest details of the skin, the lines and creases of the hands are clearly indicated. In sum, what we have here in these materializations are momentary and ephemeral creations but nevertheless perfect, anatomically and biologically living organs or organisms."[5]

In all, the evidence of the molds corroborated other observations made in the course of the séances with Kluski. The hands, while invisible, appeared to be formed from the same fluidic substance that observers had seen issuing from the medium's mouth, nose, and skin—an unknown form of living matter whose structure was subject to the ideational influences of the medium.

Geley's claims met with skepticism by those who noted what they took to be telling omissions in the IMI's report on the Kluski experiments. Charles Nordmann, the scientific editor of *La Revue des Deux Mondes,* questioned, for instance, the process by which the final castings were made, something that none of the accounts considered relevant enough to specify. What controls were applied to the production of the plaster castings? Nordmann asked. Who was responsible for making them and in the presence of whom? Who exactly was present at each particular séance? Why did so many of the participants remain anonymous in the accounts? What other methods, besides the use of an inflatable rubber hand or glove, could be used to produce such molds under the given conditions? Why did Geley not consider materials such as colloidon, cellulose, and celluloid, which were commonly used in the production of industrial castings?[6]

While Nordmann's criticisms were pointed and his position clearly skeptical, his overall attitude toward psychical research, which he developed over the course of the three articles he wrote on the subject in 1922, was far from polemical. As one commentator noted, Nordmann's discussion of the subject was distinguished by a tone and tact that readers recognized as the hallmark of a "scientific mind," one not "blinded by prejudice," as were some of the more severe criticisms in the press.[7] But in spite of the reasonableness that some attributed to Nordmann's approach, members of the IMI took his articles in *La Revue des Deux Mondes* as a slanderous attack on their credibility. In December 1922 *La Revue Métapsychique* published a rebuttal in which Richet, Santoliquido, and Gramont protested against the insinuations they perceived in Nordmann's article and reaffirmed their support for Geley as a man of science and a man of truth.[8]

If the members of the IMI responded to Nordmann's critique in polemical fashion, it was because they were already embroiled in just such an exchange with a journalist named Paul Heuzé, who in 1922 began publishing damning accounts of recent work in psychical research in the newspaper *L'Opinion.* Heuzé's engagement with psychical research had begun in 1920 with the modest intention of demonstrating that the phenomena of spiritism were far from proven facts, as was often claimed, and with the hopes of clarifying the various positions of those leading scientists whose names were often invoked in the context of such a claim. His articles and interviews, reprinted in 1921 as *Les Morts, vivent-ils?* showed the significant differences in the opinions of the leading spiritualist, Gabriel Delanne, and those of the leading psychical researcher, Gustave Geley. Scientific opinions on psychical phenomena were also shown to vary widely. While Camille Flammarion supported the spirit hypothesis, Charles Richet did not. While both of these notable scientists were motivated by their separate hypothesis, others who had participated in mediumistic séances, Marie Curie and Édouard Branly, could offer Heuzé no definite opinions about their experiences.[9]

Heuzé's most important intervention in the public debate surrounding psychical research involved the medium Eva Carrière, or "Eva C.," who was to become the subject of a series of experiments conducted at the Sorbonne in 1922. It was Heuzé who convinced the Sorbonne's Henri Piéron and George Dumas that such an investigation was in the best interests of science. The thirty-six-year-old Eva had become known prior to the war as a result of two books, one in French and one in German, which provided detailed accounts of the séances she had given between 1909 and 1913 in Paris, Biarritz, and Munich.[10] These books were the work of Juliette Bisson, the Parisian socialite and widow of the celebrated playwright Alexandre Bisson, and of her collaborator, a psychiatrist from Munich named Albert Baron von Schrenck-Notzing. Their experiments with Eva focused primarily on the phenomena of materialization and on the appearance of the substance ectoplasm (or teleplasm), which emerged from the medium's body, usually near her mouth, as a white (though occasionally gray or black) material that was cold to the touch and viscous and had a high degree of mobility. Bisson and Schrenck-Notzing observed the material advance, retract, swell like a balloon, tie itself into knots, and spread out over the medium's body like a veil. Sometimes these protrusions took the form of fingers or partially formed hands.[11] Sometimes they coalesced into figures resembling human faces.

All of these phenomena occurred in what Bisson and Schrenck-Notzing described as strict conditions of control. The medium was undressed, inspected, and given a special garment to wear to prevent her from smuggling anything into the séance room, which was itself sealed under lock and key.[12] In certain séances Eva wore a fine mesh hood enclosing her head and tied tightly around her neck through which the ectoplasm nonetheless managed to travel without producing any tears. On occasion Eva appeared nude in the *cabinet noir* with ectoplasm emerging from her breasts or her navel.[13] Against the charge that ectoplasm was simply some mundane material that had been ingested and then regurgitated during the séance (critics often likened it to muslin cloth), Eva was given blueberry jam to eat prior to the séances with the understanding that this would stain the contents of her stomach, making regurgitation evident. Eva was even examined by laryngologists, who attested that she was not a merycist (she did not have the anatomical capacity to regurgitate at will). Many of Bisson's early experiments with Eva

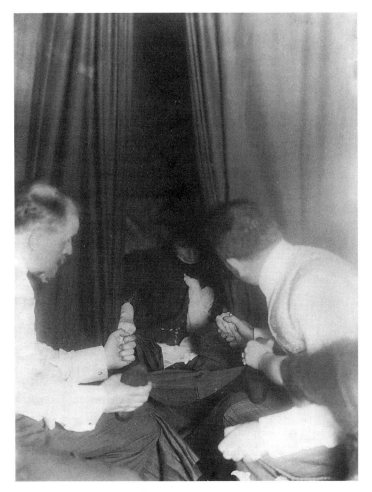

Figure 6.2. "Eva C." Date unknown. IMI 22: 2.

began with an examination of the vagina and rectum designed to discount the hypothesis that props were smuggled into the séance room using these bodily cavities.[14]

The séances with Eva C. took place in a highly charged atmosphere. Along with the production of the materializations themselves, Bisson's accounts detail disturbing instances in which the medium was struck about the face by the ectoplasmic hands or in which she seemed to be choking and unable to breathe only to emerge from her trance trembling violently and calling for help.[15] On occasion, the materializations took the form of a death's head or

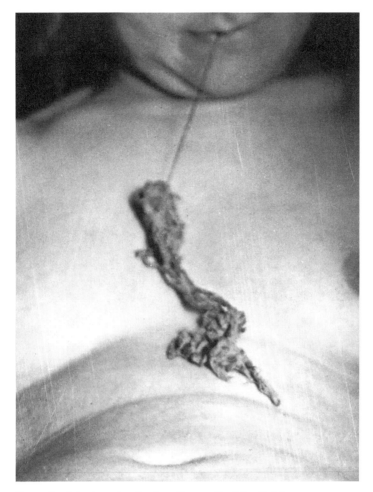

Figure 6.3. Ectoplasm issuing from the mouth of Eva C. IMI 22: 2.

they slid across Eva's body "like a reptile."[16] Eva's trance states were characterized by rapid and shallow breathing accompanied by trembling and long
and loud exhalations (behavior that Bisson compared to that of a woman in
labor).[17] The séances ended when Bisson broke Eva's trance by blowing on
the back of her neck.

From 1909 until their collaboration was interrupted in 1914 by the war,
Schrenck-Notzing and Bisson worked extensively together. In order to document the materializations they constructed a laboratory in Bisson's home
equipped with seven cameras that could be trained on the medium simul-

taneously. Eva responded by providing them with an abundance of visible phenomena. As a result, photographs became a major feature of their published accounts. Bisson's *Les Phénomènes dits de materialisation* contained over 200 photographs of the materializations and Schrenck-Notzing's *Materialisations-Phaenomene* over 150. The extensive visual record of Eva's performances effectively established her as the most photogenic medium of the period.[18] These striking documents show the medium extruding ectoplasmic materializations before a fascinated and often astonished group of observers. For the sake of propriety, photographs of the medium in various states of undress were touched up prior to their inclusion in Schrenck-Notzing's and Bisson's books.[19]

In January 1914 Bisson's book was ridiculed in the Parisian newspaper *Le Matin* on the basis of its photographic evidence. The opposition was sparked by an article published in *Psychic Magazine* claiming that the spirit faces materialized in the course of Eva's séances and featured in the photographs of the two Eva books were nothing more than portraits clipped from the pages of the pictorial magazine *Le Miroir* and crudely altered with penciled-in hair, beards, and mustaches. The side-by-side resemblances between Eva's materializations and the magazine's portraits of Woodrow Wilson, Raymond Poincaré, Paul Deschanel, and Ferdinand I of Bulgaria were taken as a clear indication of fraud. The clippings, critics argued, had simply been folded and smuggled into the séances unbeknownst to the controllers and produced during the séances as the various "materializations." This conclusion was corroborated by a photo taken inside the *cabinet noir* by a camera positioned behind the medium in which the large block letters making up the front-page title of *Le Miroir* ("M-I-R-O") were visible.

Schrenck-Notzing argued in response that the resemblance of the images might just as easily be accounted for by the phenomenon of "ideoplasty," in which the medium gave ectoplasmic form to images that she had recently seen and whose traces (the letters of the title, the creases of the paper) had been registered in her memory and reproduced in exact detail in the materializations. Schrenck-Notzing supported his hypothesis by making efforts to reproduce the images like those he and Bisson featured in their books using the fraudulent method claimed by skeptics. The resulting photographs showed only low-contrast images with none of the detail evident in the actual séance photos. Under close inspection with a loupe, the fake photographs showed the half-tone linescreen typical of the newsprint photo, a characteristic that was not visible in the actual séance photos.[20] Schrenck-Notzing's explanation, which was corroborated by affidavits from the expert photog-

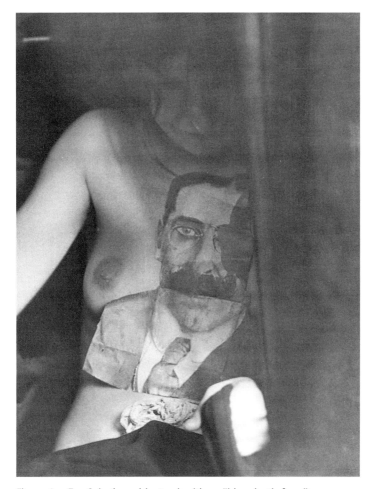

Figure 6.4. Eva C. in the *cabinet noir* with an "ideoplastic form" or a clipping of Woodrow Wilson's portrait from *Le Miroir*. IMI 22: 2.

raphers he worked with in Paris and Munich, no doubt exceeded the technical knowledge and interest of those for whom the resemblances between the séances' photographs and the pictures from *Le Miroir* were an obvious indication of foul play.[21]

The exchange over the images taken by Bisson and Schrenck-Notzing was typical of those that were to continue to surround the career of Eva C. in the interwar period. The growing polemic was in many ways a realization of the intensified hostility toward psychical research that Oliver Lodge had forecast in Santoliquido's effort to give greater prominence to the field. In the years following the war the difficulties that had long plagued the efforts of psychical researchers to contribute to scientific knowledge were compounded by unprecedented popular interest in the field. As the interest in psychical research grew in this period, so too did scrutiny from a skeptical public that was, from the perspective of the committed psychical researcher, inexpert and ill informed. The intuitive arguments made regarding the similarities between Eva's ideoplastic faces and portraits from *Le Miroir* indicated the errors inherent in the popular conception that the reality of mediumistic phenomena could be tested by commonplace methods of observation. What seemed obvious and indisputable to the uninitiated observer was far from the case for the experienced psychical researcher.

Questions of Method

The difficulties presented by popular interest in the experiments of psychical research were especially pronounced in the study of ectoplasm, since, in contrast to the easily reproduced phenomena of table rapping, mediums with the ability to produce materializations were extremely rare, and the technical expertise claimed by those who studied them was well beyond the reach of the merely curious.[22] Those who did not have firsthand experience in the study of materialization necessarily relied on the good faith and perspicacity of those who did. For some critics, this situation constituted a serious weakness in the attempt of psychical researchers to contribute to the scientific construction of public knowledge. This criticism certainly serviced a populist resentment of psychical research that saw it as a bizarre form of scientific elitism. It also, however, fueled debate among scientists themselves as to the actual meanings of the term *science*. Drawing widely from the methodologies of natural history, clinical psychology, and physiology, the field of psychical research had developed in the last decades of the nineteenth century in a methodological no-man's-land. For some, this ambiguity meant that many of the facts that psychical researchers looked to as the basis of the future development of their field would forever lack the rigorous basis necessary to proceed with scientific certainty. Marie Curie would argue, for example (following her own inconclusive experiences with the medium Eusapia Palladino), that a "fact is not scientific until it can be followed, by oneself or others in the same fashion, in a laboratory, and produced at will with certainty."[23] Curie's definition of science would have no doubt been considered overly narrow by the clinicians, biologists, astronomers, geologists, and sociologists whose investigations led them far afield in pursuit of experiences that could not be confined to the limited surface of the laboratory bench. In fact, psychical researchers like Richet and Schrenck-Notzing often claimed solidarity with such scientists by arguing that their science was closer to that of the naturalist who observes phenomena that the observer has no power to bring about or influence.[24] On this issue the otherwise skeptical Charles Nordmann was inclined to agree that psychical research presented a methodology typical of many accepted sciences even if it did not conform to the standards indicated by Mme Curie. Nordmann concurred with Richet that limiting scientific investigation by the criteria of reproducibility represented an unjustifiable apriority. The fact that the phenomena of psychical research were rare and unpredictable did not mean that one should exclude them from scientific study any more than one should disregard the irreproducible event of a meteor falling to earth.[25]

While claiming a methodological similarity to the field sciences, psychical researchers nevertheless continued in their efforts to emulate the experimental sciences. This aspiration was, of course, continually thwarted by the field's reliance on human subjects and on the possibility that the phenomena observed were produced in the interests of deception—a possibility that would serve as the central preoccupation of the field. As Richet would note, "The other sciences do not suffer from the same plague. . . . A single preoccupation, intense and anxiety ridden, invades my every thought—'do everything to prevent being duped'—I can think of nothing but this. . . . One must always have in one's mind the dominating, obsessive idea that the medium is trying to trick you."[26] Of course, this concern had to be constantly balanced with the need to accommodate the interests of the medium, whose performance the experiments depended on for their success. Researchers agreed that an overly severe set of controls was just as likely to disrupt a genuine phenomenon as expose a false one. In the space between these two considerations, experimenters were apt to rely on a criterion that was difficult to translate into terms acceptable to science. "Good faith," they argued, adopted on behalf of the scientist in regard to the medium and on behalf of the medium in regard to the observers was essential to the success of the experiment. For critics like Charles Nordmann, this was the Achilles heel of the entire enterprise of psychical research. The problem lay, he argued, not in the issue of accurately determining either good faith or bad faith, as so many decades of psychical research had tried to do through elaborate systems of control, but in the fact that faith had any role at all to play in the experiments. The failure to apply experimental methodology to psychical research rested with

the possibility that the facts *could have been* (and not necessarily *were*) produced fraudulently. The very features of the phenomena that had interested
researchers—their indication of volition and intelligence—were exactly the
qualities that, in Nordmann's terms, disqualified psychical research from
claiming a scientific status. Until one could establish conditions in which
faith, good or bad, no longer entered into account, the facts of psychical
research would, in Nordmann's view, remain unproven.[27]

Efforts to overcome these difficulties in the interwar period and to develop psychical research into a mature science were largely ineffectual. While
Charles Richet's attempt to give the field a standard synthetic text with his
1922 *Traité de métapsychique* met with the admiration of some, the book was
ultimately unable to resolve the methodological ambiguities that continued
to undermine the legitimacy of the field. The intervention represented by
the book was significant and would become Richet's last great effort to substantiate a field to which he had committed so much of his life. Submitting
the work to the Académie des Sciences in 1922, Richet argued that the "innumerable facts observed and recorded by men such as William Crookes,
Frederic Myers, and so many other universally esteemed scientists deserve
to be taken into consideration and should not be permitted to be drowned
out by sarcasm or disdainful silence."[28] The book and its presentation was,
Nordmann agreed, a "conscientious and courageous" effort by Richet to introduce psychical research into the world of official science by producing
the "most complete and most synthetic exposé" of the field. But in spite of
its author's "beautiful act of intellectual audacity," Nordmann was ultimately
left unconvinced that Richet's *Traité* had resolved the basic methodological
uncertainties of the field.[29] Failing this, Richet's work became little more
than a catalog of phenomena of uncertain origins. The taxonomic scheme
outlined in the book, in which subjective phenomena like telepathy were
deemed proven facts and objective phenomena like materialization were
deemed still questionable, did little to impress skeptics.

Even readers who, if critical in spirit, remained open to the possibilities
of the field felt that Richet's work had missed the mark by a wide margin.
Richet's friend Pierre Janet, who otherwise found the effort "courageous,
useful," and "serious," was ultimately disappointed by its general effect.[30] In
his review of the book Janet indicated a feeling that many other readers of
the work had communicated to him. Janet argued that the sympathetic but
critical reader, rather than finding reason for greater certainty, was likely
to conclude his reading of Richet's text feeling "confused, unsatisfied, and,
without knowing why, a bit more skeptical than he might have been before."[31]

Janet found troubling Richet's effort to establish the reality of a particular class of phenomena by giving innumerable examples, none of which was described in sufficient detail. This was not, Janet noted, the method that Richet employed in revealing the facts of biology, in which a single, well-performed, and documented experiment was sufficient to expose a certain fact. Janet was perplexed by Richet's assertion that the accumulation of marginal evidence was a legitimate method for proceeding in the sciences of observation.[32] Why, he asked, does Richet so often pronounce the various observations inconclusive and then bother to encumber his book with them?[33] Janet notes that in the descriptions of specific events "one finds in every instance the hesitations and scruples of the author: this observation was poor, this other one was incomplete, this one came secondhand, that one was performed without sufficient precautions." In the general conclusions, however, he was astonished to find Richet claiming that the facts as a whole were well established.[34] Janet's measured criticism of his friend Richet echoed the more severe judgment of Henri Piéron (director of the Sorbonne laboratory of physiological psychology), who found that in reading its "innumerable anecdotes one cannot escape—or at least I could not escape—a real sense of stupor." Piéron continued: "How can one call a scientific treatise a compendium in which not a single demonstrated fact is presented."[35]

For Janet, Richet's work failed primarily as a result of its willingness to respond to the polemics that had long surrounded the field. In its inability to find an appropriate audience among readers who were uncommitted but open-minded, the *Traité de métapsychique* merely reiterated arguments of the older debates and thus failed to push understanding of the field forward. As a result, the work repeated strategies of argumentation that Janet saw as a detriment to the credibility of the field. As a field struggling to gain recognition and credibility in the late nineteenth century, psychical research had, for instance, benefited from the prominent names of its leading practitioners. In the interwar period, however, references to the field's illustrious early patrons came to seem more like part of what Janet called a "deplorable argument" for authority, one that was "dear to religions [but] absolutely without merit" for science.[36] While the recitation of the names of Crookes, Myers, James, and Lodge might have once been necessary to rescue the field from a general lack of interest, given the attention that psychical research drew in the 1920s, Janet found their reiteration in Richet's work an unnecessary justification for a field that had already generated considerable interest. In other words, Janet argued, Richet "pushes too hard against a door that is already open."[37] Addressing itself to the hard-boiled skeptic, on the one hand, and to the confirmed believer, on the other, to the elite scientist as much as the curious layman, Richet's text produced contradictions in its methods of argumentation that, to those with critical but open minds, ultimately undermined the integrity of the field that the work was trying to define and establish.

The failure of Richet's *recueil* was particularly apparent to those who looked to the writings of psychical researchers for transparent proofs of the phenomena that they had heard about but never experienced for themselves. While Richet and his colleagues at the IMI could claim firsthand experience with many of the phenomena discussed in his book, for a public that was unlikely ever to witness something as rare as mediumistic materialization, knowledge came exclusively from written accounts. For such a public, a critical approach to mediumism based on these sources naturally invoked a set of methodologies different from those that psychical researchers employed in their laboratories. If those with access to the séances continued to claim the authority of experience and of an acumen developed by decades of working with mediums, those without such access or experience were left only with the written record, the inconsistencies and incompleteness of which served as a great source of consternation and suspicion for many. Readers demanded precise transcriptions of reality, not a loose narration of events. Where such a full accounting was lacking, the possibility for error and doubt remained. As Paul Heuzé would ask regarding an episode recounted in Camille Flammarion's *Autour de la mort*, "Why instead of saying 'one day, one night, a few years afterward' didn't [he] give precise dates, names, the exact number involved, in short, all of the information necessary for the verification of the account?"[38] In his efforts to achieve clarity in regard to the written record of psychical research, the journalist Heuzé would become a champion for those who, like his correspondent in this instance, remained perplexed by the reports that they relied on for their opinions about such matters. Heuzé argued that his method, which he described as "historical," permitted greater transparency in its ability to reveal hidden relations and inconsistencies that remained obscured in the texts.[39] In his investigation of the incident vaguely reported in Flammarion's book, Heuzé determined for his reader that, in the inconsistencies in the places and dates cited in the account, Flammarion's claims in this instance were totally unfounded.

Not surprisingly, the differences in Heuzé's method of comparing texts and corroborating various accounts often led to conclusions that differed dramatically from those presented by psychical researchers. While an experimental researcher like Schrenck-Notzing could persuade himself on the basis of his experience and technical expertise that his efforts had averted fraud, Heuzé's scrutiny of the written record of psychical research gave him a much different impression, one of "vast *fumisteries* [elaborate farces]."[40] In his close reading of the accounts, Heuzé challenged the ability of psychical researchers to make the exceptional phenomena of mediumism transparent to those not in a position to observe them firsthand.

Such transparency was notoriously difficult to achieve. This was especially true of the popular accounts by which nonspecialists formed their impressions of the experiments. These accounts, often second- or thirdhand reiterations of reports drafted by the researchers themselves, consisted largely of either positive or negative impressions and truncated descriptions of experiments featuring references to certain classes of phenomena and not necessarily to specific events. Even in the firsthand accounts issued for a specialized readership, the exhaustive transcription of the experimental conditions—of the phenomena observed and of the types of controls applied—was prohibitive. Here the problem of transparency was compounded by the fact that the actual conditions in which phenomena occurred were constantly in flux. Scientists changed their procedures of control and observation in accordance with phenomena whose exact nature they could not always anticipate. When no phenomena at all occurred, conditions were changed, often in response to the medium's requests.

These concessions were not without a legitimate basis. The physiological and psychological disposition of the medium was often cited as the reason why phenomena could not be produced or why methods of control and observation had to be altered in order to accommodate the medium. The specific conditions in place at any particular moment were not always apparent in the accounts even to the most careful of readers. As a result, the observations made in the course of the experiments simply did not translate into persuasive or even consistent accounts. Heuzé, for instance, found nothing reassuring even in the lengthiest and most detailed accounts, considering Jules Courtier's otherwise reputable (and inconclusive) summary of the 1905–8 Eusapia Palladino experiments unsatisfying in its effort to accurately represent the events that had transpired. For Heuzé, Courtier's work remained a "masterpiece of imprecision."[41] For Joseph Jastrow, a psychologist working far from the Parisian séances at the University of Wisconsin, the tendency to omit crucial details regarding the methods of control was a substantial cause to doubt any conclusions offered. Jastrow, who strongly opposed the claims surrounding Eva's materializations, argued that a close analysis of the accounts of experiments revealed troubling omissions and inconsistencies, which led to blatant distortions in their subsequent reiterations in the scholarly and popular press. Jastrow found that the careful controls used in one séance were often assumed to be in place in other séances even though the account was not specific on the matter. The result was that the "rigid conditions of one séance—usually a negative one—are transferred to another most remarkable one to which they in no way apply. Thus, error and exaggeration add to the work of credulity in disguising the true mode of operation by which ectoplasm and similar beliefs arise and expand."[42]

Heuzé's approach, which inspired popular appreciation, also drew the admiration of a number of prominent figures in Parisian scientific circles. Restricting his personal expertise to the historical method, Heuzé would enlist these figures in his effort to determine, in the interest of public knowledge, the true nature of psychical phenomena. It was largely as a result of Heuzé's intervention that the psychologist Henri Piéron agreed to become involved in a series of experiments involving Eva in 1922. While Piéron excoriated Richet's *Traité* in the pages of *L'Année Psychologique,* he was charmed by Heuzé's 1922 account of mediumistic fraud, *L'Ectoplasme,* which he found "lively" and "fun to read." Heuzé's lack of scientific training did not compromise his conclusions about fraud in the practice of mediumism, which Piéron found "perfectly correct." "If he is not exactly a man of science," Piéron opined, "P. Heuzé is at least a man of good sense."[43]

Mediumism at the Sorbonne

In the early spring of 1922 Piéron was joined by the eminent George Dumas (professor of experimental psychology), Louis Lapicque (director of the physiological laboratory of the Faculté des Sciences), and Henri Laugier (assistant to Lapicque) for the purpose of investigating the materializations of the medium Eva C. at the physiological laboratories of the Sorbonne.[44]

With the agreement of Juliette Bisson and Eva, fifteen sittings were held at the Sorbonne between 20 March and 23 June. The negotiations between Bisson and the investigating committee that preceded the experiments were considerable. In the end, the committee conceded to the requirement of near or total darkness and to the construction of a *cabinet noir* in which the medium would remain during the séance. Black paper was placed over the windows, and an enclosure for the medium was built by hanging heavy black curtains from wires suspended near the ceiling of the room. To compensate for the lack of light, the scientists installed a number of red electric bulbs whose intensity they could control at any instant. The observers also equipped themselves with flashlights, which they made use of at key moments.

Upon arriving at the Sorbonne, Eva was undressed in the presence of one of the observers and carefully inspected for hidden objects (605–6). She was then put into a tight-fitting black leotard, which was kept at the lab, and led by one of the controllers to the *cabinet noir,* where she was put into a trance by Bisson. Throughout the séance her hands and legs remained outside of the cabinet and were held by controllers sitting on either side of her.

Overall, Eva's performance proved disappointing. In the fifteen sittings only twice was anything resembling ectoplasm seen. At the first séance the observers noted a substance that they took to be saliva hanging from the medium's lips. Put into contact with the wrist of Dumas, it was described as "viscous, warm, and inert" (610). Eva reabsorbed the material by inhaling abruptly and appeared to ruminate with her jaw and tongue before its appearance and after its reabsorption (610). On another occasion Bisson declared that a phenomenon was taking place. A red bulb inside the *cabinet noir* was snapped on, and Dumas penetrated the curtain with a flashlight to see a gray substance hanging from the medium's mouth. As he approached, Eva turned her head, and the substance was reabsorbed. Dumas then inspected her mouth, pushing his fingers all the way to the back of her throat to confirm that it was empty (607). In these cases the appearance of the material was preceded by gestures that resembled those characteristic of a forced attempt to vomit (610).

The report issued by the Sorbonne committee on 7 July 1922 asserted that "nothing in our observations led us to make recourse to the notion of ectoplasm. . . . Our experiments concluded with results that can only be considered as entirely negative" (611). This statement was seen as a triumph in the popular press, which hailed it as the definitive blow against the field of psychical research. Heuzé and other critics saw the Sorbonne experiments as an effort to defraud that was successfully thwarted by the scrutiny of a truly impartial group of scientists.

In August Heuzé dealt what he undoubtedly felt would be the deathblow to the mystifications of psychical research. Eva Carrière, he announced, was in fact the pseudonym of Marthe Béraud, a woman known to his readers as the notorious young medium of the Villa Carmen affair who, more than fifteen years earlier, had become the focus of a public scandal involving the good name of Charles Richet.[45] Until Heuzé exposed this fact in his column in *L'Opinion,* the identity of Eva C. and Marthe Béraud (a.k.a. Rose Dupont) had gone entirely unmentioned. Neither Bisson nor Schrenck-Notzing, investigators who worked so closely with Eva before and after the war, made any mention of this fact in their books.[46] Heuzé's discovery of the identity of the medium (later admitted without equivocation by Richet and others)

drew from the testimony of key witnesses of the 1905 séances in Algiers—
the Noëls' household cook and the coachman, Areski. The purpose behind
Heuzé's revelation was clear: to draw the more recent investigations of Eva C.
into an association with the séances of the Villa Carmen, which were widely
believed to have been discredited in spite of Richet's continued insistence to
the contrary. Revisiting the Villa Carmen affair, Richet once again rebuffed
the slanderous accusations that had been levied against him. Nonetheless,
Heuzé's good timing seemed to have paid off, as readers came to interpret the
outcome of the Sorbonne experiments in terms of their lingering memory
of the Villa Carmen.

Richet was accordingly baffled by the popular reaction to the 1922 report
on Eva C., which for him revealed a stupefying inclination of the public to
wildly exaggerate the meaning of the facts actually recorded. In reality, Richet
noted, "my eminent friends at the Sorbonne" made no mention of fraud in
their report and, on the contrary, concluded that Bisson at least had acted
with undisputed good faith. Piéron and his colleagues had only faithfully
reported that they had seen nothing, that this was "all that they said and all
that they had the right to say." Richet continued: "But from this the public
. . . has derived a conclusion that I can only leave to the mediation of poster-
ity: 'These scientists of the Sorbonne saw nothing in these fifteen séances,
meaning there was never anything there to see, not with Eva, Eusapia, Home,
Katie King [sic], Kluski, not with anyone!'"[47]

Arguing against this misreading of the report in his own rebuttal in *Figaro*, Gustave Geley noted that, in fact, only thirteen of the fifteen séances
had really failed and that in the remaining two the scientists had not "seen
nothing," as they concluded in their report. Geley continued to suggest that
the reason for the unimpressive nature of the phenomena lay with the committee's "mediocre" commitment to the investigation. Only one investigator,
he noted, followed the experiments through to their conclusion. Two others
had only participated in half of the séances. The fourth member had been
present only for the first séance. Geley asked readers to consider that among
"those who deny [the reality of the materializations], none have studied them
seriously." In contrast, the scientists who affirm their authenticity "have all
studied them for a long time, for a very long time." In contrast to the paltry
thirteen failed séances held at the Sorbonne, there were, Geley claimed, hundreds of successful ones conducted under the same conditions of control.
"Metapsychical phenomena are true," he concluded, "indisputably true."[48]

Advocates of psychical research, familiar with the capriciousness of mediumism, were not surprised that nothing noteworthy had transpired at the

Sorbonne and indicated that the lack of phenomena indicated nothing definitive. Disappointed by her medium's performance, Juliette Bisson publicly regretted that the scientists had not seen her medium in top form, indicating that Eva had been in poor health during many of the séances.[49] She also noted that conditions in the laboratory were generally disruptive and that the observers' comings and goings, noise in the neighboring lab, and the brusque projections of light made it impossible for Eva to produce the desired phenomena. In general, Bisson was disappointed that the experiments could not have continued under better conditions. Like other researchers with extensive experience working with mediums, Bisson argued that Eva's sense of physical and emotional well-being was essential to the production of phenomena, and that, given the variability of these conditions, one could not expect any predictability in the outcome of the séances. Eva herself remarked that the process was "like having a baby . . . it's often when one wants one that one cannot have one and inversely" (609). While scientists of the Sorbonne tended to suggest that Eva was quite comfortable in her surroundings (indicating that she addressed them using the familiar second-person pronoun and called them each *mon petit*), others saw in the official description of events indications that the medium had been put off her task by the disruptive behavior of Piéron and his colleagues (608). Writing in *La Revue de France,* the *académicien* Marcel Prévost would agree that a sense of confidence and of sympathy from the audience was just as crucial to Eva's success as it was to that of any opera singer. An overly critical environment (what Arthur Conan Doyle would elsewhere call the "thumb-screw methods of scientific investigators") was just as likely to stymie a medium's performance as the heckling of a crowd was likely to disturb an otherwise gifted soprano.[50] Being blinded by flashlights and having scientists probing around inside one's mouth was, Prévost suggested, sufficient cause for the medium's poor performance. In other words, Prévost concurred with those who argued that mediumistic phenomena could not be subjected to a strict requirement of reproducibility, since the unpredictable effects of the subject's emotional and mental state always had to be taken into consideration.[51] The recognition of this fact constituted both the strength and the weakness of psychical research: "its strength," Prévost argued, "because any negative results proves nothing against it . . . [and] its weakness because [when the experiments fail] laboratory scientists can always make fun, snickering, 'Your experiments only succeed among you. As soon as we bring our eyes and our scales, nothing happens.'"[52]

Prévost's contribution to the debates surrounding Eva's materializations would ultimately lead to an involvement that serves as a telling example of the kinds of transformations that could take place in those who, given their status, actually had the opportunity to witness these rarest of mediumistic phenomena firsthand. Like that of Piéron, Prévost's intervention in the question of materializations came as a result of a visit from Heuzé, who approached him with the hopes of further publicizing the ongoing debate in the pages of *La Revue de France*. Initially quite ignorant of psychical research, Prévost claimed that he had never witnessed any "extranatural phenomenon" and that his general attitude toward such matters was that of the hardheaded "old *polytechnicien*." His effort to learn more about the field and the phenomena of psychical research from reading Camille Flammarion's *Après la mort* proved useless. Indeed, Prévost distinguished himself from those who could be convinced of anything simply by reading a *procès-verbal*. His reading of the Sorbonne report on the Eva C. experiments suggested that, just as there was no conclusive evidence that materialization was a reality, neither was there any proof in the report against such phenomena. He found, rather, that the Sorbonne report was suspiciously stilted in its account of the two appearances of "ectoplasm," as unimpressive as they were. "If they perceived fraud," Prévost asked, "why didn't they just say so outright?"[53] In light of this omission, Prévost found it bizarre that journalists, who knew nothing of the field and who had seen nothing of the experiments, could view this document as a triumph of common sense over the delusional and/or fraudulent claims of expert psychical researchers. "To claim that all of these good minds are either charlatans or dupes," Prévost argued, "is simply another way of abusing our credulity."[54] But in spite of the authority Prévost attributed to expert researchers, he ultimately reserved the right to make up his own mind regarding mediumism. Where unusual facts were taken into evidence, he could find no adequate substitution for firsthand experience.

Good Faith

Speaking openly against the press's "puerile lack of good grace" in *La Revue de France*, Prévost's articles drew the interest of Gustave Geley, who in the winter of 1922 asked Prévost to participate in a demonstration of materialization organized at the IMI.[55] Geley considered Prévost an ideal representative of public interest in the debate surrounding psychical research. While Prévost was openly inclined toward skepticism, he had also proven his ability to remain open-minded in the absence of a full consideration of the evidence. This new round of séances, which began in December, was the IMI's calculated response to the blow that psychical research had suffered at the hands of Paul Heuzé and the Sorbonne committee. This was also Geley's opportunity to introduce the French public to Jan Guzik, a Polish medium whose name was free from the negative associations that had condemned Juliette Bisson's efforts at the Sorbonne. The Guzik séances were attended by over eighty people, including members of the Institut de France, professors of various faculties, and high officials of state.

The demonstrations took place under what Geley described as the most severe conditions of control. The séance room was sealed with strips of paper adhered to the door and frame bearing the signatures of Geley and other members of the investigating committee. The seals were broken only prior to the séance in the presence of the assembled witnesses. An architect's affidavit certified that the room contained no false panels or other hiding places. Prior to the séance, the medium was undressed in the presence of the observers and redressed in pajamas with no pockets. Control of Guzik's hands was maintained by physical contact and further ensured by ribbons (whose knots were secured by a lead seal bearing the initials of the IMI) tied to the wrists of the medium and his two controllers. In certain séances the floor was scattered with sawdust designed to reveal the traces of anyone moving about the room surreptitiously.[56] In contrast to other mediums, Guzik remained calm and passive throughout the séance, insuring that the control of his hands and feet was continuous and not disrupted by abrupt movements (by which mediums were known to liberate their own hands by substituting those of the controller to each side). Visual control was also greatly improved by the absence of a *cabinet noir,* which Guzik did not require. In spite of these conditions, Guzik achieved a variety of phenomena—the movement of objects (occupied chairs), faint luminous effects, sounds, and physical contact taken to be the materialization of human and animal forms.

Following these experiments, thirty-four prominent witnesses (many of them members of IMI) signed an account published *in extenso* in the newspaper *Le Matin* on 7 June 1923 that attested to the authenticity of the phenomena.[57] Prévost, one of the signatories, would later conclude in *La Revue de France* that, having maintained a positive grip on both the medium and his own sangfroid, the hypothesis of deception or of self-deception was insufficient to explain what he had witnessed. Without making definite claims, Prévost favored the hypothesis of unknown physical forces, not intelligent in themselves but directed by the medium as if by radio control.[58] The phenomena seemed to him less supernatural in origin than like "materializations of vague dreams," as if the medium had the capacity to "make the images of his dreams come to life."[59] Based on his experiences, Prévost opened the pages of *La Revue de France* to a thorough, two-sided discussion of psychical research by which the reader would "have before his eyes all the data of the problem."[60]

In the days following the publication of the statement signed by Prévost and the other witnesses of Guzik's extraordinary talents, the debate surrounding psychical research took an unusual series of turns. Championed again by the pen of Paul Heuzé, the skeptic's cause enlisted the assistance of a professional illusionist named Professor Dicksonn who on 9 June issued a proclamation on the front page of *Le Matin* claiming that the thirty-four signatories had been duped. Dicksonn's involvement in the Guzik experiments dated back to the end of May, when some of the witnesses in the séances had urged Geley to give Dicksonn a part in the control of the medium as a means of confirming their own observations that no prestidigitation was involved in the phenomena.[61] Initially acceding to their request, Geley abruptly changed his mind and proceeded to put Guzik on a train back to Warsaw, claiming that the medium had suddenly been taken ill. In his statement to *Le Matin* weeks later, Dicksonn demanded that he be allowed to participate in the control of the medium and promised that he would reveal the Guzik mediumship as a fraud. Responding to Dicksonn's challenge a week later, Geley offered a ten-thousand-franc prize to anyone who could reproduce the same phenomena as Guzik under the same conditions of control. These challengers would, for their part, have to risk an equal sum, which they would forfeit if their challenge failed.[62] For Heuzé, the response was a transparent effort to shift the burden of proof while protecting the medium from the scrutiny of an expert in mystification. Heuzé called Geley's test a "vulgar bet" and noted that in his original offer of assistance Dicksonn had said nothing about monetary reward. Moreover, Dicksonn had not volunteered to reproduce the phenomena by means of prestidigitation but to expose the phenomena presumed to be genuine as frauds. Dicksonn justified his refusal to engage in Geley's challenge by arguing that such trickery could not be achieved without advance preparation and assistance. The implication was that the fraud was perpetrated not by the medium, on whom scrutiny was focused at all times, but by members of the audience who had intermingled with more respectable observers whose good faith was not in question.[63] Dicksonn doubted that the so-called controllers, who, in fact, served to *tirer sur la ficelle* (i.e., pull the strings), would be at his disposal had he accepted Geley's challenge. In his response to this suggestion Geley argued that it was ridiculous to cast doubt on the good faith of the thirty-four signatories, an argument with which Heuzé agreed, noting that this had never been his claim. Heuzé argued that Dicksonn's involvement was only intended to shed light on the role of the other, anonymous observers present at the séances.[64]

Defenders of the IMI argued that what Heuzé had crafted to look like a defensive admission of guilt on the part of Geley was in fact a legitimate refusal to allow Dicksonn to gain control over experimental conditions in which good faith and disinterestedness were considered essential.[65] The magician's conviction that all mediums and their "barnums" were cheats was widely known. As one psychical researcher indicated to Heuzé in private, "I wouldn't want Dicksonn at my experiments . . . because I have no confidence in his good faith. He could easily simulate the discovery of some trick, bringing with him, for example, something that he could pretend to gather up from near the medium, proclaiming 'Ah! Here is your ectoplasm!'"[66]

As Charles Richet had argued in his 1922 *Traité de métapsychique,* the psychical researcher "had to be absolutely certain of the good faith of those present during the experiments."[67] For Heuzé, Nordmann, and others, it was exactly this dependence on the ability to determine good faith that signaled the failure of psychical research. Paraphrasing the physicist Édouard Branly, Heuzé remarked that a "good scientific experiment is an experiment in which the good or bad faith of the experimenters or those present can play absolutely no role."[68] For Heuzé, who described his methodology as closer to that of the historian than the scientist, faith had no objective surface; it was not a thing or an event but a subjective condition that one person attributed to another. As such, good faith could not be transposed in any meaningful way into the written accounts of the participant-observers. The potential discord between the articulated motive and the real motive meant that good faith could not be taken as the given basis of one's observations or conclusions. Even where there were reasonable assurances of the scientist's motivations, the question of faith remained operative in the rapport that comprised the intersubjective reality of the séances. Charles Nordmann, in placing the honesty and intelligence of men like Richet and Crookes beyond all suspicion, nevertheless questioned the dynamics involved in the corporate production of phenomena in psychical research:

> When scientists, to whom humanity owes the most beautiful conquests, when a Crookes, a Lodge, a Richet, a d'Arsonval, a Branly, a Curie performs an experiment of physics or physiology . . . nothing interposes itself between the experimenter and the object of experience, which nothing can deform or influence. There is in this circumstance nothing but the conditions foreseen and realized by the scientist. His experience is unmediated. If it is a question of ectoplasm, the case is entirely different. Between the illustrious and

respectable scientist and the phenomenon there are others interposed: there is the medium and the other participants. It is not Crookes alone who produces, by experimentation, ectoplasm, it is this collective personality called "Crookes-the medium-the participants."[69]

The question of subjectivity raised in the context of psychical research was thus a question of the communicability of one's true underlying meaning or purpose. For Nordmann, the mediated quality of the experience produced insurmountable conditions of indeterminacy. In the debates surrounding psychical research, affirmations of faith and suspicions of fraud continued to point to the gap between the intent manifested in language and an occulted intent that was thought to lie behind what was said. If thorough narration, enumeration, and graphic inscription could still be attributed with representative transparency, the subjective conditions that lay behind such representations remained indeterminable. Language, in other words, could not fully account for the true measure and character of desire. Where there was desire, there was doubt.

The Psychoanalytic Unconscious and the Science of Doubt

The history of the resistance to Freud's ideas in France has revealed manifold causes, ranging from straightforward xenophobia and anti-Semitism to the more subtle characteristic of French cultural identity and its influence on France's institutions of medicine and science. In her seminal work on the subject Elisabeth Roudinesco has argued that the core of the French resistance to psychoanalysis was a certain "Cartesianism" that insisted on viewing the subject as the master of language and the author of its representations. This view of the Cartesian project was understood as the inaugurating moment of the scientific project and, indeed, conformed well to the postulate of universal determinacy espoused by French science in the nineteenth century. What was objectionable about the Freudian theory of the unconscious in French circles was that it inverted the Cartesian relation by making this other agency (which Jacques Lacan would later define as "structured like a language") the author of the experience of subjectivity. Through automatism, surrealism would assert something like the Freudian conception in the formula "je suis une autre," just as Lacanian psychoanalysis would identify the relationship between language and authorship in the expression "ça parle." What the psychoanalytic unconscious would enable Lacan to do was to restore in the cogito the lack of determinacy—Descartes' foundational doubt—as the essential condition of subjectivity and knowledge. This notion of a language that possesses its own agency had been made familiar in the last two decades of the nineteenth century in investigations that hoped to use hypnosis and mediumism as means of objectifying the mechanism of the mind for purposes of scientific study.

By the turn of the century the psychological study of mediums had given way to a program that aimed to establish the objective reality of mediumistic phenomenon. This focus corresponded to a shift in attitudes about hysteria, hypnosis, and automatism, which came to be seen not as authentic representations of mental processes but as effects of suggestion and simulation. This shift would begin around 1901 with Joseph Babinski's challenge to Charcot's theories and would be formalized in 1909 with his article "Démembrement de l'hystérie traditionnelle."[70] Psychical research responded to the diminished faith in hysteria and hypnosis by seeking to substantiate its claims in the objective phenomena of materialization. With few exceptions, the study of mediumism in this period proceeded with little serious consideration of the subjective phenomena (automatic writing, cryptomnesia, disaggregation of the personality) that had initially drawn psychologists to the study of mediums in earlier decades. Whether or not one agreed that objectivity in regard to mediumistic phenomena could be achieved even in optimal conditions (i.e., by methods in which phenomena were truly isolated from subjective motivations), this emphasis on objectivity held widespread appeal for both proponents and critics alike. Even among skeptics the argument against psychical research rested ultimately not with the fact that materializations were necessarily fraudulent but with the fact that, given the psychical researcher's methodological dependence on the nonobjective condition of good faith, the phenomena themselves could not be confirmed in their absolute objectivity.

The subjective motivations that Babinski had called into account in his repudiation of hysteria and hypnosis under the name of *pithiatisme* (i.e., a state curable by persuasion) also applied handily to the phenomena of mediumism that appeared simply as more elaborate forms of simulation.[71] Ernest Dupré, the clinical psychiatrist who in 1905 had invoked the theory of mythomania during the Villa Carmen scandal, defended the Cartesian principle of authorship by arguing that the dissimulations of the hysteric were consciously motivated. To attribute the patient's lie to unconscious mechanisms risked giving way to the lie by according it another basis of truth (i.e., in the fact that, if the unconscious was an agency of dissimulation, its representations nevertheless appeared consciously true to the patient). The declining faith in unconscious processes evident in Dupré's analysis produced unfavorable consequences for psychical researchers who, even in their study of materialization, continued to argue that unconscious processes of ideation, imagination, and memory lent form to the content provided by the physiological production of ectoplasm. While ultimately unsuccessful, this effort to give material and, above all, visible form to unconscious thoughts was sufficiently appealing to draw attention away from other manifestations of the unconscious—those that Freud had identified in the reiteration of dreams or in the free associations of the analysand's speech. Without a theory of the unconscious, the manifestations of the medium or hysteric could not be viewed as efforts to assuage contradictions inherent in the life of the human individual. Rather, they became merely an exaggerated form of the same assault on the truth found in the commonplace lie. For Dupré, hysteria and mediumism constituted a contradiction to reality; they were not, as Freud would argue, the means of negotiating a reality in which contradiction is inherent.

Not surprisingly, it was the very phenomena in which Freud's thought would situate such contradiction that were so forcefully repudiated by French psychologists. Thus, where Freud would see repression and the unconscious as mechanisms resulting from the tensions between the instinctual demands of the individual and those of the species, from the problems of human sexual latency, and from the ambivalences surrounding the prohibition against incest, in France these ideas would only serve to inspire the charge of "pansexualism" among Freud's critics (and even among his would-be proponents).[72] Such had been the basis of Janet's 1913 critique, in which he simultaneously styled himself as the inventor of psychoanalysis while repudiating its fundamental insights.[73] In 1924 the philosopher André Lalande found that the earliest French responses to Freud from Pierre Janet, Emmanuel Régis, and Angélo Hesnard were particularly severe and without a great deal of consideration for the intricacies of Freud's thought.[74] Lalande similarly found Charles Blondel's 1922 summary of psychoanalytic thought "detailed" and copiously documented but "not encouraging [in its] criticism."[75] Indeed, on the sexual etiology of neurosis Blondel looked on psychoanalysis as a "scientific obscenity," a characterization confirmed in 1923 by Paul Hartenberg and in the 1922 reedition of the critical summary of Freud's ideas by Hesnard and Régis.[76] Overall, Lalande concluded that in the handful of French works on psychoanalysis published prior to 1924 "the very tone of the discussion shows how weak is the influence which Freudianism has exercised on French scientific circles."[77] If French scientists were compelled to admit with some irony the contributions of psychoanalysis (Janet compared the role to be played by Freudianism to that played by animal magnetism; Blondel saw similarities in Freud's thought to *la folie raisonnante* of the ancient vogue for phrenology), they were ultimately unwilling to accept those aspects of his thought that rooted the neuroses in conditions produced by and surrounding sexuality.

This general opprobrium for and lack of interest in psychoanalysis stood in sharp contrast to the attention given to concurrent work in psychical research. As Lalande would note in his annual review of French thought in the *Philosophical Review,* in 1922 and 1923 there was

> a strong movement . . . manifest among psychologists and psychiatrists, against all that concerns hypnosis, "secondary personalities," intelligent psychological automatism, one could almost say against all that deviates from the mental functions recognized for centuries by commonsense. To this is doubtless due the persistent lack of success of Freudianism in our country. *On the contrary,* on the part of the public at large, in the broadest sense of the term, there is to be noted a very lively success by all that touches on the marvelous, in philosophy or in psychology: occultism, telepathy, spiritism, theosophy.[78]

The *fin de siècle* preference for psychical research over psychoanalysis, demonstrated in the comparison of Flournoy's success to Freud's, continued in the postwar period. Lalande found that in 1922 and 1923 French works on psychical research as well as those translated from other languages were "extremely numerous and sell with an ease" that he found remarkable, given that the scientific publishing industry was still in the throes of a war-induced crisis. Lalande considered that, among the numerous books published on the subject of psychical research, "special mention [was] due to the *Traité de métapsychique,* by M. Charles Richet, as much because of the name and the intellectual position of the author as because of his serious effort to treat methodically and in a positive spirit so delicate a subject." Noting the moderate tone of the review by Pierre Janet and the equally moderate tone of the response by Richet, Lalande felt optimistic that the field of psychical research was approaching a stage in its development in which both skeptics and believers would be satisfied and in which greater attention to canons of evidence would lead to the formulation of widely held conclusions.[79]

Perhaps the best measure of the relative importance of psychical research in France is to be found in the domain in which psychoanalysis had its greatest influence in French thought between the wars. This was, of course, not in the fields of psychiatry and psychology but in the world of the artists and writers of the 1920s, who, as Roudinesco has suggested, "took to psychoanalysis as they had once taken to magnetism."[80] Much to the consternation of the official guardians of psychoanalysis, these lay enthusiasts did not always show the desired respect for the distinctiveness of Freud's insights and often introduced ideas from psychical research, which, if ultimately foreign to the psychoanalytic conception of the mind, were much more widely known in France.[81] Prior to 1921, when the first translations of Freud's writings began to appear in France, knowledge of psychoanalysis came primarily from the synopses and critiques provided by Régis and Hesnard and a handful of other authors.[82] This was certainly the case with André Breton, whose early understanding of psychoanalysis was shaped by the accounts available in French.[83] While Breton would recognize psychoanalysis as his principal influence in the 1924 *Manifesto of Surrealism,* the lack of fidelity between his ideas and those of Freud was painfully evident when Breton made his pilgrimage to Vienna in 1921 and found that Freud didn't understand his project. Breton's activities prior to this period and his later reflections on the early origins of the surrealist movement would further suggest that, in fact, another body of thought supplemented his limited understanding of psychoanalysis. Given the relative prominence that psychical research enjoyed in the years immediately following the war, it is not at all surprising that ideas drawn from the readily available literature in psychical research would intermingle with ideas Breton had about psychoanalysis.[84]

As Breton himself would recognize in a statement made in a radio interview given in 1951, his interest in hypnotism in the period between the end of the Dada movement and the publication of the first *Manifesto* was crucial to the development of his ideas concerning surrealism. As an assistant in the service of Babinski's neurological clinic at La Pitié, Breton was well aware of the disrepute that surrounded the ideas of Charcot and the practice of provoked somnambulism in this period. Nevertheless, Breton recalled that he "maintained a lively, even defiant, interest in that part of the psychological literature oriented by or articulated on this teaching." His interest was to be met not only by his readings in psychoanalysis but by an engagement with the ideas of the most prominent psychical researchers: "I am thinking in particular of the beautiful work of Myers: *La Personnalité humaine;* of the passionate presentations of Théodore Flournoy regarding the medium Hélène Smith: *Des Indes aux planète Mars,* etc.; indeed, of certain chapters of *Traité du métapsychique* by Charles Richet. All of this found itself linked, conjoined with my other ways of seeing to the benefit of the enthusiastic and enduring admiration that I harbored for Freud."[85] The association that formed in Breton's mind between psychical research and psychoanalysis was hardly unique. Decades earlier Myers himself had performed a similar gesture in conflating Freud's conception of the unconscious with his own theory of a subliminal self. It was perhaps this association that inspired Freud to write his two essays in 1921 and 1922 giving consideration to the phenomena of telepathy while marking out the distinction of the approach of psychoanalysis to such questions.

While Freud's thought would receive an enthusiastic reception in literary circles, its accession into France's scientific and medical establishments would be slow in coming. The situation of psychoanalysis in France would not begin to change until the 1930s, exactly in the period during which psychical research would enter into a period of institutional decline.[86] In his chronology of the general developments in French thought, Lalande would sense just such a change in French attitudes toward Freud in Roland Dalbiez's *La Méthode psychanalytique et la doctrine freudienne* (1936), which "carries out the original enough idea of expounding Freud's theories sympathetically and in the most rational way possible."[87] While Lalande agreed that Dalbiez's affirmation of the unconscious was still "somewhat disputed, in these days, by psychologists under the influence of objective experiments," he found the account of the unconscious and of the sexual etiology of neurosis a useful addition to theories of psychical dynamism.[88]

In the wake of the psychological and moral catastrophes of the Great War, a psychical research with an ambiguous relation to the doctrines of spiritism seemed to provide a means of redeeming a society disoriented by its self-conscious encounter with its own barbarism. For all the criticisms levied against it, the propositions of psychical researchers, both materialists and spiritualists, remained preferable to those suggesting that the most civilized of relations continued to be determined by impulses described by psychoanalysis. Insofar as psychical research remained a refuge in French scientific circles for the conceptualization of an unconscious, this was largely understood as a source of future liberation, creativity, and moral perfection. In the 1961 foreword to Frederic Myers's *Human Personality*, Aldous Huxley would argue that Myers had opened a path to the future achievement of man in the full integration of the self. But where Myers had looked to the edifice of the human soul and found interest "in the rooms (ordinarily locked) above street level," Freud would concern himself with the "subterranean rats and black beetles, and with all the ways in which a conscious ego may be disturbed by the bad smells and the vermin below stairs."[89] In comparison to Myers, psychoanalysis would find nothing so edifying or liberating in the unconscious, and for this, Freud's thought would bear a stigma that it would never entirely escape.

Indeterminacy and the Discourse of Tables

     In the history of the psychoanalytic movement, talking furniture has had, at least on one occasion, something quite important to say. It was in 1955, before the neuropsychiatric clinic in Vienna, that Jacques Lacan would allow himself to be figuratively upstaged by a talking desk. In the midst of a discourse disparaging the turn that psychoanalytic practice had taken since the 1930s as "ego psychology," Lacan yielded the floor to the loquacious lectern. The gesture was, of course, a stunt, an illustration of the very ventriloquism of clinical practice that his speech was calling into question. The desk speaks: "The fact remains that I who am speaking to you, mere desk though I be, am the ideal patient since with me not so much trouble has to be taken, the results are acquired at once, I am cured in advance. Since it is simply a question of substituting your discourse for mine, I am the perfect ego, since I have never had any other, and I leave you to inform me of the things to which my regulating devices do not allow you to adapt me directly."[1]

     By this little piece of vaudeville Lacan rendered the adaptive ego into the equivalent of all those talking tables that had been rapping out their discourses for the greater part of the previous century. The implication of Lacan's speech was much more specific than this. Psychoanalytic practice had, he argued, sacrificed the distinction of Freud's thought in order to secure acceptance and reward in a cultural context ruled by the dictates of happiness and success. That this context—America—was the very same in which modern tables first thought to speak is perhaps not without consequence. What mattered to Lacan was that the analyst in this setting had become a "manager of souls," and analysis had been reduced to a didacticism composed of the "opposition between someone who knows and someone who does not."[2] Lacan was calling into question the terms of what was by then a very ancient relationship. Whether this took the form of an aristocratic *magnétiseur* and his peasant somnambule, a neurologist and his hysterical patient, a psychical researcher and his medium, or an adept of ego psychology and his poorly adapted analysand, the error was to be found in the presumption that one person knew (or could know) and the other did not. It was this same presumption that informed the principle of determinacy that had oriented the development of scientific psychology since 1880 and promoted the notion that this knowledge could be used by a class of "knowers" in their efforts to "organize humanity scientifically." In the context of his speech, the point of Lacan's clinical prosopopoeia would have been quite apparent to his audience—the subject of the unconscious is not a thing to be known and mastered. The well-adapted ego cherished by the analytic community to which Lacan addressed himself demonstrated nothing more than what the talking table had demonstrated: the source of the *I* that speaks lies elsewhere.

This recognition was not altogether different from that made by the earliest spiritists. After the initial outbreak of talking tables in 1853, it was soon understood that the messages came not from the table or some animating natural fluid but from an agency "elsewhere" characterized by intelligence and will. But while the spiritist community found solace in the rapping of tables, hearing in them the voices of the dead offering comforting insight into the mysteries of the afterlife, scientists found nothing so reassuring or revealing in the messages they received or the phenomena they witnessed. Mediumistic phenomena were capricious, unreliable, and generally ill suited to the demands of experimental science. Even the increasingly objective phenomena of mediumism—the movements of objects and the materializations that preoccupied the field after 1900—did little to satisfy researchers' uncertainties. Even when the objective reality of these phenomena had been validated by every means available, the question of agency and intent remained unresolved. This question was very much like the one raised by Lacan's talking table in Vienna: "Who is speaking?" and, moreover, what is the meaning of this message?[3]

In 1886 Charles Richet had, in fact, been presented with this message in its clearest possible form. In his contribution to the Festschrift celebrating the centenary of Michel Chevreul's birth, Richet would recount one of the many experiments by which he confirmed Chevreul's historic discovery of involuntary movements, which revealed a link between physical action and ideation. The experiment involved three friends sitting in a semicircle around a small table with the participant seated in between the two others playing the part of the "medium." All were in fact simply colleagues of Richet's and had nothing about them to suggest extraordinary mediumistic talents. At some distance there was another table on which lay a large piece of cardboard with the alphabet inscribed on it. At this second table a fourth participant continuously moved his finger over the letters of the alphabet until a bell connected to the medium's table sounded, indicating that the table had been tipped. The letter that appeared under the fourth participant's finger at this instant would be recorded, and the process would continue until a violent movement of the medium's table indicated that the message was complete. The medium and two controllers at his sides could not see what was taking place at the second table, which was obscured by a small screen. Carrying on a lively conversation throughout the experiment, the three experimenters could hardly have directed their attention to the activities of their colleague at the distant table. Nor, Richet argued, could any one of them have concentrated on the formation of coherent messages. Yet, remarkably, messages with intelligible meanings continued to emerge by this technique. In fact, the messages suggested that tables were not the pliant subjects that the ventriloquist Lacan would, in his mocking caricature of ego psychology, present to his audience in Vienna seventy years later.

The sample Richet reproduced in his presentation showed a number of the messages achieved and included indications of the inversions and minor corrections made in the effort to render them intelligible. By replacing certain letters in the sequence

GHNUESSHGAUIOHVOUSNARRHVESFZBRIEN

with the letters

DI.V. .T.I.T. .+. . . . . I. .RE.A. . . .

Richet produced the message:

d i n v e s t i g a t i o h v o u s n a r r i v e r e z a r i e n [your investigations will result in nothing]

Other messages offered similar responses. For instance:

UOUS OZ NOUYE ABXFC ORFVPERIEN E KS
V. . . . M+. . . . . . . ZAVE+. .SEX. . . . . . . +.+.

vous mznnouye zavec osexperien e ks [you bore me with your experiments] and

ELBISSOOMILRZEDNAMDDSOUV [inverted to]

VOUSDDMANDEZRLIMOOSSIBLE

. . . . .E. . . . . . + . . . P. . . . . .

vousdemandez limpossible [you ask the impossible]

Amazed at the coherent nature of the messages, Richet speculated as to the mechanism, perhaps some unconscious means of perception, that might have enabled the medium and his two controllers to know what letter was indicated at the second table at any precise moment. He remained uninterested, however, in the content of the messages, which he considered "of an extreme banality . . . and more often silly, banal, and frequently crude."[4] Indeed, in their meaning the messages indicated nothing to Richet other than the obvious evasion and resistance to the researchers' efforts. Framed as his thinking was by the criteria of determinacy that he had inherited from his intellectual ancestor Claude Bernard, Richet would, like psychical research as a whole, fail to see this resistance to knowledge as the historical product of the effort by which psychology proposed to transform subjectivity into an object of scientific knowledge. This was a moment in which the desire to know gave rise to its own elusive object, and it was only in parallax view that French thought was to understand this relation for what it was. Lacan's "return to Freud" was in this respect an effort to return to the days in which psychology, confronted by such mysterious and dark facts as hysteria, hypnosis, and talking tables, was able to shed some light on the relationship within science between desire and knowledge. Continuing his speech before the psychoanalytic community gathered in Vienna, Lacan continued his ventriloquist act, this time speaking in the name of the "truth" to its would-be "lovers": "I will reach you in the mistake against which you have no refuge. . . . [O]ne's unsuccessful acts are the most successful and . . . one's failure fulfills one's most secret wish. . . . [R]iddle, it is through you that I communicate. . . . I, the truth, would be Deceit itself."[5]

If an analysis of dreams, the most unreal and immaterial of scientific objects, could authorize such statements by a French intellectual, French psychical researchers of the late nineteenth and early twentieth centuries would continue to look on the errors, failures, uncertainties, and frauds encountered in their investigations not as revelations of truth but as obstacles to be overcome in the pursuit of truth. Psychical research emerged as relevant to French thought just as older, socially limited forms of subjective knowledge were giving way to a new, democratic enthusiasm for the objective methods of experimental science. Psychical research would embody many of the antagonisms lingering from this transition from a philosophy of the mind to a science of the mind, seeking, for example, to objectify the mind in an examination of physical and physiological phenomena while insisting on the essential qualities of will, intention, and good faith. By acting as the representative of these displaced antagonisms within the field of psychology, psychical research would help to safeguard, through its contradictory methods and assumptions, indeterminacy even as the field of scientific psychology achieved an institutional base and a corresponding social utility. As scientific psychology gave rise to methods of rendering the mind knowable and making this knowledge publicly accessible and useful, psychical research would continue to mark a point of resistance within the sciences to the very universality claimed on its behalf. Psychical research in this role would fade from this position only as the indeterminacy it represented came to be refigured in other terms. In the movement of French thought that would culminate in the Lacanian "return to Freud," indeterminacy was no longer to be seen as anathema to universal knowledge but as a necessary feature of the knowing and desiring subject.

Notes

Abbreviations

Acad. Méd.	Bibliothèque de l'Académie Nationale de Médecine
Acad. Sci.	Archives de l'Académie des Sciences
APP	Archives de la Préfecture de Police
BN/NAF	Bibliothèque Nationale de France, Nouvelles acquisitions françaises
IMI	Archives of the Institut Métapsychique International

Introduction

1. Gurney, Myers, and Podmore, *Phantasms of the Living,* 5.

2. Richet, *Traité de métapsychique,* 2–3.

3. Ibid., 3.

4. Ibid., 5. See also Kardec, *Le Livre des médiums,* 11.

5. Ellenberger, *Discovery of the Unconscious.*

6. These were held in Copenhagen in 1921, Warsaw in 1923, Paris in 1927, and Athens in 1930. See Congrès International des Recherches Psychiques, *Le Compte rendu officiel; L'État actuel des recherches psychiques; Compte rendu du IIIe Congrès International de Recherches Psychiques;* and Besterman, *Transactions.* The international congresses were subject to factionalism in 1930. For a discussion of this split, see Lachapelle, "Attempting Science," 18–21.

7. Gurney, Myers, and Podmore, *Phantasms of the Living,* 5.

8. James, "The Hidden Self," 361.

9. See Brown, review of *The Elusive Science,* 1045–46.

10. For commentary on the tendency to view spiritism and psychical research in terms of the "occult," see Bensaude-Vincent and Blondel, introduction to *Des savants face à l'occulte,* 12–17; Pierssens, "Le Syndrome des tables tournantes."

11. Renan, *Qu'est-ce qu'une nation?* 28–30.

12. Renan, *L'Avenir de la science,* 37.

13. See Elwitt, *Making of the Third Republic,* 171–229; Weisz, *Emergence of Modern Universities,* 89–133.

14. Ringer, *Toward a Social History of Knowledge,* 214.

15. Ribot, *La Psychologie allemande contemporaine.*

16. Pierssens, "Novation Astray."

17. Bernard, *Introduction à l'étude de la médecine expérimentale,* 223.

18. Ibid., 284, quoted in Cryle, "Love and Epistemology," 6.

19. Mauskopf and McVaugh, *Elusive Science.* For an overview of the contemporary situation of parapsychology in France, see Méheust, "Épistémologiquement correct." On the decline of parapsychology in the United States since 1945, see Moore, *In Search of White Crows,* 204–20. Research in parapsychology does continue, however, in a variety of research settings. Internationally, the field maintains laboratories within major universities and research institutions. For a recent evaluation of parapsychology in the United States, see David J. Hess, "Disciplining Heterodoxy, Circumventing Discipline: Parapsychology, Anthropologically," in Hess and Layne, *Anthropology of Science and Technology,* 191–222.

20. See "Fantômes de vivants et recherches psychiques. Conférence faite à la Society for Psychical Research de Londres le 28 mai 1913," in Bergson, *L'Énergie spirituelle,* 70–71.

21. Flournoy, *Théodore et Léopold,* 42.

22. Freud, *Freud Reader,* 112.

23. Flournoy, *Théodore et Léopold,* 42; Freud, *New Introductory Lectures,* 84.

Chapter 1: From Religious Enthusiasm to Reluctant Science

1. Seguin, "Lettre de M. Seguin," 891–92.

2. Ibid.

3. Chevreul, *De la baguette divinatoire.*

4. See *Le Charivari,* 17, 23, and 25 May and 1, 6, 7, 9, 13, 14, 18, and 22 June 1853.

5. The detailed discussion of the improper intimacies of the mesmerist's *cabinet* was reserved for the commission's secret report to the king. See Bailly et al., "Secret Report on Mesmerism," 3–7.

6. Scott, *Only Paradoxes to Offer,* 6–7.

7. Chertok and Saussure, *The Therapeutic Revolution,* 10.

8. See Ellenberger, *Discovery of the Unconscious,* 70–76. See also Crabtree, *From Mesmer to Freud,* 109–44.

9. Harrington, *The Cure Within,* 52.

10. Ellenberger, *Discovery of the Unconscious,* 245, 886.

11. Tourette, *L'Hypnotisme,* 24–39. See also Burdin and Dubois, *Histoire académique.*

12. Husson, *Rapport sur les expériences magnétiques.*
13. Tourette, *L'Hypnotisme*, 24–39.
14. Crabtree, *From Mesmer to Freud*, 207.
15. Darnton, *Mesmerism*, 144–45.
16. Edelman, *Voyantes*, 77. It is not without coincidence that the growing importance of spirit communication in mesmerism has been attributed to the influence of Swedenborgianism on the philosophy and practice of magnetic healing. See Crabtree, *From Mesmer to Freud*, 229–31.
17. Albanese, *A Republic of Mind and Spirit*, 194–95; Taves, *Fits, Trances, and Visions*, 168.
18. Cross, *The Burned-Over District*. See also Barkun, *Crucible of the Millennium*; Johnson, *Islands of Holiness*; and Ryan, *Cradle of the Middle Class*.
19. Crabtree, *From Mesmer to Freud*, 221–32.
20. Quoted in Anonymous, *Examen raisonné*, 29.
21. Ibid., 3–4. See also Babinet, "Les Sciences occultes," 511.
22. Tocqueville, *De la démocratie en Amérique*, 3:270.
23. Monroe, *Laboratories of Faith*, 91.
24. Davis's philosophical transcriptions held none of the empirical appeal of the Fox sisters' rappings, and Davis generally regretted the attention given to what he often considered the fraudulent physical phenomena of mediums. See Moore, *In Search of White Crows*, 10, 17. See also Crabtree, *From Mesmer to Freud*, 230–32.
25. Janet, "Le Spiritisme contemporain," 413.
26. Ibid., 166.
27. Sharp, "Rational Religion," 166–67, 174.
28. Ellenberger, *Discovery of the Unconscious*, 83.
29. While the police of the Second Empire had a reputation for omniscience, most histories of the subject suggest that this was exaggerated. See, for instance, Payne, *The Police State*. On American democracy and religion, see Tyler, *Freedom's Ferment*.
30. Ladous, *Le Spiritisme*, 33.
31. Simon, *Chez Victor Hugo*, 29.
32. Richemont, *Le Mystère*, 25.
33. Ibid., 23.
34. Ibid., 18.
35. Ibid., 29, 32.
36. Sharp, *Secular Spirituality*, 1–47.
37. Ibid., 97.
38. Ibid., 59. On the rise of positivism in this period, see Charlton, *Positivist Thought*.
39. Sharp, *Secular Spirituality*, 78.
40. The book was the subject of some controversy when in 1875 Alexander Aksakof claimed in the London journal the *Spiritualist* that its content had been stolen from the somnambule Mlle Japhet. See Edelman, *Voyantes*, 81–82.

41. This emphasis on reincarnation, which remained a matter of dispute in French spirit circles, was one of the primary ways in which Kardec's teachings differed from those of the majority of American spiritualists. While Kardec attributed his theories of reincarnation to Pythagoras, direct inspiration most likely came from his reading of Fourier. See Sharp, "Rational Religion," 26.

42. Sharp, *Secular Spirituality*, 145; Monroe, *Laboratories of Faith*, 142–43.

43. Ibid., 141–42.

44. Bergé, *La Voix des esprits*, 47–55.

45. Sharp, "Rational Religion," 293.

46. Shepard, Spence, and Fodor, *Encyclopedia of Occultism and Parapsychology*, 2:714. Réné Sudre specifies 200,000 French copies in circulation in 1923 ("La Question métapsychique [II]," 292).

47. See Lorenz, *Catalogue général*.

48. APP, BA1243.

49. Sharp, *Secular Spirituality*, 53.

50. Janet, "Le Spiritisme contemporain," 440.

51. The police informant would count eight hundred people for the 1875 ceremony, which lasted an hour and featured six different speakers (APP, BA1243). A recent guide to Père-Lachaise claims Kardec's gravesite is the most frequented of the cemetery (Dansel, *Les Lieux de culte*, 253–58). Bergé similarly describes the impressive gathering of adherents at the tomb (*Voix des esprits*, 13–15).

52. Sharp emphasizes the importance of print accounts in drawing new members (*Secular Spirituality*, 56–57).

53. Spiritism thus overcame one of the primary limitations of this form of capital—the fact of its embodied state. See Bourdieu, "The Forms of Capital," 244–45.

54. Moore, *In Search of White Crows*, 60.

55. On this point, see Thurschwell, "Fantasies of Transmission."

56. Chevreul, *De la baguette divinatoire*, 185–86.

57. Celebrated in her own right, Girardin was the wife of Émile de Girardin, a pioneer in popular journalism and owner of *La Presse* and *Le Petit Journal*.

58. Vacquerie, *Les Miettes de l'histoire*, quoted in Flammarion, *Mémoires biographiques*, 227.

59. Ibid., 228.

60. Hugo, *Le Journal*, 2:275–77.

61. Gaudon, *Ce que disent*, 33–53; and Simon, *Chez Victor Hugo*, 140–94.

62. Benjamin and Tiedemann, *The Arcades Project*, 334; Benjamin, *Charles Baudelaire*, 63.

63. Hugo, *Le Journal*, 2:275–77.

64. Matlock, "Ghostly Politics," 66–67.

65. Napoleon III was reportedly deeply impressed by a spiritist demonstration conducted by the medium Daniel Dunglas Home in 1857. See Claretie, *La Vie à Paris*, 40–41.

66. See chapter 3, article 47 of the organization's bylaws printed in Kardec, *Le Livre des médiums*, 463. The Société Parisienne des Études Spirites was recognized by a decree of 13 April 1858 issued by the prefect of police and authorized by the minister of the interior and of public safety.

67. Monroe, *Laboratories of Faith*, 156–57.

68. Foucault, *Histoire de la folie;* and Foucault, *Discipline and Punish.*

69. For a detailed discussion of the Buguet trial, see Monroe, "*Cartes de visite* from the Other World"; and Monroe, *Laboratories of Faith*, 162–98.

70. APP, BA1243.

71. Leymarie, *Procès des spirites;* and Tourette, *L'Hypnotisme*, 404, 476–80.

72. APP, BA1243.

73. Quoted in Boutry et al., *Du roi très chrétien*, 168.

74. Prior to this, attempts to prosecute under the Code Pénal were theoretically limited to article 405 (prohibiting fraud) or the rarely enforced articles 479 and 480 (prohibiting divination) (*Bulletin des lois de l'Empire français*). By the mid-nineteenth century commentaries on the law explicitly included magnetic healing, even when performed by doctors (Gilbert, *Codes d'instructions criminelle*, 611–12).

75. Ball and Chambard, "Somnambulisme naturel," 325–26. See also Tourette and Richer, "Hypnotisme." Azam claims priority in the repetition of Braid's experiments in France and recounts the means by which he encountered the phenomenon in the historical introduction of his *Hypnotisme et double conscience*, 3–12.

76. Azam apparently learned of the subject as a result of Ernest Bazin's February 1858 reading before the Société de Médecine de Bordeaux of William Benjamin Carpenter's *précis* of Braid's work in Robert Bentley Todd's *Cyclopaedia of Anatomy and Physiology*. See the summary of Bazin's letter in *Comptes Rendus Hebdomadaires des Séances de l'Académie des Sciences*, vol. 49 (1859): 946.

77. Broca, "Sur un nouveau procédé." Broca's findings were compared to the better-known effect of bright lights on epileptics.

78. Azam, *Hypnotisme et double conscience*, 4.

79. Braid's 1843 *Neurypnology* was later translated in 1883 by Jules Simon. Prior to this Braid's work remained rare even in the original version. Unable to procure the book even among Braid's associates in Manchester, Charcot finally acquired a copy as part of a collection of materials given to him by Azam in 1878. While eager to claim precedence, Azam was happy to cede ownership of hypnosis and its future development to Charcot (ibid., 10).

80. Figuier, *Histoire du merveilleux*, 4:308.

81. Quoted from a letter addressed to Azam in *Hypnotisme et double conscience*, 4.

82. Richet, "Du somnambulisme provoqué," 348. Pierre Janet would revisit this statement in his 1923 review of Richet's book *Traité de métapsychique* and recognize the legitimacy of Richet's self-proclaimed courage ("À propos de la métapsychique," 9).

83. Wolf, *Brain, Mind, and Medicine*, 26–27; Ellenberger, *Discovery of the Unconscious*, 74, 85, 90, 751. Ellenberger also credits Richet with the scientific attention

given to automatic writing (524). Réné Sudre provides an earlier account of Richet's influence in the matter of hypnotism ("La Question métapsychique [II]," 298).

84. *Comptes Rendus Hebdomadaires des Séances de l'Académie des Sciences* 94 (1882): 403–5.

85. Pascal Le Maléfan has studied in detail the connections drawn between the practice of spiritism and the etiologies of mental illness in the late nineteenth century and early twentieth century in *Folie et spiritisme*.

86. Charcot and Harris, *Clinical Lectures,* 198–206.

87. Ibid., 206. See also Le Maléfan, *Folie et spiritisme,* 58.

88. Janet would argue, in reference to Charcot's account, that "the faculty of the medium must depend on a morbid state particularly analogous to that which can emerge later as hysteria or alienation: mediumism is a symptom and not a cause" (*L'Automatisme psychologique,* 406).

89. Le Maléfan, *Folie et spiritisme,* 60–65.

90. Duhem's 1904 doctoral thesis in medicine, "Contribution à l'étude de la folie chez les Spirites," earned him a reputation as an expert on the subject. See "Société Médico-Psychologique: Séance Solennelle du 29 Avril 1907," *Annales Médico-Psychologique* (1907): 83.

91. See Duhem, "Délire mystique," 84.

92. See Camescasse, *Souvenirs.*

93. *La Presse,* 21 August 1882.

94. Tourette, *L'Hypnotisme,* 418.

95. Under articles 291 to 294 of the penal code and the law of 10 April 1834, an association made up of more than twenty people was required to have police authorization. Tourette argues that no more than three spiritist groups in Paris had such authorization (ibid., 480–81).

96. APP, DB215.

97. Tourette, *L'Hypnotisme,* 449.

98. *La Presse,* 12 July 1895.

99. *L'Éclair,* 12 July 1895.

100. Ibid.

Chapter 2: The Development of Psychical Research in France, 1882–1900

1. Janet, "Note sur quelques cas," 193–95.

2. The experiments lasted three weeks, between 24 September and 14 October 1885 (ibid., 190–98).

3. On one occasion Gibert had imparted a mental suggestion that she walk in the garden of the house with an open umbrella. Léonie went into the garden several times in an agitated state but refused to take an umbrella because of the clear weather. "Why did you make me walk all about the garden . . . I looked foolish . . . if

the weather was still like yesterday's . . . but today I would have seemed completely ridiculous" (ibid., 197).

4. Janet, "Deuxième note," 222–23.

5. Ellenberger, *Discovery of the Unconscious*, 338. Membership included Théodule Ribot, Paul Janet, Charles Féré, Charles Richet, Julian Ochorowicz, Paul Richer, and J.-M. Charcot. Ochorowicz discusses the reaction to the presentation of Janet's paper in *De la suggestion mentale*, 118.

6. Bergson, "De la simulation inconsciente," 531.

7. Janet, "Deuxième note," 223; Janet, "Autobiography," 125.

8. Janet, "Autobiography," 125. Janet's autobiography mistakenly dates the experiments with Léonie to 1882. Janet did not transfer to Le Havre from his first teaching appointment in Chateauroux until February 1883, and he did not begin his experiments with Léonie until September 1885 (Ellenberger, *Discovery of the Unconscious*, 336).

9. Boutroux, *Notice sur Paul Janet*; Picot, *Paul Janet*.

10. Goldstein, *The Post-Revolutionary Self*, 154.

11. Carroy, Ohayon, and Plas, *Histoire de la psychologie*, 18.

12. Espinas, "Être ou ne pas être," 449. See also Deploige, *Le Conflit*, 266.

13. Espinas, "Les Études sociologiques en France," 566.

14. Deploige, *Le Conflit*, 267. The censoring of Espinas's thesis is also alluded to in the second edition of Espinas, *Des sociétés animales*, 313 n. 1.

15. Janet, *La Philosophie française contemporaine*, 14.

16. Ibid., 15–16.

17. Carroy, Ohayon, and Plas, *Histoire de la psychologie*, 22.

18. Janet, "Autobiography," 124.

19. See Carroy and Plas, "How Pierre Janet Used Pathological Psychology," 231–40.

20. Janet, "Autobiography," 124.

21. Roudinesco and Plon, *Dictionnaire de la psychanalyse*, 535–36.

22. Richet, "Du somnambulisme provoqué," 348–77. See also Ellenberger, *Discovery of the Unconscious*, 85.

23. Richet, "La Suggestion mentale."

24. Janet, *L'Automatisme psychologique*, 404–13.

25. Janet would use the term *inconscient* in his 1889 thesis, "L'Automatisme psychologique." He would adopt the term *subconscient* four years later in *L'État mental des hystériques* (Roudinesco and Plon, *Dictionnaire de la psychanalyse*, 536).

26. Chevreul, "Lettre à M. Ampère," 258–66.

27. Ibid., 260–61.

28. Ibid., 265.

29. Chevreul, *De la baguette divinatoire*, 192.

30. Ibid., 229.

31. Chevreul, "Lettre à M. Ampère," 261.

32. In 1784 the magnetizer Charles d'Eslon had complained that the Franklin commission's report left the critical term *imagination* undefined: "What is imagination? The commissioners refer to it a great deal, but they do not define it" ("Observation sur les deux rapports," 17).

33. Chevreul, "Lettre à M. Ampère," 266.

34. Ibid.

35. Ibid., 266.

36. Richet, "Les Mouvements inconscients," 79–80.

37. Ibid., 81.

38. Ibid., 82.

39. Chevreul, "Lettre à M. Ampère," 254.

40. Comte, *Catéchisme positiviste*, 157.

41. Williams, *The Physical and the Moral*, 185–87.

42. Janet, *L'Automatisme psychologique*, 391. See also Brooks, *The Eclectic Legacy*, 191.

43. Janet, *L'Automatisme psychologique*, 390.

44. Ibid.

45. Ibid.

46. Ibid.

47. Describing the early influences on his intellectual development, Janet would observe the importance of the two competing tendencies that continued to orient his thought. Besides his amateur's interest in botany and the rigors of observation and classification, he noted "another tendency that was never satisfied. . . . At the age of eighteen I was very religious, and I have always retained mystical tendencies, which I have succeeded in controlling" ("Autobiography," 123).

48. Janet, *L'Automatisme psychologique*, 376.

49. Janet, "Le Spiritisme contemporain," 441–42.

50. Janet, *L'Automatisme psychologique*, 391.

51. Janet, "Le Spiritisme contemporain," 441.

52. Janet, "Société Internationale de l'Institut Psychique," 3–4.

53. Janet, "Le Spiritisme contemporain," 434.

54. Ibid., 414.

55. The work was translated in 1891 and published by Alcan as *Les Hallucinations télépathiques* with a preface by Charles Richet.

56. Dariex was an ophthalmologist practicing at the Hôpital des Quinze-Vingt in Paris. On the evolution of *Les Annales des Sciences Psychiques*, see Lachapelle, "Attempting Science," 4–5.

57. Richet, "Des phénomènes psychique," 5. Richet was approached by Dariex in 1890 with the idea of founding *Les Annales des Sciences Psychiques*. While hesitant, he eventually agreed, and the journal appeared the following year from the presses of Felix Alcan. The journal presented a discussion of somnambulism and spiritism for a more popular audience than the one sought by *La Revue Philosophique*. While

Les Annales des Sciences Psychiques included articles written by notables from the field of psychology such as Richet and Cesare Lombroso, the contributions were considerably shorter in length and less erudite than those presented in Ribot's journal. For a brief note on Richet's relationship with Dariex, see Wolf, *Brain, Mind, and Medicine,* 59.

58. Richet, "Des phénomènes psychique," 5.

59. Prévost, *Janet, Freud et la psychologie clinique,* 12; Prévost, *La Psycho-philosophie,* 15.

60. Ribot, *La Psychologie allemande contemporaine,* v.

61. See Binet, *Introduction,* 9.

62. Prévost, *Janet, Freud et la psychologie clinique,* 18. In 1893 the lab's annual budget was increased from 500 francs to the *somme modeste* of 800 francs. By contrast, Wundt's Leipzig lab received 1,875 francs annually for new equipment acquisitions alone (Binet, *Introduction,* 3, 10). Binet placed hypnotism and hysteria in the category of *psychologie morbide,* which he argued could only be legitimately studied in the Faculty of Medicine. His interest remained "la psychologie expérimentale de l'individu sain"—a definition of experimental psychology that would have excluded most of the phenomena of mediumism (ibid., 2).

63. Brooks, *The Eclectic Legacy,* 67–68.

64. Ibid., 92.

65. The chair was created on the initiative of Renan, the institution's director, and Louis Liard, the director of higher education. In spite of his ideological opposition to Ribot's emphasis on physiology Paul Janet defended the appointment publicly in "Une chaire de psychologie expérimentale." On the specifics of Ribot's appointment to the Collège, see Nicolas and Charvillat, "Introducing Psychology."

66. Ribot notes with satisfaction that the excluded terms had, nonetheless, "subsequently prevailed" ("La Psychologie," 40). The International Congress of Physiological Psychology (Congrès International de Psychologie Physiologique) occurred in Paris in 1889. The International Congress of Experimental Psychology took place in London in 1892. See also Piéron, "Histoire."

67. Janet, "De la suggestion," 84–85.

68. Ribot, "La Psychologie," 42.

69. Brooks, *The Eclectic Legacy,* 67–69.

70. See Goldstein, "Mutations of the Self," 111.

71. The membership included a variety of other celebrities, including Taine, Binet, Beaunis, Sully-Prudhomme, Magnan, Moreau de Tours, Ebbinghaus, Helmholtz, Wundt, Hake Tuke, William James, Lombroso, and Moreselli (Plas, *Naissance d'une science humaine,* 54).

72. Charcot's participation in the society was minimal after 1889. See Wundt, *Hypnotisme et suggestion,* 8. See also Wolf, *Brain, Mind, and Medicine,* 59; and Plas, *Naissance d'une science humaine,* 54–55. Both Wolf and Plas indicate that it was Richet's emphasis on the "marvelous" that alienated Charcot. Plas cites Joseph-Pierre Durand

de Gros, *Le Merveilleux scientifique* (Paris: Alcan, 1894), 6. Janet would retrospectively note a lack of moral and material support as the cause of the failure of the organization ("Allocution," 137).

73. William James would report on the 1889 congress, naming those most active in the discussion of psychical research: Marillier, Binet, Pierre Janet, Bertrand, Espinas, Bernheim, Liégeois, Ochorowicz, Delboeuf, Galton, Sidgwick, and Myers ("Report").

74. Janet, "Une chaire de psychologie expérimentale," 518–49, cited in Brooks, *The Eclectic Legacy*, 94.

75. Goldstein, "The Advent of Psychological Modernism in France," 202–4. See also Brooks, *The Eclectic Legacy*, 163.

76. Brooks, *The Eclectic Legacy*, 173–74.

77. See Janet's preface to Grasset, *Le Spiritisme*, xii–xiii.

78. Ibid., xi.

79. Ibid.

80. Janet, *La Philosophie française contemporaine*, 170–76.

81. Ibid., 170.

82. André Lalande would note in 1905 that *La Revue Philosophique* was "designed from the first to be the very original organ of a strictly scientific psychology, which, however, did not seek to separate from philosophy but rather to impart to it, at all points where they came into contact, the character of substantial knowledge that it sought itself to realize" ("Philosophy in France," 443). See also Brooks, *The Eclectic Legacy*, 82.

83. Janet, *La Philosophie française contemporaine*, 177. Brooks notes that Ribot found Janet jealous of his initiative in founding *La Revue Philosophique*. Ribot confided to Espinas in 1879 that Janet had "raged against him" because of his positivist leanings (Brooks, *The Eclectic Legacy*, 69, 271).

84. Wundt tends to overstate the case when he argues that "the authors occupied with these questions are convinced of the reality of their magical results and insist that they are, at least, worthy of being discussed and thoroughly verified" (*Hypnotisme et suggestion*, 13). Wundt notes the absence of similar attention to matters of psychical research in German philosophical and psychological periodicals in contrast to *La Revue Philosophique*.

Chapter 3: The Measure of Uncertainty

1. Janet, "Le Spiritisme contemporain," 414.

2. Schultz, *Henry Sidgwick*. The moral conflict between faith and agnosticism that led Sidgwick to psychical research was a prominent feature of Victorian intellectual life. See also Oppenheim, *The Other World*, 111–23.

3. Schultz, *Henry Sidgwick*, 275–78.

4. London Dialectical Society, *Report on Spiritualism*, vi.

5. Gauld, *The Founders of Psychical Research,* 64. Walter Leaf cotranslated the *Iliad* (1883) along with Andrew Lang and Myers's brother Ernest.

6. Sidgwick's former mentor at Rugby, Edward Benson, was married to Mary Sidgwick and served as the archbishop of Canterbury from 1882 until his death in 1896. Sidgwick married Eleanor Mildred Balfour, the sister of his former student Arthur Balfour. Balfour's sister Evelyn was, in turn, married to John William Strutt (Lord Rayleigh), who had joined the Sidgwick group in their early informal investigations of spirit phenomena in the mid-1870s. As Gauld notes, "To say that the Sidgwicks had friends in high places would be an enormous understatement" (*The Founders of Psychical Research,* 116). On Eleanor Sidgwick's achievements and personal associations, see Mauskopf and McVaugh, *Elusive Science,* 14; Oppenheim, *The Other World,* 120–21. Sidgwick himself was a member of the exclusive and enormously influential Cambridge Apostles. Sidgwick delivered this address on 17 July 1882; see Society for Psychical Research, *Presidential Addresses,* 6.

7. Society for Psychical Research, *Presidential Addresses,* 6. See also Oppenheim, *The Other World,* 135; Mauskopf and McVaugh, *Elusive Science,* 15.

8. Gauld, *Founders of Psychical Research,* 339.

9. Janet, "Allocution," 133. Youriévitch was recognized as the founding force behind what would become the Institut Général Psychologique. His enthusiasm for the organization invited a certain measure of derision. For instance, Théodore Flournoy, while publicly supportive of the institute, was privately critical of Youriévitch. He commented in a letter to William James that such a grandiose idea was the product of "the megalomaniac naïveté of a slavic brain, over-excited by the atmosphere of Paris" (Le Clair, *Letters of James and Flournoy,* 104). Youriévitch was born in Paris and spent much of his life there. As an artist he became an associate of Auguste Rodin and exhibited his work in many prominent forums, including the Tate Gallery in London. See Mourey, *Youriévitch, 24 Photos;* and Youriévitch and Mourey, *Serge Youriévitch.* His works include a bust of Charles Richet that the Académie des Sciences attempted to purchase in 1936 without success (Acad. Sci., Dossier Richet, Robert-Charles).

10. Janet, "Société Internationale de l'Institut Psychique," 1–2.

11. Ibid.

12. The first issue of the *Bulletin de l'Institut Psychique* appeared in July 1900 and listed members of the international organizational committee: Hippolyte Ribot, F. W. H. Myers, Jacques-Arsène d'Arsonval (member of the Académie des Sciences and the Académie Nationale de Médecine), Charles Bouchard (member of the Académie des Sciences and the Académie Nationale de Médecine), Émile Duclaux (member of the Académie des Sciences and the Académie Nationale de Médecine and director of the Institut Pasteur), Étienne-Jules Marey (member of the Académie des Sciences and the Académie Nationale de Médecine), René-François Sully-Prudhomme (member of the Académie Française), Cesare Lombroso, and Théodore Flournoy. Janet, Richet, and Murray acted as the provisional executive committee,

with Youriévitch as the general secretary and Felix Alcan as treasurer. Excused from the *réunion constitutive*, which took place on 30 June 1900, were Hippolyte Bernheim, Émile Boirac, Armand de Gramont, Jules Liégeois, and Albert von Schrenck-Notzing, among others. The provisional offices were established at 19, rue de l'Université.

13. Ribot, "La Psychologie," 42.

14. Ibid.

15. Régine Plas has argued that the organization of the section, which placed discussions of hypnosis alongside presentations from spiritualists, was already a sign of the diminished currency of hypnosis in experimental and therapeutic practice (*Naissance d'une science humaine*, 40).

16. Those who took an active part in the discussion of psychical research were Marillier, Gley, Binet, Pierre Janet, Bertrand, Espinas, Bernheim, Liegois, Ochorowicz, Danilewsky, Grote of Moscow, Delboeuf, Forel, Galton, Sidgwick, and Myers. See *Mind* 14 (October 1889): 615.

17. Le Clair, *Letters of James and Flournoy*, 103.

18. Vogt, "Contre le spiritisme," 656.

19. Ibid.

20. Ibid.

21. Le Clair, *Letters of James and Flournoy*, 103.

22. Janet, *IVe Congrès International de Psychologie*, 661–62.

23. Ibid., 643.

24. Ibid.

25. Ibid.

26. Ibid., 662–63.

27. Ibid., 663.

28. Ochorowicz, "De l'Institut Psychologique," 137. Ochorowicz was known in France for his translation of Ribot's writings into Polish and as a contributor to *La Revue Philosophique*. He seems to have been one of the initiators of the International Congresses of Psychology, the idea for which he presented in an 1881 article published in *La Revue Philosophique*. See Domanski, "Julian Ochorowicz (1850–1917)."

29. Ochorowicz, "De l'Institut Psychologique," 137.

30. Le Clair, *Letters of James and Flournoy*, 103.

31. Ibid., 102.

32. James, *Essays, Comments, and Reviews*, 56. See also Le Clair, *Letters of James and Flournoy*, 103.

33. On Janet's change of attitude, see Maxwell, *Les Phénomènes psychiques*, 12.

34. Youriévitch, "M. Émile Duclaux," 334.

35. Ibid.

36. Flournoy, "Observations psychologique," 102–3; Le Clair, *Letters of James and Flournoy*, 103.

37. Le Clair, *Letters of James and Flournoy*, 103.

38. Ibid.

39. The name changes have caused confusion for at least one historian well known for his archival diligence. Henri Ellenberger mentions the Institut Psychique International in his chapter on Janet but seems not to have been able to follow the organization's transformation into the Institut Général Psychologique: "The history of that *Institut Psychologique* has never been written; it would be interesting to know why it did not develop further but disappeared a few years later" (*Discovery of the Unconscious*, 342–43). The use of the term *general psychology* was, as John I. Brooks has noted, a way of expanding the scope of experimental psychology to include both normal and pathological psychology and objective and subjective approaches (*The Eclectic Legacy*, 172).

40. Janet, "Société Internationale de l'Institut Psychique," 5. But he later came to doubt that the "American" model would be easily applied in France, where the wealthy and educated had, on the one hand, become accustomed to endowing "useless" academic prizes and, on the other, only funded research with obvious practical applications. See Janet, "Allocution," 135.

41. Janet, "Société Internationale de l'Institut Psychique," 5.

42. Janet, "Allocution," 136–38.

43. Janet, "Objet," 84.

44. Ibid., 85.

45. Ibid., 89.

46. Janet, "Allocution," 134–35.

47. Janet, "Objet," 87.

48. Le Clair, *Letters of James and Flournoy*, 104.

49. Janet, "Allocution," 135.

50. Ibid., 136–38; and Janet, "Objet," 91–94.

51. Janet, "Allocution," 138.

52. Ibid.

53. Ibid.

54. Ibid., 144.

55. Parot, "Cents ans," 6.

56. Le Clair, *Letters of James and Flournoy*, 104.

57. Vesme, "L'Institut Psychologique International," 325. My thanks to Renaud Evrard for this reference.

58. Ibid., 326.

59. Ibid.

60. Sage, introduction, 17.

61. Janet, "Allocution," 137. See also Carroy, Ohayon, and Plas, *Histoire de la psychologie*, 47.

62. Vesme, "L'Institut Psychologique International," 324.

63. Le Clair, *Letters of James and Flournoy*, 104.

64. Ellenberger, *Discovery of the Unconscious*, 338. Janet's frustration over the way in which his work with Léonie was publicized lingered in his later years ("Autobiography," 125).

65. This change was formalized in March 1902, when the name of the *Bulletin* was changed and when the assets of the Institut Psychologique International (11,523 francs) were made available to the Institut Général Psychologique. See "Assemblée générale du 24 mars 1902," *Bulletin de l'Institut Général Psychologique* 2, no. 3 (December 1902): 178–79; Louis Herbette, "Allocution de M. Louis Herbette," *Bulletin de l'Institut Psychologique International* 2, no. 1 (January–February 1902): 9.

66. "Assemblée générale du 24 mars 1902," 174.

67. Ibid., 174–75.

68. Scott, *Republican Ideas*, 161–63.

69. Surkis, *Sexing the Citizen*, 144–45.

70. Seigel, *The Idea of the Self*, 512–15.

71. Fouillé, "Les Grandes Conclusions," 790.

72. Scott, *Republican Ideas*, 171.

73. Ibid., 179–81.

74. Surkis, *Sexing the Citizen*, 144.

75. Flournoy, *Esprits et médiums*, 211.

76. Ibid.

77. Marey was among the first few members after Duclaux to join the IGP, and his involvement in the Groupe d'Étude des Phénomènes Psychiques was understood by his colleagues to represent both his general openness to new scientific questions and his eagerness to see his apparatus and methods applied to the study of phenomena, the reality of which he was generally doubtful. Marey presided over the meeting during which the group resolved to bring Eusapia Palladino to Paris for a series of experiments. Marey died shortly before these experiments came about. See "Nécrologie: Émile Duclaux," *Bulletin de l'Institut Général Psychologique* 4, no. 3 (May–June 1904): 318–20.

78. Bergson offered an ultimately ineffectual counterweight to the approach represented by the physiologists, which was championed primarily by Marey. Bergson and Marey had differed on other relevant occasions. For instance, while Marey had supported the candidacy of Janet's rival, Alfred Binet, for Ribot's chair at the Collège de France during the faculty deliberations, Bergson had undertaken, with greater success, the defense of Janet (Ellenberger, *Discovery of the Unconscious*, 343).

79. "Groupe d'Étude des Phénomènes Psychiques," *Bulletin de l'Institut Psychologique International* 2, no. 1 (January–February 1902): 4.

80. Ibid.

81. Bachelard, *Le Nouvel Esprit scientifique*, 64.

82. Jacques-Arsène d'Arsonval, "Les Basses Températures," *Bulletin de l'Institut Général Psychologique* 2, no. 2 (March–April 1902): 73–74.

83. "Groupe d'Étude des Phénomènes Psychiques: Séance du 28 décembre 1903," *Bulletin de l'Institut Général Psychologique* 4, no. 1 (January–February 1904): 25–30.

84. Alfred Fouillé, "Télépathie et télégraphie sans fil," *Bulletin de l'Institut Général Psychologique* 4, no. 2 (May–June 1904): 317.

85. "Groupe d'Étude des Phénomènes Psychiques: Organisation d'un laboratoire," *Bulletin de l'Institut Général Psychologique* 2, no. 3 (December 1902): 328.

86. Even into old age Palladino would most often be referred to by her given name, a fact that I take to be an indicator of the class differences between herself and those for whom she performed.

87. Courtier, "Rapport sur les séances d'Eusapia Palladino," 479. Hereafter cited parenthetically in the text.

88. Jules Bois, "L'Authenticité des fantômes," *Le Gaulois*, 6 January 1905. Over the course of her career more than two hundred publications were devoted to the *phénoménologie palladienne*. For a bibliography, see Morselli, *Psicologia e spiritismo*.

89. Flournoy, *Esprits et médiums*, 404. See also Sudre, "La Question métapsychique (II)," 302.

90. Oppenheim, *The Other World*, 150–51.

91. *New York Times*, 5 December 1909.

92. Flournoy, *Esprits et médiums*, 406.

93. Ibid., 403–6.

94. The séances with Eusapia occurred in three separate series: thirteen were held in 1905, sixteen in 1906, and fourteen in 1907. Youriévitch mentions forty-five séances (Courtier, "Rapport sur les séances d'Eusapia Palladino," 415, 554, 70).

95. "Nécrologie: Pierre Curie," *Bulletin de l'Institut Général Psychologique* 6, no. 2 (April–June 1906): 172. On 17 September 1894 Pierre explained his interest in a letter to Marie: "I am also very intrigued by these spiritist phenomena. I believe that there is in them questions with relevance to physics. There is an unknown agent in these phenomena. Isn't this just 'free' magnetism [*le magnétisme libre*]?" (Bibliothèque Nationale de France, *Pierre et Marie Curie*, 20). A few days before his death Curie wrote a letter expressing his belief that the materializations of Eusapia had a basis in reality and were not the result of deception. See Christine Blondel, "Eusapia Palladino: La Méthode expérimentale et la 'diva des savants,'" in Bensaude-Vincent and Blondel, *Des savants face à l'occulte*, 154.

96. Courtier was the director of research at the lab. In keeping with the spirit of the division of labor that was developing in research science, Courtier and Binet cooperated closely on a number of projects and publications.

97. "Assemblée générale du 21 décembre 1908," *Bulletin de l'Institut Général Psychologique* 9, no. 2 (March–April 1909): 254.

98. Ibid., 250.

99. "Assemblée générale du 23 mars 1906," *Bulletin de l'Institut Général Psychologique* 6, nos. 3–6 (1906): 187–209.

100. Édouard Branly, "Le Biomètre et ses indications," *Bulletin de l'Institut Général Psychologique* 2, no. 2 (March–April 1902): 106–11.

101. "Assemblée du 23 décembre 1907," *Bulletin de l'Institut Général Psychologique* 7, no. 5 (1907): 357.

102. On the potentially erotic nature of these controls, see Thurschwell, "Fantasies of Transmission," 47–48.

103. From an untitled 1938 article by Pierre Devaux in Acad. Sci., Dossier Arsonval, Arsène d'.

104. She was fifty-five when the IGP séances concluded in 1908.

105. Flournoy, *From India to the Planet Mars*, 263.

106. Flournoy, *Esprits et médiums*, 425, 424.

107. According to the journalist Paul Heuzé, Branly would later object to misrepresentations of his statements regarding mediumistic phenomena. "I have myself been cited as having attested to the facts," Branly is quoted as saying. "In reality, I attested to nothing" (*Ouest Éclair* [Rennes], 26 July 1923).

Chapter 4: The Master and His Double

1. See Janet, "Note sur quelques cas" and "Deuxième note."

2. Éphèyre, *Soeur Marthe*, 404.

3. Ibid., 405.

4. Ibid., 389.

5. Ibid.

6. Surkis, *Sexing the Citizen*, 54–55, 181.

7. In this respect I would modify Jacqueline Carroy's argument, which sees in Richet's career more fluidity between the fields of science and literature than the polemics of the "two cultures" would suggest ("Playing with Signatures"). While these fields were indeed interlinked, the complementary nature of their relationship was, nevertheless, predicated on their ascribed differences.

8. The name Richet remains a prominent one in the history of French medicine. Charles Richet's own son and grandson would occupy positions at the Parisian Faculty of Medicine and the National Academy of Medicine, respectively.

9. Wolf, *Brain, Mind, and Medicine*, 30–33. Most of Richet's formal training in physiology occurred in the labs of Étienne-Jules Marey (Richet, *Souvenirs*, 18–19). On Richet's various achievements, see also "L'Académie de médecine et les savants de dix nations ont fêté hier le Jubilé du Professeur Richet, gloire de la science française," *Le Matin*, 23 May 1926; Frederic L. Holmes, "Richet, Charles Robert," in *Dictionary of Scientific Biography*, ed. Charles Coulston Gillispie (New York: Scribner, 1975), 11:425–32; Jean Louis Fauré, "Discours: Funérailles de Charles Richet," *Notices et discours: Académie des Sciences* (1937), 1:626–33; André Mayer, "Notice nécrologique sur M. Charles Richet (1850–1935)," *Bulletin de l'Académie de Médecine* (1936): 51–64; F. Saint Girons, "Charles Richet (1850–1935)," *La Revue Générale des Sciences Pures et*

Appliquées (1935): 677–79; Marilisa Juri, "Charles Richet physiologiste (1850–1935)," *Zürcher Medizingeschichtliche Abhandlungen* no. 34 (Zürich, 1965); Acad. Sci., Dossier Richet, Robert-Charles.

10. As Pasteur Vallery-Radot would assert in his eulogy to Richet in *La Revue des Deux Mondes,* 15 December 1935.

11. Charles Richet, "Mémoire sur moi et les autres: Années d'agregé, 1878–87," manuscript, Fonds Richet, Acad. Méd., 225.

12. On Richet's choice of careers, see Charles Richet, "Mémoire sur moi et les autres: Années d'étudiant," manuscript, Fonds Richet, Acad. Méd., 134.

13. Works published under the name Charles Éphèyre would not be widely attributed to Richet until 1892 (Carroy, "Playing with Signatures," 228).

14. *Jubilé du Professeur Charles Richet* (Paris: L. Maretheux, 1912), 43–44.

15. Max Dessoir, *Buch der Erinnerung* (Stuttgart: F. Enke, 1946), 122, quoted in Ellenberger, *Discovery of the Unconscious,* 330–31.

16. Jules Bois, "L'Authenticité des Fantômes," *Le Gaulois,* 6 January 1906.

17. Jean-Louis Faure, "Paroles prononcées aux obsequies de Charles Richet," *La Presse Médicale,* 11 December 1935.

18. René Sully-Prudhomme, preface to Charles Richet, *Fables et récits pacifiques* (Paris: Giard et Brière, 1904), 5–6.

19. Harry Paul has argued that the divide between the "two cultures" was not absolute but still "sufficiently close to the truth to make it useful as a generalization" ("The Debate," 306).

20. Ribot, "Philosophy in France," 386.

21. See, for instance, Taine's critique of eloquence in "M. Cousin écrivain," in *Les Philosophes classiques,* 79–103. See also Ringer, *Fields of Knowledge,* 81–83.

22. Felix Ravaisson, *La Philosophie en France au XIXe siècle* (Paris, 1904), quoted in Simon, "The 'Two Cultures,'" 52–53 n. 29.

23. Ringer, *Toward a Social History of Knowledge,* 214.

24. Quoted in Ringer, *Fields of Knowledge,* 229–30. See Lavisse, *L'Éducation de la démocratie,* 48. On the relationship between Croiset's 1903 address to the social division of labor advocated by Durkheim, see Lepenies, *Between Literature and Science,* 51.

25. See Théodule Ribot's preface in *La Revue Philosophique,* January–June 1876, 1–2.

26. Janet, *La Philosophie française contemporaine,* 178.

27. Ribot, "Philosophy in France," 386.

28. Ribot's preface, 3.

29. Ribot, *La Psychologie allemande contemporaine,* v–vi.

30. Ibid., v. Gustave Le Bon defined introspection in 1911 as the oldest psychological method by which a thinker, "shut in his *cabinet d'études,*" produced "think books" from his meditations that no one wanted to read (*Les Opinions,* 11).

31. Zola, *Le Roman expérimental.*

32. Richet, "Démoniaques d'aujourd'hui," 346.

33. Ibid., 346–47. The expression *document humain* was reputedly coined by Jules and Edmond de Goncourt (Segalen, *L'Observation médicale*, 17–18).

34. Richet, "Démoniaques d'aujourd'hui," 347.

35. Ibid., 348, cited in Goldstein, "The Uses of Male Hysteria," 139.

36. This tendency to draw on art for examples of pathological types was not limited to literary characterization. Objective descriptions of hysterical symptoms were also culled from visual representations. See Charcot and Richer, *Les Démoniaques dans l'art.*

37. Ellenberger, *Discovery of the Unconscious,* 144; Goldstein, "The Uses of Male Hysteria," 135; and Foster, *Compulsive Beauty,* 50.

38. The incident was recounted in a letter to George Sand (1 May 1874) and to Mme Roger des Genettes (1 May 1874) (Flaubert, *Correspondence,* 7:134–38). On frequent occasions his friend, the doctor Raoul Fortin, referred to him as "a big hysterical girl," a fact that he repeated in a letter to his niece Caroline (25 April 1879) (Flaubert, *Correspondence,* 8:261).

39. Richet, "Démoniaques d'aujourd'hui," 344. Interestingly, it is this "luxury" of details that serves as one of the distinguishing features of Flaubert's realism, according to Roland Barthes' essay "L'Effet du reel," in Barthes et al., *Littérature et réalité,* 82.

40. Richet, "Démoniaques d'aujourd'hui," 344.

41. Rudolf Wittkower notes that the concept of genius as madness was not fully buttressed until the nineteenth century by authors like Lombroso, Jacques-Joseph Moreau de Tours, and Paul Julius Mobius ("Genius"). As one of those resistant to this idea, Ribot would insist on the priority of the "directive principle that organizes and imposes unity" over the dreamlike incoherence of automatic inspiration (*Essai sur l'imagination créatrice,* 46–47).

42. Charles Richet, preface to Lombroso, *L'Homme de genie,* x.

43. Ibid., viii. Richet would hesitate over the term and propose *progénéré* instead.

44. Frederic Myers provides some noteworthy examples in his discussion of genius in *Human Personality,* 70–120. For a full account of the relationship between literary creativity and somnambulism, dreams, and hallucinations in the nineteenth century, see James, *Dreams, Creativity, and Madness.*

45. Richet, preface to Lombroso, *L'Homme de genie,* xiii.

46. Ibid., xvi.

47. Ibid.

48. Ibid., xvii.

49. Goldstein, "Mutations of the Self," 114.

50. On Richet's "doubling," see Carroy, *Les Personnalités doubles et multiples,* 114–24.

51. Carroy-Thirard, "Hystérie, théâtre, littérature," 312.

52. Richet, "L'Amour," 160.

53. Ibid., 162.

54. Ibid.

55. Richet, "De quelques phénomènes," 649; *Le Figaro*, 9 October 1905.

56. For a more detailed account of Carmencita Noël's biography, see Le Maléfan, "Richet chasseur des fantômes," 179–82.

57. Ibid., 179.

58. Rouby, "Bien-Boà et Ch. Richet," 490.

59. Ibid., 491.

60. Ibid.

61. Richet, "De quelques phénomènes."

62. Quoted in Flournoy, *Esprits et médiums*, 220.

63. *Le Matin,* 3 January 1906.

64. Quoted in Paul Dramas, "Dans les mondes des fantômes," *La Petite République*, 7 January 1906. See also Flournoy, "À propos des phénomènes."

65. Paul Valentin, "Apparitions et mystifications: Les Fantômes de la villa Carmen," *La Vie Normale,* 25 December 1906.

66. Le Maléfan, "Richet chasseur des fantômes," 186–87.

67. For biographical details on Rouby and his critique of Richet, see ibid., 182–86.

68. Richet refuted Rouby's evidence in the March edition of *Les Annales des Sciences Psychiques.* See Le Maléfan, "La Psychopathologie confrontée aux fantômes."

69. Le Maléfan speculates that it was on the instigation of Miguel Bombarda, a Portuguese alienist who had previously published his own critique of Richet in Valentin's *La Vie Normale,* that Rouby was invited to present his case in Lisbon. Bombarda was the secretary-general of the 1906 congress. See Le Maléfan, "La Psychopathologie confrontée aux fantômes." See also Miguel Bombarda, "Farfadets et fantômes," *La Vie Normale,* 20 January 1906; Rouby, "Bien-Boà et Ch. Richet," 516.

70. Rouby, "Bien-Boà et Ch. Richet," 465. Bien-Boa's beard was thought to resemble the *chevelures* that women of the era used to augment their natural hair.

71. Ibid., 480.

72. Ibid., 493.

73. Ibid., 492.

74. Ibid., 511. See Enrico Carreras, "Le sedute di villa Carmen," *Luce e Ombra,* November 1905, 552–59.

75. Rouby, "Bien-Boà et Ch. Richet," 511.

76. Ibid., 492.

77. Richet, *Traité de métapsychique,* 648–49.

78. Ibid., 649.

79. Rouby, "Bien-Boà et Ch. Richet," 511.

80. Ibid., 515.

81. Ibid.

82. From the discussion following Rouby's presentation of "Bien-Boà et Ch.

Richet," 516. The importance of the question of *mythomanie* to the scenarios of psychical research has been highlighted by Le Maléfan in "Richet chasseur des fantômes," 193–94. The word was coined by Dupré in 1905 in "La Mythomanie, étude psychologique et médico-légale du mensonge et de la fabulation morbide," *Bulletin Médical*, 25 March, 1 and 8 April 1905.

83. Mounier, *Traité du caractère*, 381.

84. Le Bon, *Les Opinions et les croyances*, 324.

85. Ibid., 323.

86. Ibid., 325.

87. Ibid.

88. Ibid., 326.

89. Ibid., 327.

90. Flournoy, "Esprits et médiums," 370.

91. Roudinesco, *La Bataille de cent ans*, 251. On the place of Flournoy in the history of the development of psychoanalysis, see Flournoy, *Théodore et Léopold*.

92. Sonu Shamdasani, "Encountering Hélène," in Flournoy, *From India to the Planet Mars*, xv, xxiv. For a discussion of this concept, see Ellenberger, *Discovery of the Unconscious*, 314.

93. On the subject of Hélène Smith's glossolalia, see Todorov, *Theories of the Symbol*, 255–70.

94. Ibid., 381. Mme Noël described Bien Boa as "noble, reserved, correct, a Mentor of the highest morality," in *La Revue Spirite*, 1902–3, 269.

95. Flournoy, "Esprits et médiums," 382.

96. Ibid., 383. Rouby described Brauhauban as "Rabelaisian" in Rouby, "Bien-Boà et Ch. Richet," 485.

97. Flournoy, "Esprits et médiums," 382–84.

98. Flournoy, *Théodore et Léopold*, 25–26.

99. Richet, *Traité de métapsychique*, 642 n. 1.

Chapter 5: In the Wake of War

1. Doyle had written an early piece on spiritism for the journal *Light* in 1887. Doyle's son died in England of pneumonia while recovering from wounds sustained in the Somme.

2. Lodge, *Raymond*, 83.

3. Harry Houdini, "A Magician among the Spirits," in Murchison, *The Case For and Against Psychical Belief*, 361.

4. Lodge, "Aux Affligés de toutes nations," 55.

5. Ariès and Duby, *A History of Private Life*.

6. *Daily Mail*, 17 November 1919, quoted in *La Revue Spirite*, January 1920, 2–3.

7. Baraduc, *Mes morts*.

8. *Ouest Éclair* (Rennes), 26 July 1923. Bricout was the director of *La Revue du Clergé Français*.

9. See Véga, *Les Présences invisibles.*

10. Georges Goyau, "Les Présences invisibles," *Libre Belgique,* 31 January 1923.

11. The bibliographic citation for the consulted work lists Pierre Monnier as the author (*auteur douteux*) and Cécile as the editor (*editeur scientifique*). See Monier and Monier, *Lettres de Pierre,* v. My attention was drawn to this work by Vernette, *L'Au-delà,* 113.

12. Monier and Monier, *Lettres de Pierre.*

13. Ibid., 3, 8.

14. See Becker, *La Guerre et la foi;* Mosse, *Fallen Soldiers;* and Winter, *Sites of Memory.*

15. In 1929 Jean Norton Cru claimed that the tale was "the only heroic legend born during the war which enjoys a general notoriety" (*War Books,* 28). As a bilingual postcard depicting one such incident seems to suggest, the legend was not particular to any one national experience (Laffin, *World War I in Postcards,* 96).

16. Dorgelès, *Le Réveil des morts,* 298.

17. For Gance's novelized version of this sequence, see Gance, *J'accuse,* 102–8.

18. Gance, *Prisme,* 206.

19. Vesme, "Armées."

20. Jacques Lourbet, "La Métapsychique," *Le Flambeau* (Saint Girons), 224.

21. Ibid.

22. Vesme, "Armées," 10.

23. Eugene Tardieu, "La Défilé de la victoire: La Décoration de la voie triomphale dans ses grandes lignes," *Echo de Paris,* 10 July 1919.

24. "Les Fêtes de la Victoire: M. Deschanel et M. Clemenceau les évoquent à la Chambre," *Echo de Paris,* 16 July 1919.

25. *La Revue Spirite,* January 1920, 2.

26. See Société d'Études et de Publications Industrielles, *Ceux qui font la presse,* 2:462, 315.

27. *La Revue Spirite,* January 1920, 2.

28. Ibid., 4.

29. Jules Gaillard, "Première Conférence de l'Union Spirite Française: Le Spiritisme en l'an 1919," *La Revue Spirite,* January 1920, 20.

30. *La Revue Spirite,* January 1920, 5.

31. Santoliquido was a parliamentary deputy in Rome, the director general of public health of Italy, administrative director in the Italian Ministry of the Interior, *conseiller d'état* for Italy, and a representative for the Red Cross at the League of Nations. See Eugène Osty's eulogy to Santoliquido in *La Revue Métapsychique,* November–December 1930, 465–70.

32. IMI 3: 8 *Lettres,* Santoliquido to Richet, October 1918.

33. *La Revue Métapsychique,* November–December 1930, 465–70.

34. IMI 3: 8 *Lettres,* Lodge to Richet, 16 October 1918.

35. IMI 3: 8 *Lettres,* Santoliquido to Richet, November 1918.

36. Ibid.

37. Gustave Geley et al., "Les Études métapsychique," *L'Âme Gauloise*, 12 November 1920. The original resolution can be found in IMI 3: 8 *Réunions*, meeting of 10 July 1919.

38. Gustave Geley, "Comment faire progresser les études psychiques? Quelques voeux et projets," extrait des *Nouveau horizons de la science et de la pensée*, 1905. See Stephan Chauvet, "Les Premiers Stades d'une science nouvelle: La Métapsychie," *Gazette des Hôpitaux*, 3 July 1919.

39. Chauvet, "Les Premiers Stades." See also Sudre, "La Question métapsychique (III)," 580.

40. Sudre, "La Question métapsychique (III)," 581.

41. Ibid., 590.

42. Ibid., 695.

43. Réné Sudre, "Une science nouvelle: La Métapsychie," *L'Avenir*, 31 July 1919.

44. On the military service of Richet's sons, see BN/NAF 13556: 46–47. On the death of his son Albert, see BN/NAF 16015: 126, "Papiers Poincaré tome XXIV, Lettres adressées à Raymond Poincaré; René-Rivoire."

45. The IMI's annuity from the Fondation Jean Meyer was 30,000 francs. Initial operating budget for the first year and a half was 45,000 francs. The budget for 1920 increased to 52,000 francs due both to savings from the initial year and the collection of over 13,000 francs in membership fees. Enrollment for the initial year of operation was 183 members and adherents of various ranks. Expenditure for honoraria to mediums was 1,900 francs. For the fiscal year 1920–21 6,000 francs were budgeted for the acquisition of laboratory equipment, and 5,000 francs were allocated for mediums—five times more than that to be spent on the acquisition of books for the library and only half that to be spent on the combined salaries of the director, the concierge, and the librarian. See IMI 3: 8 *Réunions*, meeting of 10 July 1919.

46. For a discussion of these facilities, see ibid. Much of this work was still in progress as of December 1919 (see *J'ai Vu*, 26 December 1919) but was reaching completion by the spring of 1920 (see *L'Information*, 21 April 1920). For a discussion of photographic equipment and lighting, see Geley's report in IMI 3: 8 *Réunions*, meeting of 18 June 1919.

47. "L'Institut des prodiges," *J'ai Vu*, 26 December 1919. While some reveled in the elegant surroundings, others felt that the location offered little advantage. Sudre felt that it was too remote, both geographically and symbolically, from the academic district of the Latin quarter. He considered the avenue Niel location temporary and predicted that the IMI would, in good time, find its proper place among the Vieux Sorbonne and the Palais de Radium. See Sudre, "Une science nouvelle."

48. "L'Institut des prodiges."

49. Members of the institute were not averse to publicizing their work in popular forums, including those provided by the spiritist and occultist organizations. Gustave Geley, for instance, would present research findings before the Société Théosophique in February 1922. See *Le Message Théosophique et Social*, 7 March 1922.

50. See IMI 3: 9 "Coupures presse" and IMI 14: 5 "Argus presse."

51. Paul Abram, "Un institut métapsychique," *L'Horizon* (Brussels), 31 January 1920.

52. Gustave Krafft, "Spiritisme," *La Cooperation,* 16 June 1921.

53. Ibid.

54. Quoted in ibid.

55. Lachapelle, "Attempting Science," 9–10.

56. Ibid., 10–11.

57. Ibid., 12.

58. Ibid.

Chapter 6: The Limits of Method

1. Paul Heuzé reports that one observer involved in the Kluski experiments counted more than twenty spirits talking and wandering about the séance room ("L'Énigme métapsychique," 156).

2. Some skeptical commentaries indicated the obscene nature of what they took to be Kluski's deception. Joseph Bricout, reminding his readers of Père Lucien Roure's account in *Le Spiritisme d'hier et d'aujourd'hui* (Paris: Beauchesne, 1923) of the *malodorante* fraud perpetrated by the Norwegian medium Ejner Nielsen, who used his rectum as "theater and instrument," also notes Paul Heuzé's "shocking" pages describing an incident in which Kluski "dropped . . . his pants and placed his buttocks in the paraffin." "Voilà," Bricout concluded, "a mold, a 'spirit face' to preserve, n'est-ce pas?" (*Ouest Éclair* [Rennes], 26 July 1923).

3. These experiments are discussed in Marcel Laurent, "Vous qui ne croyez point, voyez ces moulages, touchez. . . ." *Le Courrier du Mexique,* 7 September 1920. See also Sudre, "La Question métapsychique (III)," 579–80.

4. IMI 3: 8 *Réunions,* meeting of 11 July 1921.

5. Ibid.

6. Nordmann, "Les Mystères de l'ectoplasme," 460–61.

7. Gabriel Gobron, "Une opinion sur la question de l'ectoplasme," *L'Âme Gauloise,* 14 January 1923.

8. "La Campagne d'injures et de mensonges," *La Revue Métapsychique,* November–December 1922, 1.

9. Nordmann found the title of Heuzé's exposé ("Les Morts, vivent-ils?") unfortunate, since psychical research could be conducted independently of any hypothesis of survival. Nor did disproving the phenomena scrutinized by psychical researchers prove anything in regard to the immortality of the soul. In other words, these propositions were independent variables: "There are other happy consolations for troubled souls than the spiritualist solutions to the problem of survival" (Nordmann, "Spiritisme," 466).

10. Bisson, *Les Phénomènes;* and Schrenck-Notzing, *Materialisations-Phaenomene.*

11. See Sudre, "La Question métapsychique (III)," 574.

12. Sudre, "La Question métapsychique (II)," 284; and Sudre, "La Question métapsychique (III)," 573.

13. Bisson, *Les Phénomènes,* 54, 70.

14. See G. L. Duprat's review of Bisson's book in *La Revue Philosophique,* January–June 1915, 564–66. See Bisson, *Les Phénomènes,* 40; and Richet, *Traité de métapsychique,* 651.

15. Bisson, *Les Phénomènes,* 17, 48, 52, 174, 204.

16. Ibid., 63, 65, 73.

17. Ibid., 200, 245.

18. See also IMI 22: 2–3.

19. See Bisson, *Les Phénomènes,* 166–67. The vast majority of the photos were taken in the private sittings involving only Eva and Bisson. See Jastrow, "Ectoplasm."

20. Sudre, "La Question métapsychique (III)," 577.

21. See Schrenck-Notzing, *Phenomena of Materialisation.*

22. Charles Nordmann notes that Eva was the only French medium with this ability ("Les Grands Médiums," 938).

23. Sudre, "La Question métapsychique (II)," 277.

24. See Schrenck-Notzing, *Les Phénomènes physiques,* 7.

25. Nordmann, "Pour aborder la métapsychique," 941.

26. Richet, *Traité de métapsychique,* 593, quoted in Janet, "À propos de la métaphysique," 20.

27. Nordmann, "Spiritisme," 459.

28. "M. Charles Richet présente son livre: *Traité de métapsychique,*" *Comptes Rendus de l'Académie des Sciences,* January–June 1922, 429–30.

29. Nordmann, "Pour aborder la métapsychique," 937.

30. Janet, "À propos de la métapsychique," 5–6.

31. Ibid., 27.

32. Ibid., 28.

33. Ibid.

34. Ibid., 29.

35. Henri Piéron, review of *Traité de métapsychique, L'Année Psychologique* (1922): 602.

36. Janet, "À propos de la métapsychique," 27.

37. Ibid., 10.

38. Heuzé, *Les Morts, vivent-ils?* 227.

39. Ibid., 228.

40. Heuzé, "L'Énigme métapsychique," 167.

41. Ibid., 165.

42. Jastrow, "Ectoplasm."

43. Piéron, review of *Traité de métapsychique,* 604.

44. Lapicque et al., "Rapport." Hereafter cited in the text. The report originally appeared in *L'Opinion,* 8 July 1922. The committee's conclusions are also reproduced

in Prévost, "La Question métapsychique." See also Parot, "Psychology Experiments," 22. As with all aspects of Eva's career, the Sorbonne experiments drew international attention. See, for instance, "Sorbonne Scientists Find No Ectoplasm after Experiments in Fifteen Séances," *New York Times*, 8 July 1922.

45. Paul Heuzé, "Les Morts, vivent-ils?" *L'Opinion*, 4 August 1922.

46. Joseph Jastrow ("Ectoplasm") argues that Schrenck-Notzing was aware of Eva's identity. The identity of Eva and Marthe Béraud is admitted in Charles Richet's preface to the 1925 French translation of Schrenck-Notzing, *Phénomènes physiques*, viii.

47. Quoted in Sudre, "La Question métapsychique (II)," 273.

48. Gustave Geley, "Science Nouvelle," *Figaro*, 26 July 1923.

49. The Sorbonne report indicated that on one occasion Eva had canceled a meeting because of a menstrual cycle that made her "irritable" (Lapicque et al., "Rapport," 609–11).

50. Prévost, "La Question métapsychique," 13; Conan Doyle, *History of Spiritualism*, 2:102.

51. Prévost, "La Question métapsychique," 14.

52. Marcel Prévost, "La Vie d'a-present. Pénombres," *Intransigeant*, 19 July 1922.

53. Prévost, "La Question métapsychique," 7.

54. Ibid., 14.

55. Ibid.

56. Gustave Geley, "Les Expériences de l'Institut Métapsychique International avec le medium Jean Guzik," *Travaux du IIe Congrès International*, 28–41.

57. The newspaper *Le Matin* provided extensive coverage of the debates surrounding psychical research and even launched a contest promising 50,000 francs to any medium capable of moving a pencil without touching it (Heuzé, "L'Énigme métapsychique," 165).

58. Prévost, "La Question métapsychique," 20–22.

59. Ibid., 22.

60. Preface to Sudre, "La Question métapsychique (II)," 269. See also "Le Mystère des médiums. M. Marcel Prévost réclame une enquête impartiale," *Le Matin*, 11 January 1924.

61. Details of the exchange between Dicksonn and Geley appeared in the pages of *Le Matin* and *L'Opinion* and also circulated in the provincial press. See, for example, *Dépêche* (Brest), 20 June 1923; *Ouest Éclair* (Rennes), 26 July 1923.

62. Gustave Geley, "Spiritisme ou prestidigitation? L'Institut Métapsychique lance un defi de 10.000 francs au prestidigitateur Dicksonn," *Le Matin*, 16 June 1923. See also Sudre, "La Question métapsychique (II)," 274–76.

63. *Le Matin*, 17 June 1923.

64. Heuzé, "Questions métapsychiques."

65. The excerpt from Dicksonn's letter to *Le Matin*, 21 June 1923, is reproduced in *La France*, 22 June 1923.

66. Heuzé, "Questions métapsychiques."

67. Quoted in Nordmann, "Les Mystères de l'ectoplasme," 456.

68. Heuzé, "Questions métapsychiques."

69. Nordmann, "Les Mystères de l'ectoplasme," 457.

70. Joseph Babinski, "Démembrement de l'hystérie traditionnelle. Pithiatisme," *Semaine Médicale* 29 (1909): 3–8. See Mark S. Micale, "On the 'Disappearance' of Hysteria: A Study in the Clinical Deconstruction of a Diagnosis," *Isis* 84 (September 1993): 496–526. See also Ellenberger, *Discovery of the Unconscious*, 785–86.

71. As Marcel Boll would affirm in his 1924 denunciation of psychical research for *Mercure de France*, Babinski and Dupré had demonstrated that hypnotism and hysteria were due to deception. It was thus natural to conclude, as Dupré had in 1912, that "since hypnosis is only a simulation (mythomania), any medium that makes recourse to hypnosis must be considered capable of mystification" (Marcel Boll, "La lamentable histoire de la métapsychique," *Mercure de France*, 15 February 1924, 125).

72. See G. Marinesco, "Introduction à la psychanalyse. 2e critique des théories de Freud," *La Revue Générale des Sciences Pures et Appliquées* (1890): 510–20.

73. See Janet, "La psychanalyse." On the question of Janet's priority, see Ellenberger, *Discovery of the Unconscious*, 539.

74. Lalande, "Philosophy in France, 1922–1923," 558; Régis and Hesnard, *La Psychanalyse*. This work was an extension of an article that appeared in *L'Encéphale* in 1913 entitled "La Doctrine de Freud et de son école." See Roudinesco, *Bataille de cent ans*, 274.

75. Lalande, "Philosophy in France, 1922–1923," 558; see Blondel, *La Psychanalyse*.

76. Roudinesco, *Bataille de cent ans*, 254–55, 278, 283.

77. Lalande, "Philosophy in France, 1922–1923," 558.

78. Ibid., my emphasis.

79. Ibid.

80. Roudinesco, *Bataille de cent ans*, 282.

81. Freud's own enthusiasm for matters openly taken up by psychical research is well documented and posed its own danger to psychoanalytic doctrine. See Jones, *Life and Work*, 3:375–407. Indeed, it was Jones who, along with Max Eitingon, managed to contain Freud's enthusiasms for "occult" phenomena in order not to jeopardize the legitimation of psychoanalysis among the larger medical and scientific communities. Freud was persuaded to suppress publication of his 1921 essay on the subject, "Psychoanalysis and Telepathy," which would not appear until 1941. The essay "Dreams and Telepathy" was first published in *Imago* in 1922. A 1925 note on "The Occult Significance of Dreams" was written for inclusion in *The Interpretation of Dreams* and appeared as an appendix to the *Gesammelte Schriften* reedition of Freud's pioneering book. Freud would return to the subject once again in 1933 with the chapter "Psychoanalysis and Telepathy," in *The New Introductory Lectures on Psychoanalysis*. For a history of Freud's vacillating attitude toward "occult" phenomena, see Roudi-

nesco and Plon, *Dictionnaire de la psychanalyse,* 1051–54. Freud was evidently quite aware of the work being conducted in psychical research. He notes in "Dreams and Telepathy" (18:199) that, as a corresponding member of both the Society for Psychical Research and the American Society for Psychical Research, he received the major journals in the field. Freud was also given a copy of Charles Richet's 1922 work, *Traité de métapsychique,* by Eitingon (Jones, *Life and Work,* 3:391).

82. The French translation of Freud's *Introduction à la psychanalyse* that appeared in 1921 was considered by one reviewer "a mediocre ambassador of Freudianism in France, where we like clear ideas, well-ordered systems, and precise verbiage" (*La Revue Philosophique,* January–June 1923, 460–61).

83. Breton would have encountered a discussion of Freud in Régis, *Précis de psychiatrie,* which he read while a medical assistant for the Second Army at Saint-Dizier in 1916, and in Régis and Hesnard, *La Psychanalyse* (Bonnet, *André Breton,* 104). For dates of the translations of Freud's various works, see Roudinesco, *Bataille de cent ans,* 477–79.

84. The most developed statement of the connection between Breton's ideas and those derived from the field of psychical research is Starobinski, "Freud, Breton, Myers." Starobinski's implication is that Breton's definition and practice of surrealism acted not on the Freudian conception of the unconscious but rather on Myers's very different concept of the "subliminal self." These arguments draw evidence from the meeting between Freud and Breton in 1921, from the nonpsychoanalytic provenance of the term *automatism* (which was applied to the earliest experiments in automatic writing and which Breton preserved in his later definition of surrealism), and on later statements made by Breton showing his familiarity with the work of Myers, Richet, and Flournoy. Starobinski's conclusions have been rejected by Marguerite Bonnet primarily on the basis of his skewed chronology. Whatever the merits of Bonnet's arguments, her defense of the psychoanalytic provenance of surrealism reveals a lack of appreciation for the role that psychical research played in developing and sustaining theories of unconscious processes in French thought. She also disregards the complexity of the field as a whole and makes the familiar false assumption that it was rooted in the belief in spirits. Thus, Bonnet suggests that Breton's clear refusal of "spirits" (in 1922 and in 1933) signifies a refusal of the ideas of psychical research as a whole (*André Breton,* 104–5). Repeated consideration of the work of Myers, Richet, and Flournoy in Breton's published writings would suggest otherwise. Starobinski's position finds support in my own research showing that psychical research and the IMI in particular were indeed part of Breton's intellectual universe. The archives of the IMI, for instance, place Breton at a demonstration by the clairvoyant Pascal Forthuny, who also happened to be the art editor for *Le Matin* (IMI 20: 3–4 "Séances de Forthuny: #1204 bis, 7 January 1927, sur André Breton occupant la chaise 65"). A survey of the surrealist group's publications shows Breton and Paul Éluard addressing a 1933 questionnaire on "chance" to Flammarion, Richet, and Eugène Osty, all leading members of the IMI (*Minotaure* 3–4 [1933]: 101–13).

85. Breton et al., *Oeuvres complètes,* 3:474. Bonnet reasserts in her annotation to this passage that the reading of these works was not concomitant with the experiments in automatic writing and that Breton has himself presented a skewed chronology. This is clearly the case with Richet's work, which did not appear until 1922, three years after the initial experiment resulting in "Les Champs magnétiques." On the role that surrealism played in bringing Freudian thought to France, see Roudinesco, "Le Surréalism au service de la psychanalyse," in *Histoire de la psychanalyse,* 2:19–49.

86. See Lachapelle, "Attempting Science," 4–5.

87. Lalande, "Philosophy in France, 1935–1936," 27; Dalbiez, *La Méthode psychanalytique.*

88. Lalande, "Philosophy in France, 1935–1936," 28.

89. Myers, *Human Personality,* 7.

Conclusion

1. Lacan, "The Freudian Thing," 136.

2. Ibid., 115.

3. Ibid., 123.

4. Richet, "Les Mouvements inconscients," 90.

5. Lacan, "The Freudian Thing," 121–23.

Bibliography

Primary Sources

Agathon. *L'Esprit de la nouvelle Sorbonne: La crise de la culture classique, la crise du français.* Paris: Mercure de France, 1911.

Anonymous. *Examen raisonné des prodiges récents d'Europe et d'Amérique, notamment des tables tournantes et répondantes. Par un philosophe.* Paris: Vermot, 1853.

Arago, François. *Oeuvres complètes de François Arago.* Paris: Gide et J. Baudry, 1854.

——. "Remarques de M. Arago à l'occasion de cette communication." *Comptes Rendus Hebdomadaires des Séances de l'Académie des Sciences* 36 (1853): 893.

Azam, Eugène. *Hypnotisme et double conscience: Origine de leur étude et divers travaux sur des sujets analogues.* Paris: Alcan, 1893.

Babinet, Jacques. "Les Sciences occultes au XIXe siècle: Les tables tournantes et les manifestation prétendus surnaturelles considérées au point de vue de la science d'observation." *La Revue des Deux Mondes,* April–June 1854, 510–32.

Bailly, Jean Sylvain, et al. "Secret Report on Mesmerism, or Animal Magnetism" (1784). In *The Nature of Hypnosis: Selected Basic Readings,* edited by Ronald E. Shor and Martin T. Orne, 3–7. New York: Holt, Rinehart and Winston, 1965.

Ball, Benjamin, and Ernest Chambard. "Somnambulisme naturel ou spontanté." In *Dictionnaire encyclopédique des sciences médicales,* edited by Amédée Dechambre, series 3, vol. 10, SIR–SPE, 322–62. 1864; Paris: Asselin, 1881.

Baraduc, Hippolyte. *Mes morts, leurs manifestations, leurs influences, leurs télépathies.* Paris: Leymarie, 1908.

Baudelaire, Charles. "Madame Bovary par Gustave Flaubert." In *Curiosités esthétiques: L'Art romantique, et autres oeuvres critiques,* edited by Henri Lemaître, 641–51. Paris: Bordas, 1990.

Bautain, Louis-Eugène-Marie. *Avis aux chrétiens sur les tables tournantes et parlantes. Par un ecclésiastique.* Paris: Devarenne and Pérrisse Frères, 1853.

Bennett, Edward T. *La Société Anglo-Américain pour les recherches psychiques,* translated by Michel Sage. Paris: Lucien Bodin, 1904.

Bergson, Henri. "De la simulation inconsciente dans l'hypnotisme." *Revue Philosophique de la France et de l'Étranger,* July–December 1886, 525–31.

———. *L'Énergie spirituelle.* Paris: Presses Universitaires de France, 1949.

Bernard, Claude. *Introduction à l'étude de la médecine expérimentale.* 1865; Paris: Delagrave, 1898.

Berthelot, Marcelin, et al. *Hommage a Monsieur Chevreul à l'occasion de son centenaire, 31 août 1886.* Paris: Alcan, 1886.

Besterman, Theodore, ed. *Transactions of the Fourth International Congress for Psychical Research, Athens, 1930.* London: Society for Psychical Research, 1930.

Bibliothèque Nationale de France. *Pierre et Marie Curie.* Paris: Bibliothèque Nationale de France, 1967.

Bibliothèque Sainte-Geneviève. *Victor Hugo et le spiritisme: Exposition, 12 juin–30 juillet 1985, Bibliothèque Sainte-Geneviève.* Paris: Bibliothèque Sainte-Geneviève, 1985.

Binet, Alfred. *Introduction à la psychologie expérimentale.* Paris: F. Alcan, 1894.

Bisson, Juliette Alexandre. *Les Phénomènes dits de materialisation. Étude experimental.* Paris: Alcan, 1914.

Blondel, Charles. *La Psychanalyse.* Strasbourg: Istra, 1922.

Boutroux, Émile. *Notice sur Paul Janet.* Paris: Cerf, 1900.

Breton, André. *Bibliothèque de la Pléiade.* Vol. 3 of *Oeuvres complètes,* edited by Marguerite Bonnet. Paris: Gallimard, 1999.

Broca, Paul. "Sur un nouveau procédé, l'hypnotisme, pour obtenir l'anesthésie." *Comptes Rendus Hebdomadaires des Séances de l'Académie des Sciences* 49 (1859): 902–5.

Bulletin des lois de l'Empire français. 4th series, vol. 12, no. 277 bis (August 1810), 118. Paris: Imprimerie Imperial, 1810.

Burdin, Charles, and Frédéric Dubois. *Histoire académique du magnétisme animal: Accompagnée de notes et de remarques critiques sur toutes les observations et expériences faites jusqu'à ce jour.* Paris: J.-B. Baillière, 1841.

Camescasse, Valentine. *Souvenirs de Madame Camescasse.* Paris: Plon, 1924.

Capron, Eliab Wilkinson. *Modern Spiritualism, Its Facts and Fanaticisms, Its Consistencies and Contradictions.* Boston: B. Marsh, 1855.

Charcot, Jean-Martin. "Sur les divers états nerveux déterminés par l'hypnotisation chez les hystériques." *Comptes Rendus Hebdomadaires des Séances de l'Académie des Sciences* 94 (1882): 403–5.

Charcot, J.-M., and Paul Richer. *Les Démoniaques dans l'art: Avec 67 figures intercalées dans le texte.* Paris: Delahaye et Lecrosnier, 1887.

Charcot, J.-M., and Ruth Harris. *Clinical Lectures on the Diseases of the Nervous System.* New York: Routledge, 1990.

Chevreul, Michel Eugène. *De la baguette divinatoire du pendule dit explorateur et des tables tournantes, au point de vue de l'histoire de la critique et de la méthode expérimentale.* Paris: Mallet-Bachelier, 1854.

———. "Lettre à M. Ampère sur une classe particulière de mouvemens musculaires." *La Revue des Deux Mondes,* April–June 1833, 258–66.

Claretie, Jules. *La Vie à Paris, 1897.* Paris: Charpentier, 1898.

Compte rendu du IIIe Congrès International de Recherches Psychiques à Paris, septembre–octobre 1927. Paris: Institut Métapsychique International, 1928.

Comte, Auguste. *Catéchisme positiviste; ou, sommaire exposition de la religion universelle, avec une introduction et des notes explicatives.* 1852; Paris: Garnier, 1909.

Conan Doyle, Arthur. *History of Spiritualism.* 2 vols. 1926; San Diego: Book Tree, 2007.

Congrès International des Recherches Psychiques. *Le Compte rendu officiel du premier Congrès International des Recherches Psychiques à Copenhague, 26 août–2 septembre 1921,* edited by Carl Vett. Copenhagen: Secrétariat International des Comités pour les Recherches Psychiques, 1922.

Courtier, Jules. "Rapport sur les séances d'Eusapia Palladino à l'Institut Général Psychologique en 1905, 1906, 1907 et 1908. Lecture et discussion." *Bulletin de l'Institut Général Psychologique* 8, nos. 5–6 (1908).

Crookes, William. *Researches in the Phenomena of Spiritualism.* London: J. Burns, 1874.

Dalbiez, Roland. *La Méthode psychanalytique et la doctrine freudienne.* Paris: Desclée de Brouwer, 1936.

Deploige, Simon. *Le Conflit de la morale et de la sociologie.* Louvain: Institut Supérieur de Philosophie, 1912.

d'Eslon, Charles. *Observations sur les deux rapports de MM. les Commissaires nommés par Sa Majesté, pour l'examen du Magnétisme animal, 6 septembre 1784.* Paris: Cloussier, 1784. Reprinted in *The Nature of Hypnosis: Selected Basic Readings,* edited by Ronald E. Shor and Martin T. Orne. New York: Holt, Rinehart and Winston, 1965.

Dorgelès, Roland. *Le Réveil des morts.* Paris: A. Michel, 1923.

Dubrac, F. *Traité de jurisprudence médicale et pharmaceutique.* Paris: Baillière, 1882.

Duhem, Paul. "Délire mystique cause par les pratiques du magnétiseur Philippe." *Annales Medico-psychologique,* July 1906, 79–84.

Durkheim, Émile. *De la division du travail social.* Paris: Presses Universitaires de France, 1991.

Durkheim, Émile, Neil Gross, Robert Alun Jones, and Andrâe Lalande. *Durkheim's Philosophy Lectures: Notes from the Lycée de Sens Course, 1883–1884.* New York: Cambridge University Press, 2004.

Éphèyre, Charles. "Soeur Marthe." *La Revue des Deux Mondes,* May–June 1889, 384–431.

Espinas, Alfred Victor. *Des sociétés animales, 2 éd., augmentée d'une introduction sur l'histoire de la sociologie en général.* Paris: G. Baillière, 1878.

———. "'Être ou ne pas être' ou du postulat de la sociologie." *La Revue Philosophique,* January–June 1901, 449–80.

———. "Les Études sociologiques en France. Les colonies animales." *La Revue Philosophique,* January–June 1882, 565–607.

L'État actuel des recherches psychiques d'après les travaux du IIme Congrès International tenu à Varsovie en 1923 en l'honneur du Dr. Julian Ochorowicz avec une préface du professeur Charles Richet. Paris: Presses Universitaires de France, 1924.

Ferenczi, Sandor. "Spiritisme." In *Les Écrits de Budapest.* Paris: Broché, 1997.

Figuier, Louis. *Histoire du merveilleux dans les temps modernes,* vol. 4. Paris: L. Hachette, 1860.

Flammarion, Camille. *Mémoires biographiques et philosophiques d'un astronome.* Paris: E. Flammarion, 1911.

Flaubert, Gustave. *Correspondence: Nouvelle et augmentée, 1873–76.* Vols. 7–8 of *Oeuvres complètes de Gustave Flaubert.* Paris: L. Conard, 1930.

———. *Madame Bovary: Backgrounds and Sources,* edited and translated by Paul de Man. New York: Norton, 1965.

Flournoy, Théodore. "À propos des phénomènes de 'matérialisation' du prof. Richet." *Archives de Psychologie* 5 (1906): 388–93.

———. "Esprits et médiums." *Bulletin de l'Institut Général Psychologique,* June–July 1909, 357–90.

———. *Esprits et médiums. Mélanges de métapsychique et de psychologie.* Geneva: Librairie Kündig, 1911.

———. *From India to the Planet Mars.* Princeton, N.J.: Princeton University Press, 1994.

———. "Observations psychologique sur le spiritisme." In Janet, *IVe Congrès International de Psychologie.*

Fouillé, Alfred. "Les Grandes Conclusions de la psychologie contemporaine: La conscience et ses transformations." *La Revue des Deux Mondes* 17 (1891): 789–816.

Freud, Sigmund. "Dreams and Occultism" (1933). In *The Standard Edition of the Complete Psychological Works of Sigmund Freud,* translated by James Strachey, 22:31–56. London: Hogarth Press, 1954.

———. "Dreams and Telepathy" (1922). In *The Standard Edition of the Complete Psychological Works of Sigmund Freud,* translated by James Strachey, 18:195–220. London: Hogarth Press, 1954.

———. *The Freud Reader,* edited by Peter Gay. New York: Norton, 1989.

———. *New Introductory Lectures on Psychoanalysis,* translated by James Strachey. New York: Norton, 1965.

———. "Occult Significance of Dreams" (1925). In *The Standard Edition of the Com-*

plete Psychological Works of Sigmund Freud, translated by James Strachey, 19:135–38. London: Hogarth Press, 1954.

———. "Psychoanalysis and Telepathy" (1921). In *The Standard Edition of the Complete Psychological Works of Sigmund Freud,* translated by James Strachey, 18:175–93. London: Hogarth Press, 1954.

Freud, Sigmund, and C. G. Jung. *The Freud/Jung Letters: The Correspondence between Sigmund Freud and C. G. Jung,* edited by William McGuire, translated by Ralph Manheim and R. F. C. Hull. Cambridge, Mass.: Harvard University Press, 1974.

Gance, Abel. *J'accuse: D'après le film d'Abel Gance.* Paris: Éditions de la Lampe Merveilleuse, 1922.

———. *Prisme.* Paris: Gallimard, 1930.

Gaudon, Jean. *Ce que disent les tables parlantes; Victor Hugo à Jersey.* Paris: J.-J. Pauvert, 1963.

Gilbert, Pierre, ed. *Codes d'instructions criminelle, pénal et forestier.* Vol. 3 of *Les Codes annotés de Sirey.* Paris: Cosse et Marchal, 1858.

Gurney, Edmund, Frederic William Henry Myers, and Frank Podmore. *Phantasms of the Living.* London: Society for Psychical Research, 1886.

Hahn, Louis, and L. Thomas. "Spiritisme." In *Dictionnaire encyclopédique des sciences médicales,* edited by Amédée Dechambre, 278–94. 1864; Paris: Asselin, 1883.

Heuzé, Paul. "L'Énigme métapsychique. Où en est-on?" *La Revue de Paris,* 1 January 1924, 150–75.

———. *Les Morts, vivent-ils?* Paris: La Renaissance du Livre, 1921.

———. "Questions métapsychiques. La Querelle Dickson-Geley." *L'Opinion,* 3 August 1923.

Hugo, Adèle. *Le Journal d'Adèle Hugo, 1853,* vol. 2. Paris: Minard, 1971.

Hugo, Victor. *Correspondance (1849–1866),* vol. 2. Paris: INALF, 1961.

———. *Oeuvres complètes. Édition chronologique publiée sous la direction de Jean Massin,* edited by Jean Massin, vol. 9 (1853–55). Paris: Club Français du Livre, 1968.

Husson, Henri-Marie. *Rapport sur les experiences magnétiques faites par la Commission de l'Académie Royale de Médecine lu dans les séances des 21 et 28 juin 1831.* Paris, 1831.

James, William. *Essays, Comments, and Reviews.* Cambridge, Mass.: Harvard University Press, 1987.

———. "The Hidden Self." *Scribner's Magazine* 7 (January–June 1890): 361–73.

———. *Memories and Studies.* 1911; New York: Longmans, Green, Reader and Dyer, 1917.

———. "Report on the Congress of Physiological Psychology." *Mind* 14, no. 56 (1889): 614–16.

Janet, Paul. "Une chaire de psychologie expérimentale." *La Revue des Deux Mondes,* March–April 1888, 518–49.

———. "De la suggestion dans l'état d'hypnotisme." *Revue Politique et Littéraire,* nos. 4, 5, 6, 7 (1884).

————. *État mental des hystériques: Les accidents mentaux.* Paris: Rueff, 1894.

————. "Introduction à la science philosophique. I. La Philosophie est-elle une science?" *Revue Philosophique de la France et de l'Étranger,* January–June 1888, 337–53.

————. *La Philosophie française contemporaine.* Paris: Calmann Lévy, 1879.

Janet, Pierre. "Allocution de M. Pierre Janet." *Bulletin de l'Institut Psychologique International,* May 1901, 133–39.

————. "À propos de la métapsychique." *La Revue Philosophique,* July–December 1923, 5–32.

————. "Autobiography of Pierre Janet." In *A History of Psychology in Autobiography,* vol. 1, edited by Carl Allanmore Murchison and Edwin Garrigues Boring, 122–33. Worcester, Mass.: Clark University Press, 1930.

————. *L'Automatisme psychologique: Essai de psychologie expérimentale sur les formes inférieures de l'activité humaine.* Paris: Alcan, 1889.

————. "Deuxième note sur le sommeil provoqué à distance." *La Revue Philosophique de la France et de l'Étranger,* July–December 1886, 212–23.

————. "Note sur quelques cas de somnambulisme." *La Revue Philosophique de la France et de l'Étranger,* January–June 1886, 190–98.

————. "Objet de l'Institut Psychologique." *Bulletin de l'Institut Psychologique International,* April 1901, 83–90.

————. "La Psychanalyse." In *XVIIth International Congress of Medicine,* 13–64. London, 1913.

————, ed. *IVe Congrès International de Psychologie, tenu à Paris, du 20 au 26 août 1900 sous la présidence de Th. Ribot.* Paris: Alcan, 1901.

————. "Société Internationale de l'Institut Psychique." *Bulletin de l'Institut Psychique International,* July 1900, 3–7.

————. "Le Spiritisme contemporain." *La Revue Philosophique de la France et de l'Étranger,* January–June 1892, 413–42.

Jastrow, Joseph. "Ectoplasm, Myth or Key to the Unknown?" *New York Times,* 30 July 1922.

Jubilé du Professeur Charles Richet. Paris: L. Maretheux, 1912.

Kardec, Allan. *Le Livre des esprits.* Paris: Didier, 1867.

————. *Le Livre des médiums.* Paris: Didier, 1863.

Krafft, Gustave. "Spiritisme." *La Cooperation,* 16 June 1921.

Lacan, Jacques. "The Freudian Thing." In *Écrits: A Selection.* New York: Norton, 1977.

Lalande, André. "Philosophy in France." *Philosophical Review* 14 (July 1905): 429–55.

————. "Philosophy in France, 1922–1923." *Philosophical Review* 33 (November 1924): 535–59.

————. "Philosophy in France, 1935–1936." *Philosophical Review* 46 (January 1937): 1–29.

Lapicque, Louis, Georges Dumas, Henri Piéron, and Henri Laugier. "Rapport sur des expériences de contrôle relative aux phénomènes dits ectoplasmique." *L'Année Psychologique* (1922): 604–11.

Lavisse, Ernest. *L'Éducation de la démocratie: Leçons professées à l'École des Hautes Études Sociales.* Paris: Alcan, 1903.

Le Bon, Gustave. *Les Opinions et les croyances: Genèse, évolution.* Paris: E. Flammarion, 1911.

Léchopié, Alfred, and Charles Floquet. *Droit médical; ou, code des médecins, docteurs, officiers de santé, sages-femmes, pharmaciens, vétérinaires, étudiants, etc.* Paris: Doin, 1890.

Le Clair, Robert, ed. *The Letters of William James and Théodore Flournoy.* Madison: University of Wisconsin Press, 1966.

Levaillant, Maurice. *La Crise mystique de Victor Hugo (1843–1856): D'après des documents inédits.* Paris: J. Corti, 1954.

Lewis, E. E. *A Report of the Mysterious Noises Heard in the House of Mr. John D. Fox in Hydesville, Arcadia, Wayne County.* Canandaigua, N.Y.: Shepard and Reed, 1848.

Leymarie, P.-G. *Procès des spirites.* Paris: Librairie Spirite, 1875.

Lodge, Oliver. "Aux affligés de toutes nations." *Les Annales des Sciences Psychiques,* March 1916, 55.

———. *Raymond, or Life and Death.* New York: G. H. Doran, 1916.

Lombroso, Césare. *L'Homme de genie.* Paris: Alcan, 1889.

London Dialectical Society. *Report on Spiritualism of the Committee of the London Dialectical Society, Together with the Evidence, Oral and Written, and a Selection from the Correspondence.* London: Longmans, Green, Reader and Dyer, 1871.

Lorenz, Otto. *Catalogue général de la librairie française depuis 1840,* vols. 1–13. Paris, 1867.

Maxwell, Joseph. *Les Phénomènes psychiques.* Paris: Alcan, 1903.

Monnier, Pierre, and Cécile Monnier. *Lettres de Pierre,* vol. 1. 1922; Paris: Fernand Lanore, 1980.

Morselli, M. *Psicologia e spiritismo: Impressionni e note critiche sui fenomeni medianici di Eusapia Paladino.* Turin: Bocca, 1908.

Mounier, Emmanuel. *Traité du caractère.* 1946; Paris: Seuil, 1961.

Mourey, Gabriel. *Youriévitch, 24 Photos.* Paris: Librairie de France, 1928.

Murchison, Carl, ed. *The Case For and Against Psychical Belief.* Worcester, Mass.: Clark University, 1927.

Myers, Frederic William Henry. *Human Personality and Its Survival of Bodily Death.* 1903; New Hyde Park, N.Y.: University Books, 1961.

Nordmann, Charles. "Les Grands Médiums à ectoplasme." *La Revue des Deux Mondes,* 15 October 1922, 930–41.

———. "Les Mystères de l'ectoplasme." *La Revue des Deux Mondes,* 15 November 1922, 453–64.

———. "Pour aborder la métapsychique." *La Revue des Deux Mondes,* 15 June 1922, 935–46.

———. "Spiritisme, métapsychique, ectoplasme." *La Revue des Deux Mondes,* 15 September 1922, 458–69.

Ochorowicz, Julian. *De la suggestion mentale.* Paris: Doin, 1887.

———. "De l'Institut Psychologique." In Janet, *IVe Congrès International de Psychologie.*

Picot, Georges. *Paul Janet: Notice historique lue en séance publique le 6 décembre 1902.* Paris: Hachette, 1903.

Prévost, Marcel. "La Question métapsychique." *La Revue de France,* 1 November 1923, 5–25.

Ravaisson, Felix. *La Philosophie en France au XIXe siècle.* 1867; Paris: Hachette, 1904.

Régis, Emmanuel. *Précis de psychiatrie.* 1906; Doin: Paris, 1914.

Régis, Emmanuel, and Angélo Hesnard. *La Psychanalyse des névroses et des psychoses.* Paris: Alcan, 1914.

Renan, Ernest. *L'Avenir de la science: Pensées de 1848.* Paris: Calmann Levy, 1890.

———. *Qu'est-ce qu'une nation?: Conférence faite en Sorbonne le 11 mars 1882.* Paris: Calmann Levy, 1882.

Ribot, Théodule. *Essai sur l'imagination créatrice.* Paris: Alcan, 1900.

———. "Philosophy in France." *Mind* 2, no. 7 (1877): 366–86.

———. *La Psychologie allemande contemporaine.* Paris: G. Baillière, 1879.

———. "La Psychologie de 1896 à 1900." In Janet, *IVe Congrès International de Psychologie.*

Richemont, Eugène Panon Desbassayns, comte de. *Le Mystère de la danse des tables dévoilé par ses rapports avec les manifestations spirituelles d'Amérique. Par un catholique.* Paris: Devarenne and Pérrisse Frères, 1853.

Richer, Paul. *L'Art et la médecine.* Paris: Gaultier Magnier, 1900.

Richet, Charles. "L'Amour, étude de psychologie générale." *La Revue des Deux Mondes,* March–April 1891, 135–67.

———. "Démoniaques d'aujourd'hui. Étude de psychologie pathologique." *La Revue des Deux Mondes,* January–February 1880, 340–72.

———. "De quelques phénomènes dits de la matérialisation." *Les Annales des Sciences Psychiques,* November 1905, 649–71.

———. "Des phénomènes psychique. Lettre à M. Dariex." *Les Annales des Sciences Psychiques* 1 (1891): 1–8.

———. "Du somnambulisme provoqué." *Journal de l'Anatomie et de la Physiologie Normale et Pathologiques de Homme et des Animaux* 15 (1875): 348–77.

———. *Fables et recits pacifiques.* Paris: Giard et Brière, 1904.

———. "Les Mouvements inconscients." In *Hommage à Monsieur Chevreul à l'occasion de son centenaire, 31 août 1886,* by M. Berthelot et al. Paris: Alcan, 1886.

———. *La Sélection humaine.* Paris: Alcan, 1919.

———. *Souvenirs d'un physiologiste.* Joigny, Yonne: J. Peyronnet, 1933.

———. "La Suggestion mentale et le calcul des probabilities." *La Revue Philosophique de la France et de l'Étranger,* July–December 1884.

———. *Thirty Years of Psychical Research.* New York: Macmillan, 1923.

———. *Traité de métapsychique.* Paris: Alcan, 1922.

Rouby, Hippolyte. "Bien-Boà et Ch. Richet." *XVe Congrès International de Médecine, Lisbonne, 19–28 avril 1906.* Lisbon: Adolpho de Mendoça, 1906.

Sage, Michel. Introduction to Edward T. Bennett, *La Société Anglo-Américain pour les recherches psychiques,* translated by Michel Sage. Paris: Lucien Bodin, 1904.

Schrenck-Notzing, Albert von. *Materialisations-Phaenomene: Ein Beitrag zur Erforschung der mediumistischem Teleplastie.* Munich: E. Reinhardt, 1914.

———. *Phenomena of Materialisation: A Contribution to the Investigation of Mediumistic Teleplastics.* New York: Dutton, 1920.

———. *Les Phénomènes physiques de la médiumnité,* translated by E. Longaud. Paris: Payot, 1925.

Segalen, Victor. *L'Observation médicale chez les écrivains naturalistes.* Bordeaux: Y. Cadoret, 1902.

Seguin, Marc. "Lettre de M. Seguin aîné, sur des expériences relatives à la faculté attribuée aux êtres animés de développer, dans des corps inertes, une électricité particulière." *Comptes Rendus Hebdomadaires des Séances de l'Académie des Sciences* 36 (1853): 890–93.

Simon, Gustave. *Chez Victor Hugo: Les tables tournantes de Jersey.* Paris: L. Conrad, 1923.

"Société Médico-psychologique: Séance Solennelle du 29 avril 1907." *Annales Medico-psychologique* (1907): 83.

Society for Psychical Research. *Presidential Addresses to the Society for Psychical Research, 1882–1911.* Glasgow: Society for Psychical Research, 1912.

Sudre, Réné. "La Question métapsychique (II)." *La Revue de France,* 15 November 1923, 269–303.

———. "La Question métapsychique (III)." *La Revue de France,* 1 December 1923, 558–90.

———. "Une science nouvelle: La Métapsychie." *L'Avenir,* 31 July 1919.

Taine, Hippolyte. *De l'intelligence.* 1870; Paris: Hachette, 1897.

———. *Les Philosophes classiques du XIXe en France.* Paris: Hachette, 1888.

Tocqueville, Alexis de. *De la démocratie en Amérique,* vols. 2–3. Paris: Pagnerre, 1848.

Tourdes, Gabriel, and Edmond Metzquer. *Traité de médecine légale théorique et pratique.* Paris: Asselin et Houzeau, 1896.

Tourette, Georges Gilles de la. *L'Hypnotisme et les états analogues au point de vue médico-légal: Les États hypnotiques et les états analogues, les suggestions criminelles, cabinets de somnambules et sociétés de magnétisme et de spiritisme, l'hypnotisme devant la loi.* Paris: E. Plon, Nourrit, 1887.

Tourette, Georges Gilles de la, and Paul Richer. "Hypnotisme." In *Dictionnaire en-cyclopédique des sciences médicales,* edited by Amédée Dechambre, 67–132. 1864; Paris: Asselin, 1889.

Tours, Jacques-Joseph Moureau de. *Du hachisch et de l'aliénation mentale, études psychologiques.* Paris: Fortin et Masson, 1845.

Vacquerie, Auguste. *Les Miettes de l'histoire.* Paris: Pagnerre, 1863.

Véga, Alice, *Les Présences invisibles.* Paris: Perrin, 1923.

Vesme, César de. "Armées, flottes et combats fantômiques." *Les Annales des Sciences Psychiques,* January 1916, 1–10.

———. "L'Institut Psychologique International." *Revue d'Études Psychique* 11 (November 1901): 322–30.

Vogt, Oskar. "Contre le spiritisme." In Janet, *IVe Congrès International de Psychologie.*

Wallace, Alfred Russel. *Miracles and Modern Spiritualism.* 1875; New York: Arno Press, 1975.

———. *My Life: A Record of Events and Opinions.* 1905; Westmead, Farnborough, Hants: Gregg International, 1969.

Wallace, Alfred Russel, and James Marchant. *Alfred Russel Wallace: Letters and Reminiscences.* New York: Harper, 1916.

Wundt, Wilhelm Max. *Hypnotisme et suggestion: Étude critique.* Paris: Alcan, 1893.

Youriévitch, Serge. "M. Émile Duclaux." *Bulletin de l'Institut Général Psychologique,* July–August 1904, 334.

Youriévitch, Serge, and Gabriel Mourey. *Serge Youriévitch: American Creations, 1929–1930.* New York: D. Jacomet, 1930.

Zola, Émile. *Le Roman expérimental.* 1880; Paris: Charpetier et Fasquelle, 1894.

Secondary Sources

Albanese, Catherine L. *A Republic of Mind and Spirit: A Cultural History of American Metaphysical Religion.* New Haven, Conn.: Yale University Press, 2007.

Bachelard, Gaston. *Le Nouvel Esprit scientifique.* Paris: Presses Universitaires de France, 1934.

Balakian, Anna Elizabeth. *André Breton, Magus of Surrealism.* New York: Oxford University Press, 1971.

Barkun, Michael. *Crucible of the Millennium: The Burned-Over District of New York in the 1840s.* Syracuse, N.Y.: Syracuse University Press, 1986.

Barthes, Roland, et al. *Littérature et réalité,* edited by Gérard Genette and Tzvetan Todorov. Paris: Seuil, 1982.

Becker, Annette. *La Guerre et la foi: De la mort à la mémoire, 1914–1930.* Paris: A. Colin, 1994.

Benjamin, Walter. *Charles Baudelaire: A Lyric Poet in the Era of High Capitalism,* translated by Harry Zohn. New York: Verso, 1983.

Benjamin, Walter, and Rolf Tiedemann. *The Arcades Project*, translated by Howard Eiland and Kevin McLaughlin. Cambridge, Mass.: Harvard University Press, 1999.

Bensaude-Vincent, Bernadette, and Christine Blondel. *Des savants face à l'occulte: 1870–1940, sciences et société*. Paris: Découverte, 2002.

Bergé, Christine. *La Voix des esprits: Ethnologie du spiritisme*. Paris: Éditions Métailié, 1990.

Bilous, Daniel. "Écrits sur tables: Les au-delà intertextuels de l'exil." In *Idéologies hugoliennes: 23, 24 et 25 mai 1985, colloque Université de Nice, Centre de Recherche et d'Histoire des Idées*, edited by Anne-Marie Amiot, 95–105. Nice: Éditions Serre, 1985.

Bloch, Marc. *Les Rois thaumaturges: Étude sur le caractère surnaturel attribué à la puissance royale particulièrement en France et en Angleterre*. 1924; Paris: Gallimard, 1983.

Blumenberg, Hans. *The Legitimacy of the Modern Age*, translated by Robert M. Wallace. Cambridge, Mass.: MIT Press, 1985.

Bonnet, Marguerite. *André Breton: Naissance de l'aventure surréaliste*. Paris: Corti, 1975.

Bourdieu, Pierre. "The Forms of Capital." In *Handbook of Theory and Research for the Sociology of Education*, edited by John G. Richardson, 241–58. New York: Greenwood Press, 1986.

Boutry, Philippe, Jacques Le Goff, René Rémond, and Philippe Joutard. *Du roi très chrétien à la laïcité républicaine, XVIIIe–XIXe siècle: L'Univers historique*. Vol. 3 of *Histoire de la France religieuse*. Paris: Seuil, 1991.

Breton, André, Marguerite Bonnet, Philippe Bernier, Étienne-Alain Hubert, and José Pierre. *Oeuvres complètes II, Bibliothèque de la Pléiade*. Paris: Gallimard, 1992.

Brooks, John I. *The Eclectic Legacy: Academic Philosophy and the Human Sciences in Nineteenth-Century France*. Newark: University of Delaware Press, 1998.

Brown, Richard. Review of *The Elusive Science: The Origins of Experimental Psychical Research* by Seymour H. Mauskopf and Michael R. McVaugh. *American Historical Review* 87, no. 4 (1982): 1045–46.

Carroy, Jacqueline. *Hypnose, suggestion et psychologie: Invention du sujet*. Paris: Presses Universitaires de France, 1991.

———. *Les Personnalités doubles et multiples: Entre science et fiction*. Paris: Presses Universitaires de France, 1993.

———. "Playing with Signatures: The Young Charles Richet." In *The Mind of Modernism: Medicine, Psychology, and the Cultural Arts in Europe and America, 1880–1940*, edited by Mark S. Micale, 217–49. Stanford: Stanford University Press, 2004.

Carroy, Jacqueline, Annick Ohayon, and Régine Plas. *Histoire de la psychologie en France, XIXe–XXe siècles*. Paris: La Découvert, 2006.

Carroy, Jacqueline, and Régine Plas. "How Pierre Janet Used Pathological Psychology to Save the Philosophical Self." *Journal of the History of the Behavioral Sciences* 36 (Summer 2000): 231–40.

Carroy-Thirard, Jacqueline. "Hystérie, théâtre, littérature au 19e siècle." *Psychanalyse à l'Université* 7 (March 1982): 299–317.

Charlton, D. G. *Positivist Thought in France during the Second Empire, 1852–1870.* New York: Oxford University Press, 1959.

Chertok, Léon, and Raymond de Saussure. *The Therapeutic Revolution: From Mesmer to Freud,* translated by R. H. Ahrenfeldt. New York: Brunner/Mazel, 1979.

Cottom, Daniel. "On the Dignity of Tables." *Critical Inquiry* 14 (Summer 1988): 765–83.

Crabtree, Adam. *From Mesmer to Freud: Magnetic Sleep and the Roots of Psychological Healing.* New Haven, Conn.: Yale University Press, 1993.

Cross, Whitney. *The Burned-Over District: The Social and Intellectual History of Enthusiastic Religion in Western New York, 1800–1850.* Ithaca, N.Y.: Cornell University Press, 1950.

Cru, Jean Norton. *War Books: A Study in Historical Criticism,* translated and edited by Stanley Pincetl, Jr., and Ernest Marchand. San Diego: San Diego State University, 1976.

Cryle, Peter. "Love and Epistemology in French Fiction of the Fin-de-Siècle: In Search of the Pathological Unknown." *Dix-Neuf: Journal of the Society of Dix-neuvièmistes* 3 (September 2004): 55–74.

Dansel, Michel. *Les Lieux de culte au cimetière du Père-Lachaise.* Paris: Trédaniel, 1999.

Darnton, Robert. *Mesmerism and the End of the Enlightenment in France.* New York: Schocken, 1970.

Didi-Huberman, Georges, and J.-M. Charcot. *Invention of Hysteria: Charcot and the Photographic Iconography of the Salpêtrière.* Cambridge, Mass.: MIT Press, 2003.

Domanski, Cezary W. "Julian Ochorowicz (1850–1917) et son apport dans le développement de la psychologie du XIXe siècle." *Psychologie et Histoire* 4 (2003): 101–14.

Edelman, Nicole. *Voyantes, guérisseuses et visionnaires en France: 1785–1914.* Paris: A. Michel, 1995.

Ellenberger, Henri F. *The Discovery of the Unconscious: The History and Evolution of Dynamic Psychiatry.* New York: Basic Books, 1970.

Elwitt, Sanford. *The Making of the Third Republic: Class and Politics in France, 1868–1884.* Baton Rouge: Louisiana State University Press, 1975.

Fichman, Martin. *Alfred Russel Wallace.* Boston: Twayne Publishers, 1981.

———. *An Elusive Victorian: The Evolution of Alfred Russel Wallace.* Chicago: University of Chicago Press, 2004.

Flournoy, Olivier. *Théodore et Léopold: de Théodore Flournoy à la psychanalyse.* Neuchâtel: à la Baconnière, 1986.

Foster, Hal. *Compulsive Beauty.* Cambridge, Mass.: MIT Press, 1993.

Foucault, Michel. *Discipline and Punish: The Birth of the Prison,* translated by Alan Sheridan. New York: Vintage, 1977.

———. *Histoire de la folie à l'âge classique.* Paris: Gallimard, 1972.

Fox, Robert, and George Weisz, eds. *The Organization of Science and Technology in France, 1808–1914.* New York: Cambridge University Press, 1980.

Gauld, Alan. *The Founders of Psychical Research.* New York: Schocken Books, 1968.

Gay, Maurice. *Victor Hugo, spiritualiste.* Paris: G. Nizet, 1955.

Goldstein, Jan. "The Advent of Psychological Modernism in France: An Alternative Narrative." In *Modernist Impulses in the Human Sciences, 1870–1930,* edited by Dorothy Ross, 190–209. Baltimore, Md.: Johns Hopkins University Press, 1994.

———. "Mutations of the Self in Old Regime and Post-Revolutionary France: From Ame to Moi to Le Moi." In *Biographies of Scientific Objects,* edited by Lorraine Daston, 86–116. Chicago: University of Chicago Press, 2000.

———. *The Post-Revolutionary Self: Politics and Psyche in France, 1750–1850.* Cambridge, Mass.: Harvard University Press, 2005.

———. "The Uses of Male Hysteria: Medical and Literary Discourse in Nineteenth-Century France." *Representations* 34 (Spring 1991): 134–65.

Grasset, Joseph. "Hystérie." In *Dictionnaire encyclopédique des sciences médicales,* edited by Amédée Dechambre, 240–352. 1864; Paris: G. Masson, 1889.

———. *Le Spiritisme devant la science.* Montpellier: Coulet, 1904.

Grillet, Claudius. *Victor Hugo spirite.* Lyon: Librairie Emmanuel Vitte, 1929.

Hall, Trevor H. *The Spiritualists: The Story of Florence Cook and William Crookes.* New York: Helix Press, 1963.

Harrington, Anne. *The Cure Within: A History of Mind-Body Medicine.* New York: Norton, 2008.

Hazelgrove, Jenny. *Spiritualism and British Society Between the Wars.* New York: St. Martin's Press, 2000.

Hecht, Jennifer Michael. *The End of the Soul: Scientific Modernity, Atheism, and Anthropology in France.* New York: Columbia University Press, 2005.

Hess, David J., and Linda Layne, eds. *The Anthropology of Science and Technology.* Vol. 9 of *Knowledge and Society.* Greenwich, Conn.: JAI Press, 1992.

Horne, Janet R. *A Social Laboratory for Modern France: The Musée Social and the Rise of the Welfare State.* Durham, N.C.: Duke University Press, 2002.

James, Tony. *Dreams, Creativity, and Madness in Nineteenth-Century France.* New York: Oxford University Press, 1995.

Johnson, Curtis D. *Islands of Holiness: Rural Religion in Upstate New York, 1790–1860.* Ithaca, N.Y.: Cornell University Press, 1989.

Jones, Ernest. *The Life and Work of Sigmund Freud,* 3 vols. New York: Basic Books, 1953–57.

Keeley, James P. "Subliminal Promptings: Psychoanalytic Theory and the Society for Psychical Research." *American Imago* 58, no. 4 (2001): 767–91.

Kottler, Malcolm Jay. "Alfred Russel Wallace, the Origins of Man, and Spiritualism." *Isis* 65 (June 1974): 145–92.

Kuhn, Thomas S. *The Structure of Scientific Revolutions.* Chicago: University of Chicago Press, 1996.

Lachapelle, Sophie. "Attempting Science: The Creation and Early Development of the Institut Métapsychiques International in Paris, 1919–1931." *Journal of the History of the Behavioral Sciences* 41 (Winter 2005): 1–24.

———. "A World Outside Science: French Attitudes Toward Mediumistic Phenomena, 1853–1931." PhD diss., University of Notre Dame, 2002.

Ladous, Régis. *Le Spiritisme.* Paris: Cerf, 1989.

Laffin, John. *World War I in Postcards.* Gloucester, UK: Alan Sutton Publishing, 1988.

Lefort, Claude. "The Death of Immortality?" In *Democracy and Political Theory,* translated by David Macey, 256–82. Minneapolis: University of Minnesota Press, 1989.

Le Maléfan, Pascal. *Folie et spiritisme: Histoire du discours psychopathologique sur la pratique du spiritisme, ses abords et ses avatars, 1850–1950.* Paris: L'Harmattan, 1999.

———. "La Psychopathologie confrontée aux fantômes: L'Épisode de la villa Carmen." *Psychologie et Histoire* 5 (2004): 1–19.

———. "Richet chasseur des fantômes: L'Épisode de la villa Carmen." In *Des savants face à l'occulte, 1870–1940,* edited by Bernadette Bensaude-Vincent and Christine Blondel, 173–200. Paris: Découverte, 2002.

Lepenies, Wolf. *Between Literature and Science: The Rise of Sociology.* New York: Cambridge University Press, 1988.

Lusardy, Martine. *Art spirite, mediumnique, visionnaire, messages utre-monde: Une exposition de la Halle Saint-Pierre, du 13 septembre 1999 au 27 février 2000.* Paris: Hoëbeke, 1999.

Matlock, Jann. "Ghostly Politics." *Diacritics* 30, no. 3 (2000): 53–71.

Mauskopf, Seymour H., and M. R. McVaugh. *The Elusive Science: Origins of Experimental Psychical Research.* Baltimore, Md.: Johns Hopkins University Press, 1980.

Méheust, Bertrand. *Le Choc des sciences psychiques.* Vol. 2 of *Somnambulisme et médiumnité (1784–1930).* Le Plessis–Robinson: Institut Synthélabo, 1999.

———. "Épistémologiquement correct." *Alliage* 28 (Fall 1996): 15–24.

Micale, Mark S. "On the 'Disappearance' of Hysteria: A Study in the Clinical Deconstruction of a Diagnosis." *Isis* 84 (September 1993): 496–526.

Monroe, John. "*Cartes de visite* from the Other World: Spiritisme and the Discourse of *Laïcisme* in the Early Third Republic." *French Historical Studies* 26 (Winter 2003): 119–53.

———. *Laboratories of Faith: Mesmerism, Spiritism, and Occultism in Modern France.* Ithaca, N.Y.: Cornell University Press, 2008.

———. "Making the Séance 'Serious': *Tables Tournantes* and Second Empire Bourgeois Culture, 1853–1861." *History of Religions* 38 (February 1999): 219–46.

Moore, R. Laurence. *In Search of White Crows: Spiritualism, Parapsychology, and American Culture.* New York: Oxford University Press, 1977.

Mosse, George. *Fallen Soldiers: Reshaping the Memory of the World Wars.* New York: Oxford University Press, 1990.

Nicolas, Serge, and Agnès Charvillat. "Introducing Psychology as an Academic Discipline in France: Théodule Ribot and the Collège de France (1888–1901)." *Journal of the History of the Behavioral Sciences* 37 (Spring 2001): 143–64.

Offen, Karen. "Depopulation, Nationalism, and Feminism in Fin-de-Siècle France." *American Historical Review* 89, no. 3 (1984): 648–76.

Oppenheim, Janet. *The Other World: Spiritualism and Psychical Research in England, 1850–1914.* New York: Cambridge University Press, 1985.

Owen, Alex. *The Darkened Room: Women, Power, and Spiritualism in Late Victorian England.* Philadelphia: University of Pennsylvania Press, 1990.

Parinet, Elisabeth. *La Librairie Flammarion: 1875–1914.* Paris: IMEC Éditions, 1992.

Parot, Françoise. "Cents ans de Société de Psychologie en France." *Psychologie Française* 45, no. 1 (2000): 3–11.

———. "Psychology Experiments: Spiritism at the Sorbonne." *Journal of the History of the Behavioral Sciences* 29 (January 1993): 22–28.

Paul, Harry. "The Debate over the Bankruptcy of Science in 1895." *French Historical Studies* 5 (Spring 1968): 299–327.

Payne, Howard C. *The Police State of Louis Napoleon Bonaparte, 1851–1860.* Seattle: University of Washington Press, 1966.

Perrot, Michelle, ed., and Arthur Goldhammer, trans. *From the Fires of Revolution to the Great War.* Vol. 4 of *A History of Private Life,* edited by Phillippe Ariès and Georges Duby. Cambridge, Mass.: Belknap Press, 1990.

Piéron, Henri. "Histoire des congrès internationaux." *Année Psychologique* 54 (1954): 397–405.

Pierssens, Michel. "Novation Astray." *SubStance* 62–63 (1990): 157–67.

———. "Le Syndrome des tables tournantes: Crise du savoir et 'sciences psychiques' au XIXe siècle." *Temps Modernes* 528 (July 1990): 91 n. 5.

Plas, Régine. *Naissance d'une science humaine: La Psychologie, les psychologues et le "Merveilleux Psychique."* Rennes: Presses Universitaires de Rennes, 2000.

Prévost, Claude M. *Janet, Freud et la psychologie clinique.* Paris: Payot, 1973.

———. *La Psycho-philosophie de Pierre Janet: Économies mentales et progrès humain.* Paris: Payot, 1973.

Ringer, Fritz K. *Fields of Knowledge: French Academic Culture in Comparative Perspective, 1890–1920.* New York: Cambridge University Press, 1992.

———. *Toward a Social History of Knowledge: Collected Essays.* New York: Berghahn Books, 2000.

Roudinesco, Elisabeth. *La Bataille de cent ans.* Vol. 1 of *Histoire de la psychanalyse en France.* Paris: Seuil, 1986.

———. *Histoire de la psychanalyse en France, 1925–1985,* vol. 2. Paris: Fayard, 1994.

Roudinesco, Elisabeth, and Michel Plon. *Dictionnaire de la psychanalyse.* Paris: Fayard, 1997.

Ryan, Mary. *Cradle of the Middle Class: The Family in Oneida County, New York, 1790–1865.* New York: Cambridge University Press, 1981.

Schneider, William. "Charles Richet and the Social Role of Medical Men." *Journal of Medical Biography* 9 (November 2001): 213–19.

Schultz, Bart. *Henry Sidgwick, Eye of the Universe: An Intellectual Biography.* New York: Cambridge University Press, 2004.

Scott, Joan Wallach. *Only Paradoxes to Offer: French Feminists and the Rights of Man.* Cambridge, Mass.: Harvard University Press, 1996.

Scott, John A. *Republican Ideas and the Liberal Tradition in France, 1870–1914.* New York: Octagon, 1966.

Seigel, Jerrold. *The Idea of the Self: Thought and Experience in Western Europe since the Seventeenth Century.* New York: Cambridge University Press, 2005.

Sharp, Lynn L. "Rational Religion, Irrational Science: Men, Women, and Belief in French Spiritism, 1853–1914." PhD diss., University of California, Irvine, 1996.

———. *Secular Spirituality: Reincarnation and Spiritism in Nineteenth-Century France.* Lanham, Md.: Lexington Books, 2006.

Shepard, Leslie, Lewis Spence, and Nandor Fodor. *Encyclopedia of Occultism and Parapsychology.* Detroit: Gale Research, 1984.

Shor, Ronald E., and Martin T. Orne. *The Nature of Hypnosis: Selected Basic Readings.* New York: Holt, Rinehart and Winston, 1965.

Simon, W. M. "The 'Two Cultures' in Nineteenth-Century France: Victor Cousin and Auguste Comte." *Journal of the History of Ideas* 26 (January–March 1965): 45–58.

Société d'Études et de Publications Industrielles. *Ceux qui font la presse, dictionnaire biographique des personnalités du monde de la presse Langue Français.* Paris: Société d'Études et de Publications Industrielles, 1979.

Starobinski, Jean. "Freud, Breton, Myers." *L'Arc* 34 (1968): 87–96.

Surkis, Judith. *Sexing the Citizen: Morality and Masculinity in France, 1870–1920.* Ithaca, N.Y.: Cornell University Press, 2006.

Taves, Ann. *Fits, Trances, and Visions: Experiencing Religion and Explaining Experience from Wesley to James.* Princeton, N.J.: Princeton University Press, 1999.

Thurschwell, Pamela N. "Fantasies of Transmission: Psychical Research and the Mediation of Intimacy, 1880–1916." PhD diss., Cornell University, 1998.

Todorov, Tzvetan. *Theories of the Symbol,* translated by Catherine Porter. Ithaca, N.Y.: Cornell University Press, 1982.

Turner, Frank M. *Between Science and Religion: The Reaction to Scientific Naturalism in Late Victorian England.* New Haven, Conn.: Yale University Press, 1974.

Tyler, Alice Felt. *Freedom's Ferment: Phases of American Social History to 1860*. Minneapolis: University of Minnesota Press, 1944.

Veith, Ilza. *Hysteria: The History of a Disease*. Chicago: University of Chicago Press, 1965.

Vernette, Jean. *L'Au-delà*. Paris: Presses Universitaires de France, 1998.

Weisz, George. *The Emergence of Modern Universities in France, 1863–1914*. Princeton, N.J.: Princeton University Press, 1983.

———. *The Medical Mandarins: The French Academy of Medicine in the Nineteenth and Early Twentieth Centuries*. New York: Oxford University Press, 1995.

Williams, Elizabeth A. *The Physical and the Moral: Anthropology, Physiology, and Philosophical Medicine in France, 1750–1850*. New York: Cambridge University Press, 1994.

Williams, Raymond. *Keywords: A Vocabulary of Culture and Society*. New York: Oxford University Press, 1985.

Wilson, Elizabeth Ann. *Neural Geographies: Feminism and the Microstructure of Cognition*. New York: Routledge, 1998.

Winstanley, D. A. *Later Victorian Cambridge*. Cambridge: Cambridge University Press, 1947.

Winter, Alison. *Mesmerized: Powers of Mind in Victorian Britain*. Chicago: University of Chicago Press, 1998.

Winter, Jay. *Sites of Memory, Sites of Mourning*. New York: Cambridge University Press, 1995.

Wittkower, Rudolf. "Genius: Individualism in Art and Artists." In *The Dictionary of the History of Ideas*, ed. Philip Wiener, 2:293–326. New York: Scribner, 1973.

Wolf, Stewart. *Brain, Mind, and Medicine: Charles Richet and the Origins of Physiological Psychology*. New Brunswick, N.J.: Transaction Publishers, 1993.

Index

M. BRADY BROWER is an assistant professor of history at Weber State University.

The University of Illinois Press
is a founding member of the
Association of American University Presses.

Designed by Kelly Gray
Composed in 10.5/13 Adobe Minion Pro
with Serifa and Meta display
by Jim Proefrock
at the University of Illinois Press
Manufactured by Sheridan Books, Inc.

University of Illinois Press
1325 South Oak Street
Champaign, IL 61820-6903
www.press.uillinois.edu